Understanding Video Activism on Social Media

"If you want to understand the power of video activism not just as a political tool but as a social force, please read this book. The authors manage to analyze in depth the historical, rhetorical, aesthetical, and other aspects of video activism and how it is enmeshed in the distribution logic of social media. Due to its geopolitical scope combined with a broad analytical framework, *Understanding Video Activism on Social Media* is an eye-opener for students, scholars, and activists alike."
José van Dijck, Professor of Media and Digital Society at Utrecht University, co-author of *The Platform Society*

"This rich analysis of video activism shows how activists use video production and platform technologies to create often impressive public engagement for their causes. The authors examine an intriguing variety of cases that reveal the challenges and opportunities facing movements in increasingly noisy communication environments. In addition, the book places video activism in the larger contests of platforms, power, and geopolitics. Students of social movements, democracy, and media will find this a valuable resource that changes how we think about activist communication."
W. Lance Bennett, Senior Research Fellow, Centre for Journalism, Media & Democracy; Emeritus Professor of Political Science and Communication, University of Washington

"This book offers a thorough and engaging review of the changing contexts, practices and forms of video activism. It is alert to shifts in technology and aesthetics as well as to changing modes of access and engagement, framing these within broader political and economic factors. Clear and provocative, it will refresh and stimulate the debate about what media 'activism' now means and what it could mean in the settings of both vigorous platform capitalism and increasing tendencies to authoritarian restriction."
John Corner, Visiting Professor in Media and Communication, University of Leeds; Emeritus Professor, University of Liverpool; Fellow of the Royal Society of Arts

"This book offers valuable insights into the evolving role of video in activism. The authors discuss video activism across various time periods and media forms, from documentary films to TikTok videos. They provide a unique perspective on the continuity and specificities in how videos are deployed to champion causes and mobilize collective action. By incorporating relevant concepts and theories, the authors enrich the discussion with a strong analytical framework. Rich with both historical and contemporary case examples, this book will be a useful resource for media communication scholars and students."
Jing Zeng, Professor of Computational Social and Communication Science, University of Zurich

Understanding Video Activism on Social Media

Jens Eder, Britta Hartmann, and Chris Tedjasukmana

intellect
Bristol, UK / Chicago, USA

First published in the UK in 2025 by
Intellect, The Mill, Parnall Road, Fishponds, Bristol, BS16 3JG, UK

First published in the USA in 2025 by
Intellect, The University of Chicago Press, 1427 E. 60th Street,
Chicago, IL 60637, USA

A catalogue record for this book is available from the British Library.

Copy editor: MPS Limited
Cover designer: Christina Chalkidou
Cover manager: Tanya Montefusco
Cover image: Collage of protesters holding up their phones. 2024.
Pictures by Imad Alassiry and Koshu Kunii (Unsplash) and Sides Imagery (Pexels).
Production manager: Debora Nicosia
Typesetter: MPS Limited

Hardback ISBN 978-1-83595-082-1
Paperback ISBN 978-1-83595-083-8
ePDF ISBN 978-1-83595-085-2
ePUB ISBN 978-1-83595-084-5

This publication was funded by the Volkswagen Foundation.

VolkswagenStiftung

The manuscript for this book was completed at the end of 2023;
later developments could therefore not be taken into account.

To find out about all our publications, please visit our website.
There you can subscribe to our e-newsletter, browse or download our current
catalogue and buy any titles that are in print.

www.intellectbooks.com

This is a peer-reviewed publication.

Contents

Figures

Acknowledgments

Let's start at the end of this book, where we develop the idea of diversity in solidarity, a collaborative practice that welcomes and promotes the plurality of democratic activists, their different concerns and strategies in their joint struggle for progressive social change. This theoretical idea also corresponds to a practical guiding principle that has inspired our work from the very beginning. This book was not only co-authored by three authors, but also owes much to many attentive readers, commentators, partners, and supporters, and is thus ultimately the result of a collectively shared practice. As the authors of this book, we are grateful to the many individuals and institutions that have supported this publication in various ways (while recognizing that any errors the book may still contain are our own).

First and foremost, we would like to thank the Volkswagen Foundation for funding this publication and the research projects on which it is based, "Video Activism between Social Media and Social Movements" (2016–18) and "Attention Strategies of Video Activism on the Social Web" (2018–23). For critical activists reading this book, it is perhaps important to know that the Volkswagen Foundation is completely independent of the eponymous car manufacturer. The similarity in name arises solely from the fact that 60 years ago, the German state sold its shares in the car company to establish the foundation, which today is one of the most important non-profit funding organizations for academic research in Germany, known in particular for opening up spaces for innovative, socially relevant research. Our thanks also go to the publishers Dieter Bertz and Katrin Fischer, who made it possible for us to develop this book on the basis of a small German-language predecessor: the booklet *Bewegungsbilder: Politische Videos in Sozialen Medien*, published in 2020 by Bertz + Fischer in Berlin. Our British publisher Intellect, two anonymous reviewers, and above all the ever-obliging and patient Julia Brockley and Debora Nicosia have made it possible to turn the original German manuscript into a thoroughly revised, updated, and expanded book of twice the size—we thank them very much.

Our sincere thanks also go to Tobias Gralke and Maurice Lahde, who scrutinized and critically reviewed the manuscript at various stages and generously shared their helpful suggestions with us. Tobias also contributed insightful analyses of the use of video in the Russian war against Ukraine, some of which have been integrated into Chapter 7. Stephen Lowry, our esteemed academic colleague and careful translator of the book, shed new light on many of our thoughts during the editing process. Joana da Silva, Raphael Flechtner, Ashley Gould, Amelie Gradaus, Neal Graham, Jonathan Guggenberger, Dana Rostek, Jakob Schlußmeier, and Simon Schneider supported us in countless cases throughout the research and editorial process.

Moreover, we would especially like to thank Leonhard Balk, Anja Breljak, Christine Noll Brinckmann, Katja Crone, Tom Divon, Leopold Lippert, and many others for their stimulating thoughts on parts of the manuscript. In workshops, conferences, and labs, many participants provided us with helpful and inspiring ideas, among them were Angela Aguayo, Nather Henafe Alali, Naima Alam, Julia Althoff, Kari Andén-Papadopoulos, Tina Askanius, Mine Gencel Bek, Marcus Bösch, Amanda Brennan, Catalin Brylla, Robin Celikates, Christian Christensen, Yves Citton, John Corner, Tom Divon, Tobias Ebbrecht-Hartmann, Şirin Erensoy, Kathrin Fahlenbrach, Maik Fielitz, Patricia Finneran, Maike Gosch, Timo Gößler, Nanna Heidenreich, Bianca Hoffmann, Kay Hoffmann, Moritz Hohenfeld, Romy Jaster, Aya Jubeh, Guido Kirsten, Charlotte Klonk, Aslı Kotaman, Bettina Kurz, Margreth Lünenborg, Mykola Makhortykh, Concha Mateos, Sören Musyal, Tobias Nanz, Kate Nash, Ben O'Loughlin, Dana Regev, Maike Reinerth, Sandra Ristovska, Dieter Rucht, Sophija Savtchouk, Kerstin Schankweiler, Birgit Schneider, Karolin Schwarz, Sascha Simons, Gudrun Sommer, Verena Straub, Alena Strohmeier, Giacomo Tagliani, Simon Teune, Margarita Tsomou, Josepha Wessels, Claire Yorke, Manuel Zahn, and many others. We are also grateful for inspiring discussions with the students of our seminars on video activism.

And finally, a very special thanks to Rayk Anders, Florence Ayisi, bak.ma, Louisa Dellert, Sam Gregory (Witness), Stephanie Hankey and Leil-Zahra Mortada (Tactical Technology Collective), Jenny Harbauer, Samantha Iwowo, David Knight, Fynn Kröger (Ultralativ), Julia Lazarus, Leftvision, Marius Liedtke, Linke Sau, Heiko Linnemann (Greenpeace Germany), Henning Obens (Rosa Luxemburg Foundation), Jean Peters and Ronny Sommer (Peng! Collective), Sue Sudbury, Tarik Tesfu, Anne Thoma (WWF Germany), Malte Voß, Thorsten Winsel, and many other activists, filmmakers, and video creators for generously sharing their stories and expertise with us—without their insights, this book would never have been possible.

Introduction: The Power of Video Activism

What political power do videos on social media have? In what ways do they exert influence, shape publics, and change political life? And how can committed civil society actors in this field assert themselves against hegemonic discourses, commercial interests, anti-democratic agitation, and authoritarian propaganda? These questions are being debated intensely as social media increasingly dominate global information flows, and videos increasingly dominate social media. Some of the largest platforms, such as YouTube and TikTok, specialize exclusively in videos. Other major players, such as Instagram, X (formerly Twitter), Facebook, or Twitch, are actively expanding video to boost user engagement. Even usually text-centered messenger services like Telegram or WeChat are now relying more and more on audiovisual content. According to their own regularly updated statistics, the largest platforms record billions of video views every day and hundreds of hours of video uploads every minute.[1] Moving images already account for the greatest part of global internet traffic (about 65 percent of its data volume according to Sandvine 2019), and big tech corporations continue to invest significant sums in enhancing their video capacities.

Videos have also become an indispensable means of political communication because they have the potential to spread messages quickly, accessibly, and effectively, to move viewers deeply, and to motivate them to act. Political actors of all kinds take advantage of this: not only governments and oppositional parties, non-governmental organizations and grassroots initiatives, communities and corporations, journalists and artists, influencers and average users but also authoritarian regimes, conspiracy ideologues, paramilitary units, religious fundamentalists, and violent mobs. These different actors might use video to different ends: to inform or manipulate, highlight grievances or distract from them, mobilize allies or attack opponents, provide evidence, arguments, and narratives, evoke fear, outrage, or hope. Sinister political videos have attracted considerable public and academic attention. Among them are those spreading disinformation and propaganda, interference in democratic elections, far-right agitation, or the terror of self-proclaimed holy warriors. Some researchers even accuse the major communication platforms of being altogether "anti-social media" (Vaidhyanathan 2018).[2]

In view of many current developments, any naïve enthusiasm about democratic utopias of the internet would indeed be misguided. Social media and their videos are in fact highly ambivalent phenomena, designed and used for divergent purposes. But precisely for this reason, the urgent question is how to critically analyze them, identify problems, and increase general media literacy and political education to achieve better use of social media and their videos and to clarify political issues regarding the restructuring of platforms. After all, social media will certainly not simply disappear. This book therefore emphasizes the continuing potential that videos have for achieving democratic social change, forming opinions, and motivating political participation, as is also reflected in numerous recent studies (e.g., Pew Research Center 2022). We focus on actors who respect democratic processes and scientific knowledge, advocate for socially marginalized causes and groups, promote equality, and are guided by widely shared core values as expressed in the United Nations Global Goals (such as combating human rights violations, poverty, hunger, and environmental degradation). In this context, we understand video activism as the use of online video by individuals and groups in civil society who advocate for their political causes largely independently of the state, business, professional journalism, or other established institutions.[3] Video activism takes many forms and stems from various political orientations (see Chapter 5). It can be reformist or radical, progressive or conservative, and includes networked users, social and political communities, non-governmental organizations, and social movements. When NGOs publicize their actions, when protest movements organize around hashtags like #FridaysForFuture or #BlackLivesMatter, and when influencers express their political opinions in video posts, they can potentially reach more people than would ever have been thought possible before the advent of social media. Linked with other channels and profiles, integrated into multifaceted media environments, and in constant interaction with online and offline public spheres, citizen activists provide a counterforce to the established actors in politics, the media, and the economy. This is currently all the more important as global inequality continues to increase (Piketty 2014) and the social and ecological conditions for a good life with sufficient resources are under growing threat worldwide (Raworth 2017).

The importance of video activism and its role in making political grievances visible is particularly evident in the case of authoritarian states that repress large segments of their populations, significantly restrict freedom of speech, control the media, and systematically mislead the public (Reporters Without Borders 2022). But even in democratic societies with mostly free and pluralistic media, the established press and gatekeepers do not always report on relevant social problems or present every conflict adequately and fairly, and they do not grant all citizens equal access to the public sphere and its discourses. Moreover, most people in most countries have only limited time and resources to inform themselves about significant issues and to actively participate in politics. Therefore, it is extremely important that video activists draw attention to problems that many otherwise ignore—when power is abused, when human rights are violated, when people or nature are exploited, when the suffering of the most vulnerable in society is neglected, or when global problems like the climate crisis are denied.

To get a better overview of the historical development of video activism on social media, one can distinguish four main phases, each lasting about five years (for a more in-depth analysis, see Chapter 2). Video activists were active on social media very soon after they were introduced. For example, many activist YouTube channels date back to 2006. However, in this first phase (around 2005–10), their degree of organization was comparatively low. This changed in a second phase, an early peak of activism (around 2010–15), when younger people in particular used videos in the context of large protest movements with considerable impact such as the uprisings in the MENA region, Occupy, or the Indignados. Many of these videos had their origin and strongest effects in specific countries, while at the same time crossing borders and reaching international audiences. The recording of the death of demonstrator Neda Agha-Soltan during the Green Movement in Iran in 2009 shocked people around the world (Hamed Rad 2009). Since 2010 at the latest, witness videos in Syria and other Arab countries have provided evidence of state terrorism and war crimes.[4] Videos were also important in the Gezi Park protests in Turkey in 2013 and contributed to the formation of an oppositional identity. In the United States, videos have captured police violence against Black citizens and since 2013 have fueled international protest against racism under the hashtag Black Lives Matter (which gained renewed force in 2020 after the murder of George Floyd, see Chapter 6). Around 2015, a third phase of consolidation, public awareness about government and corporate surveillance (following the 2013 "Snowden leaks" and other events) increased and the struggle for attention on platforms intensified. During this period, activist channels grew in number, but commercial and entertainment videos did so even more (see Chapter 3). Nevertheless, some activist productions still stood out from the flood of moving images because of their ingenuity, reach, or influence. In 2015, for example, the Spanish civil alliance No Somos Delito ("We are Not a Crime") caused a stir by using video holograms instead of people protesting a ban on demonstrations. In the same year, in China, the web documentary 穹顶之下 (*Under the Dome*) (Chai 2015) was viewed more than a hundred million times in a few days before it was blocked, sparking debates about severe air pollution. Whether in Hong Kong, Brazil, Myanmar, or Nigeria, the worldwide growth of political protest is linked to the spread of videos on social media. In 2019, the German influencer Rezo released the video *Die Zerstörung der CDU* ("The Destruction of the CDU"), a scathing critique of the government that put it under considerable pressure (see Chapter 4). Although many of these exemplary videos were only distributed for a short time and some are already historic today, they managed to have a considerable impact on political conflicts. Since around 2020, however, existing state repression and persecution as well as measures in geopolitical internet regulation were once again clearly increasing (see Chapter 7). For example, the video blogs by Sergei Tikhanovsky in Belarus and Alexei Navalny in Russia played an important role in courageous protest movements against the ruling autocrats, but both opposition leaders were then arrested and sentenced to prison on dubious grounds. During the Iranian protests in 2022, which sparked after the murder of Mahsa Amini and in which broad sections of the population showed solidarity against the oppression of women, the state appears to have systematically analyzed videos (based on Chinese facial recognition technology) to identify and detain many protesters. Currently, the increasing state intervention on social media is particularly evident in the context of Russia's war of aggression against Ukraine. At the same time, the numerous video posts by everyday users and content creators continue to influence political conflicts and social discourses in liberating, democratic ways (Figures I.1–I.3).

FIGURE I.1: *Under the Dome*, China 2015, Chai Jing, YouTube.

FIGURE I.2: *Hologramas por la Libertad* ("Holograms for Freedom"), Spain 2015, Roca de Viñals et al., YouTube, by No Somos Delito ("We Are Not a Crime").

FIGURE I.3: An older woman in Russia protesting the war against Ukraine, Russia 2022, @aperegarom (Dama S. Peregarom), X/Twitter.

Viral videos in large political protests are certainly the most striking examples of video activism, but they ultimately reflect only a small section of this field, which includes countless more mundane posts about limited local issues in everyday politics. As we will show in this book, there are a variety of interesting and relevant video forms that contribute to shaping everyday political life. Activist videos are a powerful political force in various ways. They interact with mass media, state institutions, or interest groups and can drive political behavior, protest, and direct action.

The development of social video activism raises many questions. What are its consequences for politics, social movements, and the public sphere? What are its potentials and challenges? How does it affect people's participation in society, also considering the digital divide between the Global North and South, or between younger and older people? Such questions are discussed in different disciplines from various perspectives. In the social sciences, in particular, there is a vast amount of literature on political internet communication, online activism, and the visual communication of social movements (e.g., Terranova 2004; Fuchs 2014; Barassi 2015; Fenton 2016; Spier 2017; Dee 2018; Napoli 2019; Barendregt and Schneider 2020; Stephansen and Treré 2020). Some of this has already been condensed in handbooks, surveys, and anthologies (Dörr and Teune 2012; McLagan and McKee 2012; della Porta and Diani 2014; Atton 2015; Robertson 2015; Weibel 2015; Bruns et al. 2016; McGarry et al. 2020; Baker et al. 2021; Presence et al. 2021). From this perspective, videos are usually seen as one of many different means of political communication and activist practice. Such general work forms an important basis for our reflections in this book and we will draw on it frequently. However, we agree with Tina Askanius (2019) that we also need more nuanced studies that do justice to the intricate practices, structures, and logic of video activism on social media. Only then can we answer more specific questions: What exactly makes up the purported power of these videos? How do they attract public attention, and how do they make an impact on society? What types of political videos have been developed? Where can their historical roots be found, and what has changed since then? Who are the agents behind the videos, and what are their strategies and practices? What ethical, legal, and practical problems are involved? How are digital videos misused, manipulated, or faked, and how can their authenticity and factualness be verified? How do filmmakers ensure their own safety and protect their informants and witnesses, the privacy, and the rights of the people they catch on camera?

In view of such questions, Askanius (2019) distinguishes between three dominant strands of research on activist video, which have different focuses: its aesthetic and rhetorical form, the production and distribution infrastructure, or its use as visual evidence. The main challenge, she believes, is to integrate such perspectives within a holistic approach that takes different video practices into account. Such an approach still seems to be rare. However, there is a growing body of excellent research that addresses more specific aspects of video activism in detail. Some studies focus on certain countries or regions where video activists have played important political roles, including Syria (Wessels 2019), Turkey (Mehrabov 2010; Akser and McCollum 2018), Nigeria (Yékú 2022), Russia (Borenstein 2022; Glazunova 2022), and the United States (Robé 2023). Some authors also take a historical perspective and try to reconstruct the development of video activism in certain cultural, medial, and political contexts (Robé and Charbonneau 2020; Ristovska 2021a). Moreover, there is pioneering work on specific political issues and media contexts in the United States, like Alexandra Juhasz's (1995) study of video activism in the context of the early AIDS crisis, Alissa V. Richardson's (2020) work on smartphone-based Black witnessing, and investigations of hashtag movements from #MeToo to #BlackLivesMatter (Jackson et al. 2020).

Others concentrate on activist forms, strategies, and approaches. Several authors distinguish between different genres or functional types of videos such as mobilization videos and witness videos (Askanius 2013; Mateos and Gaona 2015; Reinsborough and Canning 2017). Among those genres, most studies concentrate not only on activist video as a means of providing evidence, which can take the form of mobile, connective camera witnessing (Andén-Papadopoulos 2014; Chouliaraki 2015; Mortensen 2015) but also on more elaborate forms of sousveillance (Reilly 2021) or counter-forensic videos (Fuller and Weizman 2021). Comprehensive studies have also explored in detail "how human rights organisations are seeking to professionalise video activism through video production, verification standards, and training" to influence powerful legal, media, and political institutions (Notley et al. 2017; Ristovska 2021). In contrast, others have turned to the use of video as an entertaining, participatory element of youth activism (Jenkins et al. 2016a, 2016b) or focus on forms of "playful activism" particularly on TikTok (Kaye et al. 2022, Chapter 3; Cervi and Divon 2023). With an even more specific focus, some researchers have looked at individual video collectives or activist groups such as Anonymous (Coleman 2015), Invisible Children (Shresthova 2016), or Reel News (Presence 2016). The influence of more recent technological developments such as deepfakes and artificial intelligence (AI) on video has also been discussed (Gregory 2022).

Building on this and further research, our book presents a more general overview of the field of video activism by clarifying basic concepts and questions that might lay the groundwork for more comprehensive answers. To this end, we evaluate existing theories and studies from various disciplines and combine them with our own case studies, which analyze discourse and videos, as well as media ethnographic interviews with activists. We incorporate results from quantitative studies but have not conducted such research ourselves. Our perspective is primarily one of film and media studies, critical theory, and hermeneutics. We consider this approach a useful complement to other research designs because it makes it possible to capture dynamic developments in video activism without much delay, keep an eye on its aesthetic and affective nuances, connect different scholarly perspectives on the field, integrate their findings and thereby gain a more holistic view.

Of course, our perspective—based on two research projects conducted between 2016 and 2023—is also limited and sets certain priorities that are intended to complement existing studies. Where others exclusively focus on the audiovisual testimonies of witnesses or the protests of social movements, we also include the video work of influencers and other content creators and of more established NGOs on social media. And while most studies focus either on the United States or on crisis areas in the MENA region, we focus primarily on Europe (as our professional and personal home region). Nevertheless, we try to deal with the diverse fields of video activism adequately and hope that some of our findings can be applied to other forms of political videos and geopolitical contexts as well. As indicated above, the social sciences and public discourses on such videos have focused mainly on the political actors and the reactions of users. Our study centers more on the videos themselves, their rhetorical and aesthetic forms, their historical models, their media environments, and their specific relationship to activist communities and publics. This book is an attempt to develop such approaches further. We hope that our work will be of interest not only to scholars but also to activists as well as media and political educators, and that it can find use in public discourses on social media politics.

This book comprises seven chapters. Chapter 1 introduces the crucial role videos play in political framing, especially in the context of social movements, and gives a brief overview of the most common video types and platform environments. Chapter 2 describes how activist videos have been shaped by the ethical and political principles of their historical predecessors in committed filmmaking, emphasizing what can be learned from them. Chapter 3 asks how activist videos achieve social impact and what role their aesthetic forms and affective qualities play in competing for attention. Chapter 4 explores related strategies for producing, designing, and disseminating videos in networked and hybrid media environments. Chapter 5 examines the principles and practices of various kinds of video activists: small media collectives, networks of influencers and other content creators, larger NGOs, as well as broad hashtag movements. Chapter 6 investigates the complex relationship between video activism and other political forms of public discourse and how it is involved in the struggle to create pluralistic, democratic public spheres. Finally, Chapter 7 offers a brief outlook on activist videos in contemporary contexts of war, oppression, and persecution. We conclude that chapter and the book with a plea for diversity in solidarity within democratic activism.

Understanding video activism seems particularly relevant at a time when the internet is undergoing fundamental disruptions. The forms, practices, and opportunities of activism depend on its media environment, which now is changing rapidly and profoundly in terms of its technological basis, ownership, legal regulations, and governmental control. Some recent developments include, for instance, the growing influence of states and corporations on information flows on the internet, often aiming at the repression of protest (Earl et al. 2022); the spread of firewalls, geoblocking, shadow banning, and other ways of hiding content (e.g., Russia's Sovereign Internet Law 2019); the growth of a political "influence industry" (The Influence Industry Project n.d.); the hiring of professional bot-farm runners and disinformation producers (Kirchgaessner et al. 2023); geopolitical friction, particularly after the rise of TikTok; the curtailment of fact-checking and ethical content moderation on X; ongoing questions concerning to what extent platforms are responsible for violent attacks when they distribute extremist videos; the attempts of states and supranational unions to regulate content (e.g., the EU Digital Services Act from 2022); and the as yet unforeseeable changes emerging through the use of AI and other emerging technologies. Our book will certainly not be able to do justice to such rapid and profound changes in media and political contexts, but we hope that it can help to assess their potential impact on activism. Internet cultures are a rapidly and constantly changing field of research. But even if the protagonists, media structures, and video practices mentioned here may well have been replaced or changed in many ways by the time this book is published or read, we hope its basic observations will remain useful and relevant.

1

The Media Logics of Video Activism: Frames, Forms, and Platforms

In the highly competitive social media environments, activists create and circulate videos of different types to generate attention for a variety of political issues. How do they frame their concerns to intervene in political conflicts? What audiovisual forms do they use? What characterizes the platform systems in which they operate? And how are their videos made to fit the specific affordances of the various platforms?

These questions suggest that video activism emerges at the intersection of three spheres, each of which has its own logic: politics and its frames, video and its forms, and social media and its platforms (van Dijck and Poell 2013). The power of video activism as a crucial practice of political communication stems from the fact that the logic of these three spheres—political framing, video aesthetics, and platform dynamics—interact dynamically and their potentials can reinforce each other. Politics, as a constant struggle for social decisions, power, and representation, drives collective action and depends on communication. Videos are a particularly effective kind of communication because of their impression of presence and evidence, their easy comprehensibility, their affective intensity, and their symbolic and cultural density. Social media platforms enable political videos to be used in a specific way: networked, interactive, fast, transnational, mobile, multimodal, partly user-generated, and partly governed by algorithms.

The interplay of these spheres makes video activism a particularly effective instrument in social struggles, and even more so for protest movements and people who do not have direct access to mass media. Videos can provide arguments in public debates, express legitimate interests and political emotions, influence public opinion, or serve as strategic weapons. As part of social media networks, they can create new publics, exert pressure on the powerful, strengthen social movements, and support a variety of political causes. This chapter provides an overview of the basic dimensions and logic of video activism. It first briefly addresses the field of politics, with a focus on social movements and political framing, then differentiates between common types of activist videos, and finally places them in the context of contemporary platform ecologies.

Political Contexts and Frames of Video Activism

Video activists take action to change society, often in response to collective experiences of crisis, degradation, suffering, or loss. They tackle all kinds of political issues, including the rights of marginalized social groups, economic inequality and poverty, state repression, democratic representation, the rule of law, environmental destruction, the climate crisis, corruption, migration, or freedom of expression. They create visibility for workers', refugees', women's, and LGBTQIA+ rights, fight racism and classism, counter the neoliberal capitalist restructuring of society, further the decolonization of white institutions, and call for climate justice. In authoritarian regimes and in war areas, activists fight under dangerous circumstances for basic possibilities of participation and against the daily violation of human rights. Engaging with such injustices can take place at the level of individuals, small groups, or local collectives, but when talking about activism, we are usually also dealing with larger social movements involved in longer-term, intense conflicts with dominant social groups. Social movements consist of many interconnected actors online and offline—from individual citizens to big NGOs—who find themselves in opposition to hegemonic power relations, institutions, and policy measures (see Chapter 5).

Most research relevant to understanding the political contexts and logic of activism has taken place within the framework of *Social Movement Studies*.[5] Social movements (and other, more limited or local forms of political action) emerge when a collective experiences social conditions as unjust, threatening, or problematic. Usually, striking events trigger a surge of collective action, which is then consolidated and guided by organizational networks, while the institutions of social control are unable to suppress it. The emergence of the movement requires sufficient resources of money, labor, time, knowledge, and social connections. Moreover, it is facilitated by cultural capital and "political opportunity structures," such as a weakening of the ruling power or the appearance of new allies (Meyer 2004). Movements often grow during particular, limited periods of time, for example, when power relations are shifting, or important events are widely reported in the media. Fridays for Future, for instance (itself a part of the larger movement for climate justice), was significantly affected by the Paris Climate Agreement of 2015 and the media presence of activist Greta Thunberg since 2018. Movements go through different phases of confrontation with opposing forces, repeatedly trying to mobilize their members and sympathizers for specific actions. In their activities and strategies, they resort to certain "repertoires of contention," including, for instance, meetings, demonstrations, petitions, strikes, roadblocks, occupation of buildings, press statements, leaflets, songs, art works and performances, as well as various kinds of online actions (della Porta 2013).

Video activism can be a crucial part of such repertoires and play important roles in all kinds and phases of political activity, which always involve processes of *framing*, that is, representing political issues in the media and in the mind (Johnston and Noakes 2005). Frames provide diagnoses and evaluations of a problem, and often also suggest solutions and causes. They function as interpretive schemata that are charged with affects and values and suggest answers to questions such as: What is in fact the problem, and why is it important? How should it be evaluated morally? How did it come about? Who is responsible? How can it be solved? Frames focus on certain aspects of an issue, highlight and assess them, and exclude others. Are protesters "terrorists" or "freedom fighters"? Are nuclear power plants guarantors of clean and cheap energy or an uncontrollable danger and burden for future generations? Is racist police brutality an unfortunate exception or a systemic problem? And how does the public perception of a demonstration change with the visual and auditory perspective—for example, when a witness's camera focuses on police violence from within the crowd of demonstrators or when a selection of images taken by police cameras draws attention to suspicious-looking demonstrators?

Dominant frames are usually tacitly accepted by most of the population and define what is considered to be normal—until they are actively put into question. Conflicts develop when various actors (the state, capital, social movements, and counter-movements) try to assert their "collective action frames" as the ones to be generally accepted (Johnston and Noakes 2005, 1–33). Whether actors are successful depends on their trustworthiness, charisma, and strategic skills, and on whether people view the suggested frame as relevant and compatible with their social identities, cultural backgrounds, everyday experiences, and belief systems. The frame's persuasive power in the media and how well it corresponds to its logic are further factors in its effectiveness.

Political actors use all kinds of media strategically to frame conflicts in public, to structure and stage them, and to organize their own actions. Three kinds of media practices have traditionally been particularly influential: professional journalism with current news, strategic communication by government press offices and corporate PR, and mass media entertainment that spreads political ideas more casually and subliminally. The power to control communication is distributed unequally: states and corporations have better access to mass media than socially marginalized groups and individual citizens. Critical journalists play an essential role in providing information and shaping public opinion by exposing wrongdoing and injustices. However, journalists often work according to specific routines and filters, and their reporting tends to be oriented toward common *news values* such as topicality, celebrity, and social or geographical proximity to the target audience (Harcup and O'Neill 2017; Scott et al. 2018). This often results in selective or biased reporting, for instance about humanitarian catastrophes. Furthermore, many news outlets are owned by powerful media corporations that pursue their own political agendas. Contrary to popular belief, journalism in most countries of the Global Northwest is by no means "left-wing," but tends to be conservative (e.g., Rupert Murdoch's News Corporation in the United Kingdom, United States, and Australia or Axel Springer SE in Germany and the United States). Even large broadcasters or newspapers that are considered "left-wing" (such as the BBC or the *Washington Post*) tend to take a liberal stance close to the political center and are by no means critical of capitalism.[6] Moreover, there is the ongoing problem of influential business lobbies that distort public opinion through pseudo-journalistic coverage. Companies also pay for click workers and sock puppets to simulate broad interest.

Such factors often influence journalistic coverage of protest movements, despite efforts to achieve unbiased reporting. Civic movements are frequently marginalized or portrayed negatively, even though they represent legitimate concerns, or their long-term goals receive only short-term attention. This is partly because social movements and their agendas often do not appeal to established journalistic reporting frames, because mass media simply reproduce the status quo, or because "merchants of doubt" are paid by businesses to spread disinformation (Oreskes and Conway 2011). In historical retrospect, for example, the anti-nuclear protests of the 1970s and 1980s and the women's and gay liberation movements in liberal democratic societies were vilified by the press for a long time before their contribution to a free and more just society was, at least partially, recognized and accepted. Communication by social movements—or more generally by socially less powerful groups and individuals—is thus a necessary counterweight to dominant public discourses (see Chapters 4 and 6). It forms counter-discourses and oppositional or alternative publics that clearly distance themselves from the prevailing interpretations of situations, set their own frames, and define their own identities (Fraser 1990; Wimmer 2015). In doing so, they must choose between adapting to mass media, attacking them, ignoring them, or producing their own alternative media products (Rucht 2004).

Most of these counter-discourses have their roots in a leftist or progressive tradition. At present, however, protest movements are also increasingly being formed by the alt-right, by conspiracy demagogues, and other anti-democratic groups, who spread so-called alternative truths, crude world views, and open hatred of those who think differently (Fielitz and Laloire 2016; Fielitz and Thurston 2019; Strick 2022). In reality, alternative publics are thus not necessarily pro-democratic, but rather strategic formations that mark a relational difference to the hegemonic power networks (see Chapter 6). Democratic activists come into conflict not only with those networks but also with numerous anti-democratic movements, including right-wing populists, religious agitators, corporate lobbyists, and state-financed troll armies that create confusion and sow fear or hatred and that increasingly rely on strategic video communication as well. Central distinguishing criteria in examining the broad range of those movements are thus their attitudes toward democracy, pluralism, equality, science, and human rights (see Chapter 7).

Moreover, progressive and pro-democracy activism itself, despite its important societal role, is not without some internal difficulties and ambivalences. Activism, by definition, is not objective, neutral, or impartial and can reinforce divisions within a society. Activists address or intensify conflicts without being able to assess the consequences for social coexistence. Organizational independence from established parties and institutions together with the associated scarcity of resources often makes long-term and sustainable political engagement difficult and favors shorter-term forms of protest. And while activists are often experts on specific grievances, they might not necessarily consider multifactorial causations. Some NGOs have become powerful intermediaries between governments and corporations (for instance by evaluating emission certificates), thereby undergoing the risk of becoming political lobbyists instead of serving as an independent, corrective voice. At the same time, however, these critical aspects do not change the basic fact that civic activism is an integral and indispensable part of political participation.

It is worth recalling this landscape of media and politics, with all its problems and power imbalances, in order to understand the serious break that the spread of social media marked after the turn of the century. Today, the internet is the most important source of information for people under 50 in many parts of the world.[7] Among the various types of online infrastructure, social media platforms have proven to be an extremely versatile and useful form of communication, particularly for marginalized social groups. On social media, users can easily reach a larger audience, bypass established gatekeepers, and protest openly or anonymously. Moreover, as systems of relationships, social movements are themselves constantly involved in processes of negotiating their own frames and associated values, emotions, and goals (della Porta and Mattoni 2015; Snow et al. 2019). In making use of social media, they are increasingly developing forms of loose, personalized participation that override spatial separation, for example, when content creators on Instagram participated in the "Blackout Tuesday" event in 2020, posting black squares and thereby declaring their solidarity with the Movement for Black Lives.

Social media are thus a crucial prerequisite for certain political frames to spread both within a community or movement and beyond. A new form of *networked activism* has developed on this basis since around 2005. It encompasses many different forms of activity: posting, liking, sharing, and commenting on political content, hashtagging, organizing spontaneous protests, setting up petitions and calls for donations, as well as forms of "hacktivism" or "digital civil disobedience" such as blocking websites through system overload (distributed denial-of-service, DDoS), counter-surveillance (sousveillance), and revealing secrets (whistleblowing) (Sauter 2014). Online activism can significantly influence the dynamics of social struggles with such activities and power (Eskjaer et al. 2015). It can shift, mitigate, accelerate, amplify, or otherwise alter existing conflicts, and it can generate new types of online/offline conflicts such as debates, scandals, callouts, image events, and image wars.

Common Forms and Types of Activist Videos

In the context of social movements and their framing practices, videos and other images circulate on ever-changing social media platforms where they serve as catalysts for political action in various ways:[8] they have an *epistemic* function in spreading knowledge, for example, about social injustices, environmental problems, or specific movements. An *affective* function can be seen in the way they evoke collective emotions such as outrage, moral indignation, or empathy and thus shape political attitudes and behavior. They can have an *appellative* function by directly calling on the viewers to take action, for example, in spontaneous street protests, online petitions, or by making donations. And they can have a *performative* function in that the mere presence of cameras might already prevent police violence, or in that political events are staged with the main goal of creating powerful images. Use of images and visual memes (Shifman 2014; Denisova 2019; Arkenbout et al. 2021), entertaining graphics, photos, image macros, or GIFs has therefore become a decisive means of communication for online activism. Videos, however, are particularly important in this context and achieve on average the highest engagement rates among users.

Video activism is a very diverse phenomenon with a wide variety of practices, forms, and genres. NGOs, grassroots organizations, hashtag movements, artists, social media influencers, and other actors use moving images in different ways (see Chapter 5). For example, eyewitnesses in brutal regimes may try to spread video evidence while protecting those affected and their own lives. Leftist collectives in liberal democratic countries document their protest actions. Environmental NGOs use powerful images to get as many people as possible to act and donate. Influencers who rely on advertising may make sporadic political statements, reaching huge crowds of followers. Individual video creators are active in many more ways, including hybrid practices such as citizen journalism and artivism (Allan 2013; Kara 2015; Kara and Møhring Reestorff 2015; Taylor 2016). Activist videos are often created within a specific community whose subcultural codes, styles, and rituals influence the audiovisual form, either as a deliberate strategy to address the audience or as an implicit part of the social lifeworld. They circulate in a specific "economy of attention" (see Chapters 3 and 4), address mostly fragmented and polarized audiences (see Chapter 6), and are often involved in image conflicts. They compete with and fight against the public relations of parties and politicians, mass media coverage, corporate PR, propaganda, and other forms of political expression (see Chapter 7).

Before social media, activist moving images were screened as 16 mm films or videotapes in community centers by leftist collectives, in court, or on open TV channels, and later they were uploaded as low-resolution digital video embedded in large amounts of text on the internet homepages (see Chapter 2). Since the advent of the social web, activist videos have found new, broader, and more diverse ways and contexts of circulation that often combine online and offline publics and communities (see Chapter 5). At the same time, new media also enable the creation of new forms (see Chapter 3). Video activists constantly adapt and redefine practices of documentation, education, criticism, agitation, self-representation, and empowerment. Recurring types and genres of activist videos that are loosely related to earlier moving images have gradually become discernible. Several authors have attempted to identify the main types of activist videos (Askanius 2013; Mateos and Gaona 2015).[9] We build on their work, but integrate, adapt, and modify their categories in light of more recent developments and according to a combination of three sets of criteria: the communicative function of the videos, their aesthetic and rhetorical form, and their practical contexts of production, dissemination and circulation on specific platforms.[10] Based on these considerations, we distinguish (without claiming to be exhaustive) *five video types* that are currently particularly relevant: witness videos, documentaries, video blogs, mobilization videos, and subversion videos.

Witness videos are camera recordings of unjust acts or human rights violations and serve to provide visible evidence. They are made in the immediate vicinity of an event and reach the public when media amateurs or organized activists upload the videos to their own channels or when they are live-streamed or passed on to journalists or lawyers. As "battle footage" they document the violence of war (like the more than three and a half million videos on syrianarchive.org), of the police (as in the context of Black Lives Matter), or of powerful groups against minorities (supported by NGOs such as WITNESS). In general, such videos are unedited, seem rough, capture the situation and the emotions of the people involved in the incident and those who witness and film it, and thus are meant to be understood as authentic. The proliferation of smartphones with cameras and broadband access along with strongly growing citizen awareness has greatly increased the number of witness videos. Videos that are long enough to have documentary quality and that are also concise and intensive enough to be compatible with current online viewing habits are particularly successful in competing for attention. Their emotional impact may arouse the public and lead to protests. In some cases, they are used as evidence in court (Ristovska 2021). Witness videos may be picked up by mass media if they gain enough attention online and then they are shown, for instance, on television news, before they are swept back into the social media networks in various forms. Such hybrid media flows often make it difficult to locate the original source. For this and other reasons, many witness videos are plagued with problems of verification and manipulation, with conspiracy theories and pseudo-forensic counter-analyses that question their authenticity. They also compete with an increasing number of cheap and deep fakes, as well as voyeuristic videos by mobile bystanders. Therefore, the credibility of witness videos increasingly depends on additional verification through the "authenticity infrastructure" (Gregory 2022), for example, fact-checking initiatives like snopes.com or media NGOs such as Forensic Architecture or WITNESS.

Documentary videos or webdocs usually have a longer and more complex form and typically follow the established conventions of documentary film or television journalism, but can also take on new or hybrid forms, including those of more recent online formats. They provide information about public affairs from political perspectives that are rarely represented in the mass media. The filmmakers can be independent citizen journalists, NGO members, representatives of social movements, or individual video amateurs. Many videos stay close to the patterns of TV reporting such as the reports by the Reel News group in the United Kingdom or Democracy Now! in the United States. Others such as the 2021 video *Putin's Palace* by the Russian vlogger and oppositional politician Alexey Navalny, who died in a labor camp, or the 2015 Chinese environmental documentary *Under the Dome* by citizen journalist Chai Jing (both reached hundreds of millions of views), are closer to documentary films. There are many more forms of online documentaries. Investigative videos like WikiLeak's *Collateral Murder* (2010)[11] create rhetorical arguments out of material provided by whistle blowers or witnesses. Archival videos like *Y'All Better Quiet Down* (LoveTapesCollective 2019), depicting queer of color activist Sylvia Rivera at a rally in 1973, recontextualize older film footage of political movements. Explanatory videos such as *Wealth Inequality in America* (Politizane) from 2012 elucidate politically relevant facts through animated data visualization. Online documentaries generally combine the presentation of facts and evidence with rhetorical argumentation, whereby the spectrum ranges from ostensive matter-of-factness to emotionalized storytelling.

Some videos also assume the form of interactive documentaries (iDocs) or involve virtual or augmented reality, for example, in the context of the democracy movement in Hong Kong since 2014.

Video blogs or vlogs, including influencer and other content creator posts, function mostly as forms of personal political commentary. They can be produced quickly, are usually opinion-oriented, and aim at influencing followers. Structurally and functionally, some resemble private diary entries or op-eds in newspapers. However, online creators turn directly to the camera, address users personally, and engage with them through live streams and comment sections. In many cases, they speak to their audience from their private homes, but at the same time consciously orchestrate the presentation of their bodies and surroundings (e.g., through graphics, props, clothing, lighting). Some content creators only sporadically comment on political issues, others run explicitly political channels such as ContraPoints (2011–present) by the leftist influencer Natalie Wynn in the United States (see Chapter 5). NGOs, but also corporations and authoritarian governments, sometimes collaborate with well-known influencers to tap into wider target groups beyond the more traditional political and mass media audiences.

Mobilization and campaign videos tend to be produced strategically by activist collectives, NGOs, or think tanks and are often embedded in broader online and offline campaigns. They aim at moving viewers to action: to sign petitions, donate money, or participate in a demonstration. To achieve this, mobilization videos are usually short and use dramatic storytelling and rhetoric aimed at evoking collective feelings such as compassion or outrage, quite often also through fictional narratives. Many producers of mobilization videos try to maximize the reach of their political persuasion and make use of professional video production companies and online marketing strategies (an example is the *Most Shocking Second a Day Video*, which will be discussed in Chapter 3). In some cases, videos are produced with considerable budgets and star power, as in the case of *A Homeless Polar Bear in London—Ft. Jude Law and Radiohead* (Greenpeace International 2012). It is not uncommon for mobilization videos to be criticized for a compromised form of strategic communication, as was the case with the viral phenomenon *KONY 2012* (Invisible Children and Russell 2012), whose political utility was widely doubted (Engelhardt and Jansz 2014; Torchin 2016).

Playful *subversion videos* or *guerrilla communication videos* attempt to subvert, mock, or ironize generic mass media material, corporate PR, political propaganda, or social media content from powerful sources. They appropriate, edit, and modify such hegemonic or popular material in playful, satirical, and innovative ways to create surprise, shock, reflection, provocation, or entertainment. Subversion videos include artivist productions, audiovisual memes, and mashups, such as the found-footage remixes by the British music and comedy duo, Cassetteboy

(2006–present), who edit politicians' speeches into pop songs. They are often produced by small collectives that follow strategies of "culture jamming" (Lasn 2000) or "tactical media" (Lovink 2002; Raley 2009). Examples include The Yes Men in the United States and the transnational Peng! Collective operating out of Berlin (see Chapter 5). They often try to reach the public in witty and provocative ways, through satirical forms, parodying conventional modes of representation, and reinterpreting cultural signs. Such forms include imitations of powerful corporations' image videos or state propaganda, as well as videos that make spectacular offline actions available to the net community in audiovisual form. Another variety of such playful approaches has developed on TikTok. There, "memetic political videos" (Kaye et al. 2022, Chapter 4; Zulli and Zulli 2022) come in many varieties. Some clips take up speeches by politicians and satirize them in lip-synching performances. Others create audio memes and pick up trending songs or sound snippets and use them as a basis for political messages. For example, during the uprising of Iranian women in 2022, activists accompanied pictures of the murdered Mahsa Amini with the song *Another Love* by Tom Odell (refrain: "And if somebody hurts you, I wanna fight," sung along passionately by a live audience), which became something of a battle chant of activism from Iran on the platform.

These most striking and widespread types of video often interact with each other and complement each other in their functions, and they are also often found as hybrid forms and combinations. The types mentioned here by no means cover the entire spectrum of activist video work, which is constantly developing new forms and becoming increasingly diverse (see Chapters 3 and 4). This process of change and adaptation is facilitated by the availability of new platforms and apps with new functions and affordances. For example, the rise of TikTok in the late 2010s enabled a novel form of low-threshold, playful, and everyday video activism. More generally, it can be said that the emergence, form, and reach of certain types of videos depend not least on the specific structures, logic, and affordances of different social media in the current platform system.

The System of Social Media Platforms

To understand what considerations are made in the production and design of the various types of videos, how they circulate on social media, how they influence their viewers, and what media conditions they are subject to, it is necessary to take a closer look at the structures of the platform system as a whole and the individual social media that make it up. The concept of "web 2.0" arose around 2005, when media entrepreneurs like Tim O'Reilly used the term to refer to a fundamental change on the internet, which was no longer made up just of static web pages and included more and more tools for social interaction. Online commerce was a driving force from the beginning, and just a few years later a handful of globally operating corporations such as Amazon and Alibaba dominated the internet and provided a broad range of services. Media scholars and social scientists have outlined the global transformation toward a "platform society" (van Dijck et al. 2018)—or "platform capitalism" (Srnicek 2016) and "surveillance capitalism" (Zuboff 2019). In this new system, large technology corporations have restructured major industries of the world economy (from material production to the service and communication sectors) as digital platforms through processes of datafication, commodification, and algorithmic selection. Particularly in the case of social media platforms, this development amounts to an extractivist logic of algorithmic exploitation of user data (Couldry and Mejias 2019). Thus, the characterization of such media as "social" does not, of course, mean that they are aimed at the common good, but that they enable interactions between users, the uploading and streaming of user-generated content, and the formation of networks.

Today, there are two dominant platform ecosystems: the US corporate capitalist system, including Google's YouTube or Meta's Facebook and Instagram, and the Chinese state capitalist system with its own social media such as iQIYI, Youku, Sina Weibo, and WeChat. The Chinese system dominates in China itself, while the US system dominates in most other countries around the world, even if it can take different forms there due to local censorship or the primacy of various US platforms. Some countries are trying to break away from both systems and develop their own—Russia, for example, has its own platforms (such as VK) and is currently trying to set up Rusnet as a separate, state-controlled internet—but these attempts have not yet progressed very far. The Chinese and US platform systems are largely isolated from each other—organizationally, legally, and linguistically. Companies that are active in both systems, despite the associated risks, offer strictly separate services. For example, the Chinese company ByteDance operates the twin video platforms Douyin (in China) and TikTok (abroad). In this book, we focus on the various US platforms and TikTok because they prevail in most countries (without ignoring the importance of other systems and region-specific constellations, see Chapter 7).

Evidently, the development of social media has had a lasting impact on the way people communicate with each other and organize their knowledge, emotions, relationships, and ways of life, including the way they conduct politics. Robert Kozinets has summarized this transformation in several principles of "networked individualism" (Kozinets 2020, 122–23, following Rainie and Wellman 2012). Accordingly, networked individuals are increasingly becoming partial members of dispersed and diverse networks and rely less on intimate and enduring connections with close partners. The internet contains some of their most important social contacts and enables them to reach out to an extended audience. The boundaries between communication and action, between the public and the private are blurring. In this context, social scientists have also identified a new "logic of *connective action*" through flexible self-organization, which complements the older "logic of collective action" in long-lasting organizations (Bennett and Segerberg 2013, emphasis added).[12] The constitution and organization of social interest groups, as well as networking among them, now occurs less in fixed, localized, and lasting structures, and more in dynamic and diverse ways, independent of location, and thus is also less organized and possibly less enduring. Some social scientists and media scholars emphasize the potential for democratizing communication, others the risk of fragmented and polarized publics as well as weakened institutions and alliances.[13] There is agreement that the influence of web-based media is still growing significantly and having an impact on the mass media system (press, radio, cinema, television). This development has led to a "hybrid media system," in which, for example, mass media pick up on internet trends, use witness videos in news reporting, or produce specific content for their own social media channels, while online media circulate mass media content, imitate television formats, or cooperate with journalistic institutions (Chadwick 2013).

In this hybrid media system, online video has emerged as a medium in its own right, alongside other media such as television or the press, from which it is distinguished by its specific constellation of technologies, forms, organizations, and practices of production, distribution, and interaction. This historically new medium creates and circulates an enormous amount of moving images, far more than cinema or television (whose material it greedily soaks up). Every few minutes, about as much audiovisual material is uploaded to YouTube as Hollywood cinema produces in a year. The technical basis for this is given by the expansion of broadband internet access, unified coding standards (MP4, etc.), widespread use of smartphones with high-resolution screens and megapixel cameras for video (e.g., Nokia N90 introduced in 2005, iPhone from 2007 on), video sharing platforms (especially YouTube, beginning in 2005), networking services (Facebook, including video since 2007), live stream functions (e.g., Facebook Live since 2015), and editing software and its embedment in apps, for instance messaging services. Social media create many new possibilities to produce and distribute videos easily, quickly, and cheaply—individually or collectively, but in any case largely free from established production norms and gatekeepers such as television stations or film funding agencies. This is a decisive factor behind the enormous variety of professional and non-professional, user-generated or user-collected and edited videos, which are usually available worldwide and free of charge. As distribution is mostly done through commercial social media, these intermediaries have become the new gatekeepers (Gillespie 2018). This development only hints at one of many problems that come with the new platform system (see below).

The *reception of videos on social media* (or social videos) differs from other audiovisual media such as cinema in that one usually watches videos incidentally, choosing from an endless flow of short image-text constellations on a small mobile screen. A major difference is also that the individual videos are embedded in human-computer interfaces (HCI), multimodal websites or apps with additional information, algorithmically generated video recommendations, autoplay functions, comment threads, advertising banners, pop-up advertising, and various possibilities for interaction. Videos can be collected in channels and playlists, liked, commented on, shared with others, streamed across diverse platforms, and picked up by mass media. Because of their small-scale formats and their short lifespans, the reception of social videos may seem less intense than cinema and television, but the variety and sheer amount of content as well as the possibilities of interactive participation turn the videos into significant elements of interpersonal communication. When viewers watch, like, share, or comment on videos, these images are transformed into personal and collective means to struggle for attention and recognition, connect with friends and followers, and build individual or collective identities and social groups. All this intensifies the emotional involvement, for example, in the form of social emotions such as the fear of missing out (FOMO), the feeling of success at being the first to "discover" a funny video, or shame at having shared a questionable video with one's friends. Circulation of videos on social media thus involves a complex interaction between the dynamics of technical networks and psychological group dynamics, between platform algorithms and tendencies in the users' behavior that they are often not even aware of (see Chapter 4).

Social video content creation is increasingly planned and optimized for the functions and algorithms of specific platforms, and even videos that are based on more traditional film or television genres are adapted to suit them (for instance, by tagging videos and tying them into social media campaigns). The presence and reach of videos depend strongly on the structures, algorithms, and moderation of platforms, which lack transparency and can change quickly. Screen interface design also affects the use of videos. Placement of the video player, advertising, and comments, as well as autoplay features and add-ons, direct users' attention. User interfaces provide some possibilities for interaction and leave out others—YouTube currently provides a "thumbs down" button, while Facebook does not. While YouTube's algorithm recommends additional content on the sidebar and offers an autoplay switch, TikTok runs those videos automatically on the user's "For You" page.

It is thus important to note that videos circulate on different, specialized, constantly evolving platforms that reach all kinds of audiences—the still widespread idea of "YouTube videos" viewed only by young people has long been proven to be fundamentally wrong. The functions, interfaces, and standards of these services, their algorithms and protocols, their handling of data and metadata, rules, and modes of regulation differ considerably from one another. A brief comparison of the currently most important social media platforms shows that they provide very different frameworks for content creators and are suited for different forms of videos. Of course, these may then also circulate on other platforms.[14]

The video-sharing platform YouTube, currently the second-most visited website overall, belongs to Google, which in turn is part of the large US corporation Alphabet. It is often used like a video search engine or archive because it offers an effective search function and organizes its videos into categories, channels, overviews, recommendation lists, and stories. YouTube channels with high subscription numbers can earn a small share of advertising revenue. Many regular YouTubers also link their videos to social donation services like Patreon. Preview images (thumbnails) focus attention and invite users to watch the videos, which the player presents in the horizontal widescreen format (16:9) common for movies and TV shows. YouTube provides for live streams as well as the upload of long videos. The average viewing time per video is longer than on other platforms, but interaction rates tend to be lower, although YouTube provides various possibilities for exchange. With YouTube Shorts (since 2021), the platform has responded to competitive pressure from TikTok and offers its own short, vertical video format (content can be up to 60 seconds long), while its unique feature as a comparably more static archive for longer videos remains intact. (The Chinese video-sharing platforms iQIYI and Youku operate in a way similar to YouTube in many respects, but are much more heavily monitored and censored by the state.)

Compared to YouTube, videos on the major social networks Facebook and Instagram, both of which belong to the giant US corporation Meta, appear primarily as part of a user's ongoing newsfeed. As a result, they are more difficult to search and find and seem more personal. Since 2018, the Facebook newsfeed privileges posts by individual "friends" over messages from "groups" (including political ones), whose visibility is reduced as a result. Facebook's algorithms favor videos uploaded directly to it over video links from competing platforms such as YouTube. Since videos are often watched on the go, on smartphones and muted, they are regularly subtitled or intertitled. And since the videos and available live streams are only watched briefly by many users, they are often designed as thumb stoppers by placing eyecatchers right at the beginning to keep viewers from scrolling further in their feed.

Compared to Facebook, typical Instagram videos tend to be more snapshot-like, casual, humorous, or situated in the context of the user's profile. However, on

IGTV (since 2018), Instagram also allows video uploads of up to one hour in length. The platform has introduced additional formats such as Reels, (Vertical) Stories, or Co-Watching, which take functions from competitors such as TikTok and Snapchat. Since Instagram and Facebook as well as the instant messaging service WhatsApp and the social networking platform Threads all belong to the Meta corporation, users can benefit from synergy effects—as does the company from exploiting their data (similar cross-connections also exist between competing platforms).

The short-form video hosting service TikTok, part of the Chinese corporation ByteDance, has been the fastest-growing social network since 2018 and was the most often downloaded app worldwide in 2020 (Koetsier 2021). TikTok originally started as a place to upload lip-synced music clips, dance challenges, and duets with other users. However, the platform is also used for activism, especially by younger users of the so-called Gen Z demographic (Literat and Kligler-Vilenchik 2023). Political protest is sometimes spread openly, but often also as a kind of smuggled goods, when for example criticism of Chinese re-education camps is found embedded in a makeup tutorial (Kuo 2019). Due to their reach and popularity, TikTok videos have played a crucial role in witnessing events during the Iran uprising since 2022 as well as the Russian war against Ukraine (see Chapter 7). However, many TikTok creators, including disabled and LGBTQIA+ activists, complain about the platform's shadow-banning practice (Reuter and Köver 2019) and, supposedly, the automated deletion of videos containing trigger words (such as "gay," "transsexual," or "government in exile") in the written overlays (Reuter and Köver 2019; Bösch and Köver 2021; Walsh 2022). Moreover, a spectacular conflict over cybersecurity between China and the United States in 2020 flared up again in 2023 when the US Congress debated a ban on TikTok (Clayton 2023).

Many videos are also disseminated, linked, and commented on via microblogging services, especially X/Twitter. Although initially for short text messages, X is now heavily used for distributing images and videos, also through links to other platforms, and X's own in-app live function allows for producing and streaming videos. The platform is particularly important in political contexts, since many journalists, politicians, NGOs, grassroots activists, and other opinion leaders use the service to disseminate their messages, thus often launching public debates in the mass media, as well as addressing, criticizing, or provoking decision-makers. However, propaganda, misinformation, and racist agitation have significantly increased on X since the takeover by billionaire Elon Musk in 2022 and the expulsion of many employees who were responsible, among other things, for moderating content (Benjamin 2022). The app fell into a credibility crisis and many users, including journalists, canceled their accounts and switched to other services like Mastodon. Musk's takeover and rebranding of Twitter is a particularly spectacular example of the unprecedented economic and political power to remodel entire communication networks for hundreds of millions of users according to personal interests.

Messaging services such as WhatsApp, Telegram, Snapchat, Signal, Line, Kakao Talk, and WeChat are also used to distribute political videos. A relevant difference to the previously mentioned platforms is that most messengers are encrypted and less public; they mainly allow private communication between individuals or semi-public communication within groups of registered users. However, many of these groups are now de facto open and some are enormous. Telegram has become an important platform for activists because so far it has largely escaped the grasp of authoritarian states like Russia or Iran (see Chapter 7). However, anti-democratic movements are also very present in messaging services. The success of right-wing extremist Jair Bolsonaro in the 2018 Brazilian presidential election was due in part to a flood of propaganda videos on WhatsApp (Herrmann 2018). Messaging services were also used intensively in various countries by right-wing extremists and COVID-19 deniers, particularly after they were banned from other video platforms. Messenger apps are also increasingly being monitored by authoritarian and democratic governments. Some are banned because they spread hate and ignore laws, others because they are used by terrorists—or government critics. In 2023, India blocked 14 services at once, including Briar, which the company said was particularly relevant for activists and journalists (Verma 2023).

In addition to messenger apps, a growing number of other services are also used politically. Amazon's gaming and live-streaming platform Twitch is a gathering place for political commentary and is also significantly used for right-wing agitation. Both right-wing and left-wing activist networks access the communication platform Discord for organizational purposes. Social news aggregators such as Reddit with more open and flexible structures are popular for activist and community organizing and informal group discussion (Forestal 2023), and some left-wing activists collect and share their videos on subreddits such as BreadTube. Videos are also uploaded to the many closed online groups, unmoderated image boards, and shock sites with videos that are blocked on other platforms, including innumerable gore videos, antisemitic messages, and conspiracy narratives (Malkowski 2017). Platforms such as Truth Social (founded by Trump Media after Donald Trump's ban from X/Twitter in 2021) and Parler, which bill themselves as supporting free speech but in fact spread vast amounts of propaganda and hate speech, are popular among Trump supporters and other political actors of the far right.

Since commercial platforms pose many problems (such as ubiquitous data capture and surveillance, removing videos and blocking channels without notice, not deleting violent content, harboring extremists, etc.) or simply as part of their political self-understanding, some video activists prefer to use their own websites or alternative non-commercial services additionally or exclusively. A veteran independent portal is Indymedia (Kidd 2021), which has been supplying the global left with video uploads since 2004. Since 2019, the streaming platform means.tv has been trying to establish itself as a leftist, anti-capitalist video-on-demand provider. However, none of these activist websites offer the reach, the interactive affordances, and the network effects of the large, commercial social platforms, and they are also frequently the target of state surveillance measures.

The overall picture is that apart from China, Russia, and other authoritarian-ruled countries, the current system of social media is still globally dominated by five major platforms: TikTok, Instagram, YouTube, Facebook, and X. These large commercial platforms are particularly relevant for political discourse and video activism because of their user numbers and engagement rates. However, they are used in different ways and in different constellations with each other and with other services in various areas of the world. For example, TikTok is currently banned in India, Facebook in Uganda; Instagram is more influential in some countries, YouTube in others. Other services such as Telegram, which is more likely to be beyond the reach of the state, can be more important than the major platforms in certain regions or conflicts (see Chapter 7). In specific contexts, a variety of smaller platforms are also relevant for video activists.

All these platforms, with their constantly changing features, differ in their individual logic and basic affordances, some of which are comparable to well-known functions of older media (Facebook as address book and event calendar, Instagram as photo album, YouTube as video library). Some focus on sharing videos, others on networking or messaging. Some are searchable, others are not. Some are predominantly public, others are based on private groups with limited access. Some are regulated relatively strictly, others hardly at all. Some platforms allow longer videos, others only short ones. Some prefer the horizontal cinema format, others the vertical or square format. Some suggest watching videos with sound, others without. The platforms differ in terms of ownership, business models, interfaces, functionality, and algorithms. They form different social networks and are involved in different political conflicts. Moreover, all these platforms interact with each other and with the mass media in complex forms of exchange and competition.

Thus, it would be important to consider the complexity of this overall system in future studies on video activism, as difficult as that may be. For a long time, many researchers have spoken of "the social media" in sweeping terms or narrowed their focus to individual platforms and generalized assessments limited to them. Our depiction of social media, however provisional and incomplete, therefore points to the need to look critically at both the specific and the overarching logic behind the individual platforms and the platform system as a whole. This includes the diverse and creative ways in which activists deal with the complex logic of the platforms. While many activists have considerable difficulty navigating the system, others are becoming increasingly aware of the various ways in which platforms operate and are learning which one to use for what purpose and how to reach specific audiences (see Chapter 5). With each change in the system, content creators adapt their tactics and invent new practices (such as the use of "algospeak," i.e., circumventing censored keywords with codes or varied punctuation). One key challenge here is the time as well as the human and financial resources required to do this. Another challenge consists of the many problems for society that social media brings forth alongside their possibilities.

The Platform System in the Age of the Splinternet

The challenges of using social media are entangled with broader, structural problems of the current platform system caused by governments and corporations alike. It is important to be aware of these challenges to understand the terrain on which video activists operate and videos circulate. Some are of a material nature but raise ethical questions, for instance concerning social and climate justice. One problem is that the production and streaming of internet videos cause about as much CO_2 emissions as a medium-sized industrial country, as organizations like The Shift Project have estimated (The Shift Project 2019).[15] Another aspect concerns the exploitative working conditions in hardware factories or coltan, cobalt, and other mines, mostly in developing countries of the Global South. Further problems include limited access to networked media and the considerable digital divide that disadvantages rural areas and regions in the southern hemisphere. The latter point also serves as a reminder that Tim Berners-Lee's very notion of the "world wide web"—once associated with the media utopia of the "global village" (McLuhan 1962, 31), the connection of people all over the world, and the free flow of ideas—has never been fully reached.

Possibly even more serious for many video activists is a complex of problems that are currently becoming increasingly drastic. The world wide web seems to be deteriorating into a "splinternet" (Searls 2008), driven by antagonistic forces and broken down into geopolitical zones with national or supranational borders, sustained by geoblocking and censorship, for example, by China's "Great Firewall" or Russia's Independent Internet Law. The tendency to fragment the internet is driven in particular by autocratic governments. Domestically, they seek to gain control over their populations' communication and impede oppositional activism through censorship and surveillance measures, tightened laws, and repressive law enforcement. Externally they pursue targeted disinformation and cyberattacks. As mentioned,

China has built its own tightly monitored and censored social media system behind the Great Firewall, with platforms such as Youku (the equivalent of YouTube), Sina Weibo (the equivalent of X/Twitter), or WeChat (which bundles more features than any Western platform). Russia operates disinformation channels on social media outside the country, while, at home, the media monitoring agency Roskomnadzor and other institutions ban US-based services like Facebook and Instagram and block sites critical of the Kremlin. They chase, arrest, torture, and imprison activists and delete activist videos like those of opposition leader Alexei Navalny and his team, who face severe penalties because of their work (Gritsenko et al. 2021). Navalny died under unclear circumstances in a Siberian prison in February 2024.

The Belarusian resistance movement against the Lukashenko dictatorship and independent video news sources such as Nexta or ePramova operate from abroad because vloggers and other oppositional activists are rigorously persecuted in the country. And similar problems apply to video activists from Russia and Turkey. In orthodox Islamic countries and regions, religious leaders are trying to regulate the use of social media through fatwas. Saudi Arabia penalizes vloggers who post videos critical of the regime with draconian corporal punishment. In Iran, internet surveillance, blockages, and threats to shut down TikTok accompanied the violent repression of the feminist protest movement which spontaneously formed in 2022. Myanmar and other countries use technological means such as limitation of software and hardware functions as well as internet slowdowns or temporary shutdowns.

Authorities drastically intervene in internet communication in several democratic countries, as well. India, Pakistan, and Indonesia have banned TikTok for hosting illicit content, while Nigeria blocked X and in Burundi, Guinea, Tanzania, and Togo internet shutdowns and blackouts at times of elections or protests have been observed. Altogether, the organizations Access Now and #KeepItOn registered at least 155 shutdowns in 29 countries in 2020 (AccessNow and #KeepItOn 2020). Government interventions that diminish internet freedom take place even in liberal democracies in the Global Northwest. In 2018, for example, the United States repealed net neutrality, one of the fundamental principles of the internet, which guaranteed the equal handling of all online traffic. Network providers are now allowed to give preferential treatment to certain (commercial) websites or services, throttle access to others, or even block them altogether and have service providers or users pay for fast lanes.

But governments are only one of the forces that restrict the free flow of information and cause fragmentation and polarization on the internet. The corporations behind social media services are themselves powerful actors who heavily influence the way billions of people communicate and push the fragmentation and polarization of online communication through both direct and indirect measures.

Platforms intervene directly in users' video communication through algorithms and content moderators who select, often in a problematic way, what becomes publicly visible and what passes unseen, as, for instance, the documentary *The Cleaners* (Block and Riesewieck 2018) shows.[16] Platforms may delete profiles and remove videos at any time. Such measures may seem justified and necessary in view of the plethora of videos spreading lies, proliferating hate speech, and depicting gross violence or terror. But platform censorship does not only affect such cases. In 2017, for instance, YouTube deleted tens of thousands of videos by Syrian citizens that were used by video activists as central sources to document human rights violations (Browne 2017). Another example concerns racist attacks on TikTok. When content creators respond to these attacks, the system tends to remove anti-racist callouts, ignoring the decisive difference between offence and defense, hate speech and counterspeech (Contreras and Martinez 2021). Deleting videos, accounts, and groups can also backfire and contribute to fragmenting the networked public sphere further, for instance when Trump supporters attempted to take over the social network Parler in 2020 and one year later founded their own, ideologically more homogeneous service, Truth Social.

Openly removing or censoring content and creators is, however, only one course of action. Machine learning systems and content moderators constantly filter and sort posts in various ways and apply more subtle and discreet mechanisms. As mentioned above, investigative journalists used leaked documents to reconstruct how TikTok shadow-banned pro-democracy protest videos from Hong Kong and content by LGBTIAQ+ and disabled creators (Hern 2019). According to this research, high-reach videos go through several reviewing levels based on company policies and national laws. With this pre-sorting, algorithms push certain videos in the feed or hide them and make them difficult or impossible to find when searching the app. In such cases, content creators can still see the videos they posted and are thus unaware that they are effectively banned.

In addition to these direct interventions, platforms have indirect but equally problematic effects on the work of video activists and online communication in general. These effects result from the very structures and operational modes of social media and again further fragmentation and polarization on the web. They are consequences of the basic business models of the corporations. According to Nick Srnicek (2016), the primary economic function of social media is to serve as "advertising platforms" that at the same time allow themselves and their partners to extract vast amounts of user data and sell it to other companies. To achieve the highest possible advertising rates and syphon off as much data as possible, they provide incentives for long periods of use and foster the emergence of "automated" or "calculated" publics (Gillespie 2018, see Chapter 6; Pasquale 2018). They encourage addictive behavior, for example, through clickbait, pop-ups, autoplay video functions, or an unending series of cross-references, as, for instance, Jeff Orlowski's documentary *The Social Dilemma* (2020) demonstrates. Another feature to ensure continuous user engagement is to micro-target users, feed them individually selected and customized content, and connect them only to like-minded users and communities—a process which has contributed to the creation of "filter bubbles" (Pariser 2011) or "echo chambers" and a distorted perception of political issues (Sunstein 2001).

However, these bubbles and chambers are not completely separate but rather conflict with each other at times. Platform algorithms favor sensationalist and opinionated messages that elicit more involvement and feedback. When users share and comment on videos, they can easily trigger cascades of emotions—waves of empathy and solidarity, but also of outrage or hate. These waves provoke "filter clashes" (Pörksen 2018, 116) both in the wide-open space of the web and on individual profiles and channels or in peer groups. This is all the more true for political videos that take up controversial topics. Combined with psychological "online disinhibition effects" (Suler 2004), they have in countless cases helped spread dis- and misinformation and fuel hatred of marginalized social groups or people with dissenting opinions. Algorithms generate recommendations that amplify these tendencies. Anyone who clicks on a right-wing extremist video on YouTube is drawn into the proverbial "rabbit hole" and encounters an entire ecosystem of far-right content. YouTube has therefore repeatedly been criticized as a "great radicalizer" (Tufekci 2018). Similar accusations could be brought against other platforms equally well (Kaiser and Rauchfleisch 2018; Ribeiro et al. 2020).

Problems also arise on platforms through artificial intelligence tools or, to be more precise, systems of "algorithmically controlled, automated decision making (ADM)" (Alfter et al. 2019, 9). ADM or AI systems have been integrated into platforms and smartphones quickly and seemingly casually in the past few years. Cameras are coupled with automatic image processing and facial recognition, and easy-to-use software makes it easier to manipulate or generate texts, sounds, and images. Thus, increasingly sophisticated deep fakes have led to an escalation of disinformation tactics, and civil society initiatives have therefore developed their own tools for recognizing deep fakes and offer recommendations for the responsible use of AI (see Chapter 7). However, AI-supported deep fake videos are not the biggest problem for the public and video activism in social media. Cheap fakes, such as videos taken out of context with lying captions, are proving to be easier and just as effective (and have been used in the wars in Ukraine and Gaza, for example). Furthermore, AI is by no means only used for video fakes, but also for algorithmic forms of influence. As a study by the US think tank Freedom House shows, authoritarian and some democratic governments also use AI tools from opaque contract service providers to automatically censor critical content and influence public opinion (Funk et al. 2023).

At the same time, AI disinformation and censorship, filter clashes, disinhibition, and rabbit hole effects also point to the heterogeneous and unpredictable reactions to political videos distributed through social media. Such heterogeneity is partly due to viewers' individual dispositions since videos generate reactions depending on the viewers' identities, self-images, and values. The comment sections on social media bear witness to this. A striking example of the polarized and ambivalent reactions to activist moving images is the WikiLeaks video *Collateral Murder* (WikiLeaks 2010/People Over Politics 2012).[17] Its original footage was leaked by Chelsea Manning and later edited by Julian Assange (both of whom were and are subject to severe state repression). The almost 18-minute-long video shows US combat helicopters gunning down a group of Iraqi civilians and two Reuters journalists in 2007. Leaking the material was supposed to provide clear evidence of a war crime. On YouTube, however, among the tens of thousands of comments listed under the original video were not only ones that conveyed disapproval and horror about the human rights violations but also comments expressing pride in the power of the US Army, fear of retribution, or aesthetic fascination (Eder 2018). The effects of online videos are difficult to determine empirically due to the complexity of political conflicts, psychological dispositions, and social media structures. They result from the dynamic interplay of video structures (the audiovisual text), user dispositions, and media-related and political contexts. Unwanted effects often occur. Videos may lead to voyeurism, insecurity, fatalism, or clicktivism (pseudo-activism aimed solely at high click and view numbers) instead of political action, or they may involve greater risks and ethical problems. In some cases, the videos exploit the people they depict, who then are forced to live with dangerous or defamatory images of themselves. They may be threatened and persecuted by right-wing trolls or made identifiable as protesters and thus exposed to state repression (Mehrabov 2016; Tufekci 2017, 223–60). To some extent, it is simply a given that posting audiovisual content has unpredictable effects, but the mechanisms of social media mean that political videos contribute significantly to further polarization on the internet and beyond.

Being able to counter such ambiguity and predict political influence and success has, in turn, become an attractive market proposition for financially potent stakeholders. As a study conducted by the Tactical Technology Collective has demonstrated, a growing "influence industry" promotes itself with the promise of being able to measure the data streams of clicks, likes, shares, followers, and conversion rates (the ratio of clicks to follow-up actions) precisely and to use them to determine the political influence on users (Hankey 2018). But such data ultimately remains shaky and unreliable. Viral audiovisual content very often circulates in numerous versions under various names at different times across several platforms, each of which represents only part of its total data and makes it impossible to verify. Moreover, the same video can reach various audiences and have very different effects. For instance, a witness video might first reach a lawyer at an NGO, be reworked by the organization's social media team and disseminated as a call for protest, then be picked up by a major media agency, and in the end stir the emotions of a large, heterogenous TV audience. At the same time, it can provoke a strong backlash from the perpetrators of the documented violence. This interplay of videos with their diverse social and media contexts generates political effects in a variety of ways, both among individuals and the public (see Chapters 3 and 4).

In addition to prognostics, other branches of the influence industry prefer a more proactive approach. Platform providers invite professional content creators, companies, and their marketing agencies to pay them for extended reach or allow external click farms and follower factories to push their preferred content to the foreground. Buying views, likes, and followers is easy and rather cheap; some companies charge only fractions of a cent for them (Lindquist 2019). Such business practices make it even more difficult for average users or video activists with ethical concerns, with no or small budgets, to gain attention for their issues (see Chapters 3 and 5). Moreover, such structural imbalances increase online fragmentation and affect the very foundations of public discourse. Follower factories and similar entities also contribute to the exploitation of click workers in the Global South who play a substantial role as buyable users and, for example, accounted for large numbers of clicks and likes in Trump's first presidential campaign in 2016 (Casilli 2016).

Another way of simulating influence and impact on platforms, misleading the public, and distorting its discourses is by creating fake NGOs—or more precisely government, party, and business-organized NGOs. These GONGOs, PANGOs, and BINGOs may have funny names, but their deceptive maneuvers need to be taken seriously both by platforms and the general public (Götz 2008). They employ greenwashing (misleading environmental marketing), astroturfing (imitation of grassroots movements), and sock puppeting (fake accounts), aiming to influence public opinion, spread disbelief of scientifically proven facts, or paralyze rational thinking with a flood of untruths and nonsense. Platforms have so far ignored these problems and benefited from the enhanced polarization that these videos and practices have caused.

The problems summarized here are not all caused directly by the social media companies themselves. However, the firms do carry a great deal of responsibility and the question of what to do in response arises. In view of increasing criticism of platform inaction in the face of growing online hate speech, dis- and misinformation, network providers have, albeit insufficiently, developed their own monitoring and flagging systems. But concerns over collateral damage through unjustified blockage of important information remains, as does that of a fundamental impairment of freedom of expression through opaque platform guidelines and censorship practices (see Chapter 7). As shown among other things by the storming of national parliaments by right-wing extremists in the United States in 2021 and Brazil in 2023, which was fueled on Facebook, Instagram, and other platforms, social media have become and continue to be a threat to democracy.

A first response to that threat would lie in a complete redefinition of content moderation, which requires much more and better-trained staff (the opposite is currently the case) as well as sufficient company guidelines and a clear legal framework. With Zuboff (2019) and others, however, one might also argue that social platforms do not fulfill their responsibility as long as they rely on the "surveillance dividend," the exploitation of as much user data as possible. On the one hand, turning away from this extractivist principle would mean a break with the platform system's business model. On the other hand, competitors have long relied on other models based on, for instance, subscription or micro payment systems. Moreover, the growing economic, social, and political influence of the "Big Five" in the United States—Alphabet (including Google and YouTube), Amazon (including Twitch), Apple, Meta (with Facebook, Instagram, and WhatsApp), and Microsoft—has led to new legislation (e.g., the EU Digital Services Act or the British Online Safety Bill), intensified discussion about regulating them (e.g., in relation to Section 230 of the US Communications Decency Act) or breaking them up entirely.

But considering the unreliability of platform providers and the ambivalent role of governments, civil society actors as a third party remain indispensable in the fight against hate speech and false information. Fact-checking initiatives such as factcheck.org and their international equivalents, human rights NGOs such as Amnesty International, as well as investigative networks and activist research collectives like Bellingcat, Forensic Architecture, and Syrian Archive all attempt in different ways to counter the spread of misinformation and the cover-up of human rights violations (Weizman 2017; Gray 2019). Fact-checking channels are also on TikTok, where they aim at educating young people and provide tools for recognizing fake news (e.g., the "Digitaler Kompass" project in Austria; @bait.faktencheck n.d.). Overall, these projects illustrate the significance of an ethical stance and continuous self-examination for video activism and civil society action, and finally of a well-thought-out use of the different video forms and strategies to reach specific user groups (see Chapter 7).

Given the multiple problems caused by governments and platform corporations, the current social media system appears to be at best a highly ambivalent terrain for video activism. While the social web initially promised enormous reach and impact, the increasing fragmentation and polarization of the internet and its tendency toward the splinternet have proven to be severe limitations to this potential. Video activists therefore must develop specific strategies and tactics on different levels to gain visibility. However, there are still many cases in which video activists succeed, at least in part, in using platform algorithms in their favor or even outsmarting them and subverting the logic of surveillance capitalism.

How to Outsmart Platforms: The Most Boring Viral Video

The Spanish-Catalonian campaign video *The Most Boring Viral Video* (Arrels fundació 2015) may be viewed as an exceptional attempt (Figure 1.1). It is several years old and has been deleted from the internet, but it keeps reappearing on individual platforms and may serve here as a shrewd example of how social activism can both use and subvert platform affordances (but also of what problems remain unsolved in the process). A hybrid of the types of mobilization and subversion video described above, it was produced and designed for disseminating on YouTube and reflects, remediates, and criticizes the specific logic of this platform. In less than two minutes, the video exposes YouTube's fundamental commercial principle and outwits it at the same time. For a campaign against homelessness, the Catalonian relief organization Arrels fundació—working with a film production company and an established advertising agency—applied a guerrilla-style communication tactic for a Robin Hood kind of action.

The video was tagged with commercially promising, positively connoted tags such as "money," "home," or "luxury" to trick YouTube's search algorithms and

FIGURE 1.1: *The Most Boring Viral Video*, Spain 2015, The Cyranos/McCann and Arrels fundació.

thus attract ads from big advertisers, who then automatically pay money to the charity every time the video is viewed. The spot thus set up a false front of feelgood factors that attracted the advertisers in order to syphon off their money and pass it on through the charity organization to the homeless on Barcelona's streets. At the same time, the video openly showed the trick involved and thus presented itself as a lesson in the techniques of resistance against the profit-driven social media that turn the users' attention into a commodity.

The Most Boring Viral Video emphasizes its David vs. Goliath approach and its criticism of consumerism through its ostentatiously "cheap" aesthetics: a piece of cloth hung up in front of a derelict house served as a green screen behind an on-screen narrator who guided the viewers through the video. A clap of the hands was used instead of an electronic clapperboard. Generic images and video clips fished from the net filled the background, with retro typefaces and graphics that looked like they were from the early days of YouTube. The narrator addressed the audience directly, using clear and simple words and gestures, and referred to the website and its contents. For example, he pointed out an embedded real estate ad by Bankia, one of the main players during the 2010s Spanish financial crisis, which led to a rise in the rate of homelessness. What was shown in the background wittily illustrated the commentator's explanations of the logic of money flows on the internet. The message was that it takes very little to trick the techno-capitalist apparatus: cute cat pictures, the right keywords, and the simple request to stay tuned in, combined with the title's paradoxical promise of presenting something extremely boring. The lure was the fun of subversion, combined with the awareness of doing good without having to do or pay anything for it. Without any effort, one gained access to a group of sophisticated, media-savvy users and could enjoy how the seemingly invincible platform capitalism is milked in its sleep.

According to reports, the video was quickly viewed up to 800,000 times, but this cannot be verified, since YouTube blocked it due to copyright violations and forced the producers to make corrections. However, the subversive media strategy also worked in a later, tamed version (which nevertheless has been removed from the internet as well). The video's wide reach was also due in part to its many awards from the advertising industry which, however, raises the question of whether this was not primarily a PR coup for the advertising agency and a case of clicktivism. In 2015, content creators on YouTube were paid around 1.60 euros per thousand viewings. Thus, the revenue from the video with its 800,000 viewings can be calculated at a mere 1,280 euros, hardly a notable amount for a charity helping the homeless in Catalonia.[18] Still, the video was able to draw public attention to the aid organization, the problem of homelessness, and the way commercial platforms work.

Considering the political frames and audiovisual forms as well as the platform structures in which they are embedded, it becomes evident that the communication revolution set off by social media has highly ambivalent effects on video activism. It empowers and disempowers activists and other users at the same time. On the one hand, video activists can quickly and easily build networks, counter and replace dominant political frames, develop new forms and strategies, and constitute publics and counterpublics. On the other hand, they are confronted with a growing plethora of misinformation, hate speech, and violence. And they become the target of global extractivist corporations that exploit their data, cooperate with governments against user interests, and massively influence and distort public discourses. For some time now, media theorists have been speaking of a new kind of "network power" that appears to be more horizontal, more open, and more inclusive, but at the same time leads to a significant loss of control for users (Galloway and Thacker 2007). Video activists are entangled in this highly complex and ambivalent system and its elusive logic as soon as they use social media (see Chapter 5). However, activists, educators, and filmmakers can also draw attention to the problems of this system in their videos. Moreover, some create videos and tools that demonstrate how one can adapt to the platform logic in order to ultimately subvert, problematize, and challenge them.

2

Trajectories of Video Activism: Past and Present

Activist videos in social media are a relatively recent phenomenon, but at the same time they are part of a longer history of political film and video work. They have emerged from the goals, strategies, and forms of various predecessors and in many respects refer back to them (Askanius 2012; Robé 2017; Ristovska 2021). A review of this history not only makes its continuities visible but also highlights what is new about video activism in social media. Furthermore, the historical perspective helps to bring to light valuable but largely forgotten bodies of knowledge and practices that could inspire current and future generations of video activists.

Contemporary forms of video activism draw on a wide range of historical precursors such as political documentaries, television journalism, agitprop, guerrilla communication, performance art and happenings, music videos, and even PR and advertising. The diversity of these roots also points to widespread conflicts of aims within political filmmaking. Political films and videos often simultaneously aim to credibly represent their concerns, educate or persuade their audiences, find answers to ethical challenges, and develop an aesthetics of resistance. The divergent intentions of educating, persuading, and creating art each suggest different strategies for film and video work. In terms of their political stance, most of the earlier film and video movements can be categorized as left-wing or progressive, and most currents of contemporary video activism are directly or indirectly linked to this tradition. They include utopian concepts of alternative communication, share an awareness of the limits of one's own power vis-à-vis the dominant social order and the interests of capital, but also a strong belief in the mobilizing power of moving images in the struggle for social change. Such concerns of collectivity and the forming of "counterpublics" (Negt and Kluge 1993) are often linked to certain aesthetic principles, favoring non-mainstream aesthetics that represent and communicate alternative views and ways of life.

These kinds of aesthetic standpoints generally involve ethical positions as well, aiming at a responsible use of images and sounds, at protecting the filmmakers and the individuals filmed from repression, and at assuring the credibility of sources and the verifiability of what the videos show and state. Crucial to this are considerations of the voice and the agency of those involved, both in front of and behind the camera. This refers to questions of who speaks, of whose views and experiences are expressed in the film, and of how the people represented in the film are involved in making it. Issues of representation, truth, perspective, ethics, and aesthetics are closely interwoven in these debates about political film practice.

Addressing such ethical and aesthetic questions has become even more difficult today due to the immensely growing number of activist videos and the much easier ways to create and distribute them on "attention capitalist" platforms (Citton 2017). The wide reach of social videos facilitates having effects or political impact on larger audiences (see Chapter 3). But what are the consequences when the various audiences of activist videos have less direct and personal contact with each other (compared to films at festivals or rallies) when they communicate primarily via social media and smartphone screens? What is the relationship between online and offline publics, between "tweets and the streets" (Gerbaudo 2012)? What new aesthetic and ethical challenges arise when videos have to compete for attention on social media platforms and are subject to their algorithmic logic? And what conclusions do activists draw from the fact that their opponents can also easily access their videos and that the public sphere they constitute is thus not a protected space? In this book, we will not be able to answer these questions comprehensively. However, we think that looking back at the history of activist film and video may be illuminating and provide critical comparisons and ways to reflect on current conditions. Our focus in some parts of this chapter is on the history of political film and media in Germany, partly because we live in this country and have a deeper knowledge of the German film and media landscape, and partly because its political film history, especially in the context of the new social movements, is particularly revealing due to the country's borderline position between East and West, capitalism and communism. We thus understand our considerations as exemplary, selective, and specifically situated. Our aim is not to constitute a definite version of history, but rather to inspire new and more diverse histories and to open new perspectives.

Demanding Representation, Criticizing Capitalism

The history of leftist film, which began in the 1920s at the latest, is a major historical trajectory leading to contemporary video activism. In particular, witness videos, documentaries, and subversion videos (see Chapter 1) relate back to social and political documentary films and their intention to represent the marginalized and those without a voice in society (Waugh 1984; Rabinowitz 1994). Documentaries of this sort address the viewers in their here and now, refer directly to their life-world, and challenge them to take a stance toward the represented reality (Chanan 2007). They attempt to capture real events in relationship to their political context, present a clear position on them, and have an influence on the viewers, so that they pay attention to and become interested in the issues, show understanding and solidarity, feel moral outrage, and then rise up, take action, and carry on with the struggles depicted on the screen in their own lives.

Political documentary relies on presenting evidence and arguments, and as a rhetorical form it aims at shaping attitudes and emotions (Nichols 2010). The films may take on the role of "reporter," "advocate" or "prosecutor," "catalyst," or that of a "guerrilla" fighting against injustice, violence, and exploitation, to refer to just some of the divergent documentary practices that Barnouw filters out (Barnouw 1993). Like "committed documentaries" (Waugh 1984), documentaries of these sorts act in solidarity with people whose suffering they hope to allay, whose struggles they support and make their own. All this describes the self-understanding of many contemporary video activists as well, who see their mission as not just to observe and describe, but to change reality.

The Workers Film & Photo League (WFPL, later renamed Film and Photo League) was one of the first organized film movements. It was founded in 1930 in the United States to support the American labor movement during the time of the Great Depression with regular documentary film work. It was funded by the Workers International Relief, founded by Lenin.[19] European countries also had comparable film movements, using film as a means of resistance against capitalism and exploitation (Alexander 1981; Hogenkamp 2013). In the context of mass unemployment, strikes, and widespread poverty, WFPL newsreels depicted, for instance, the "hunger marches" to Washington and workers protesting outside factory gates. The six-minute-long film *Detroit Workers News Special 1932: Ford Massacre* (Hurwitz 1932), for example, documented how mounted police violently broke up one such protest while the camera operator had to scurry to safety, but went on filming. Many of WFPL's silent short films (examples can be found on YouTube) can serve as early examples of witness films: they provide "battle footage" or visible evidence intended to prove injustice or violence, while also appealing for solidarity and organized resistance. Despite the different political contexts, they fulfill functions quite similar to the work done later by independent newsreel groups or video collectives in many countries, as well as to current video work in the context of movements like Black Lives Matter or NGOs such as WITNESS (see Chapters 5 and 6).

A decisive figure in the history of politically committed documentaries and audiovisual activism is the Dutch filmmaker Joris Ivens. Beginning in the 1930s, he filmed oppression, war, and revolution at sites around the world. His film *Borinage*

(*Misère au Borinage*) (Storck and Ivens 1934) denounced the social inequities in the Walloon coalfields in Belgium and condemned capitalist exploitation. The silent movie reveals typical phenomena of poverty and misery (hunger, horrible hygienic conditions, illnesses, and children's developmental disorders) in scenes developed together with working-class families. It goes on to point to possible ways of improving their lot, to be found in solidarity, unionization, and standing up together for workers' rights and communism. Fundamental elements of Iven's work that have been carried on by later film and video activist movements are the filmmaker's ethical commitment to issues where the world looks away, to unconditionally taking sides with vulnerable social groups, to changing conditions instead of merely documenting them, and to actively involving those filmed.

Whether a film can contribute to social change depends not only on its topic, the people involved, and the stance it takes, but also on its ability to gain the audience's attention and evoke longer-term public reactions (see Chapters 3, 4, and 6). Being part of larger campaigns or movements helps. Iven's documentary *Spanish Earth* (1937), for instance, was part of a campaign to inform the American public about the Spanish Civil War following Franco's fascist putsch. In particular, it was used in fundraising to support the Republican side and the International Brigades. To this day, activist films are often similarly embedded in larger campaigns to inform and mobilize people and are part of strategies to build political networks. NGOs such as Greenpeace, for example, link their videos to spectacular live actions (see Chapter 5).

Similar positions and strategies were adopted in political-emancipatory film movements, often referred to as New Left Cinema, around the world during the 1960s. The Cuban filmmaker Santiago Álvarez, for instance, inserted shots from US television news into his found footage film *Now!* (Álvarez 1965), underlined with the song of the same name by the singer, actress, and civil rights activist Lena Horne, thus expressing a harsh criticism of American racism. Films from the Brazilian Cinema Novo—programmatically accompanied by Glauber Rocha's 1967 manifesto "The Aesthetics of Hunger" (Rocha 1983)—used allegorical forms to deal with the country's colonial past, the situation during the military dictatorship and the life of the poor in the northern rural regions of postcolonial Brazil. Around the same time, the "Third Cinema" movement and the Argentine filmmakers Octavio Getino and Fernando E. Solanas (1976) and their Grupo Cine Liberacíon demanded that films be placed strictly in the service of the liberation struggles of the then so-called Third World. Their essayistic, almost four-and-a-half-hour-long film *La Hora de las Hornos* (*The Hour of the Furnaces*) (Solanas and Getino 1968) was highly influential both aesthetically and politically. It is a furious indictment of neo-colonialism, tyranny, and violence in Argentina, Latin America, and the Global South. Solanas explicitly understood it to be a "film act" (a film acting). It should not only depict and name the injustices but understand itself as a call for a political revolution. The Chilean film activist Patricio Guzmán later took up this partisan or guerrilla impulse in his three-part documentary *La Batalla de Chile* ("The Battle of Chile") (1975–79) about the brutal counter-revolution and coup against the democratically elected Socialist government.

In the same period, social-revolutionary commitment shaped the Radical Cinema movement in the United States. Emile de Antonio was one of its leading figures with films like *In the Year of the Pig* (1968), a documentary, using historical footage, about the Vietnamese liberation war, *Underground* (de Antonio et al. 1976) about the radical leftist Weather Underground group, and *Millhouse: A White Comedy* (de Antonio 1971), a bitingly satirical reckoning with the Nixon presidency. Particularly important were various newsreel collectives such as the San Francisco Newsreel Group, which made agitation films like *Black Panther a.k.a. Off the Pig* (1967), or the Chicago-based production company The Film Group, which produced the short documentary *Cicero March* (1966) as well as the feature-length documentary *The Murder of Fred Hampton* (Alk 1971) and was part of the Chicago Freedom as well as the Black Panther movements. These film collectives saw their work as directly related to the Workers Film & Photo League (Nichols 1980; Beyerle and Brinckmann 1991).[20] Similar impulses were behind the European film movements associated with the 1968 protests, such as the French *cinéma militant*, which included Marxist film collectives like the Groupe Dziga Vertov and the Groupe Medvedkine, spearheaded by filmmakers like Jean-Luc Godard, Jean-Pierre Gorin and Chris Marker, or the Collectif Cinélutte (Grant 2016; Adamson 2018; Gerhardt and Saljoughi 2018).

In the 1970s, the women's liberation and gay movements in many countries enabled feminist and queer collective film practices (Holmlund and Fuchs 1999; Waldman and Walker 1999). In *Enduring Images: A Future History of New Left Cinema* from 2018, Morgan Adamson gives an insight into Italian feminist film collectives and looks closely at influential works such as the collectively produced *L'Aggettivo donna* ("The Adjective Woman") (Daopoulos 1971). A West German example of women's collective film practice is the documentary *Wir haben lange geschwiegen* ("We Have Been Silent for a Long Time") (1975) by the Women's Film Group Munich. The interactive and reflexive film depicts typical scenes from the daily lives of women, which then are discussed in consciousness-raising groups. These critical debates form a part of the project and the film. In 1973, filmmakers Helke Sander and Claudia von Alemann founded Germany's first (and still existing) women's film festival. Since then, female filmmakers have also demanded that all funding institutions in Germany be equally staffed with women (Dietze 2019). Cornerstone feminist films included Sander's *Die allseits reduzierte Persönlichkeit—Redupers* ("The All-Round Reduced Personality—Redupers")

(1978), which combines fiction, documentary, and essay film, Helga Reidemeister's participatory documentary *Von wegen "Schicksal"* ("Is This Fate?") (1979), and Cristina Perincioli's *Für Frauen: 1. Kapitel* ("For Women: Chapter 1") (1971), a call for a women's strike. Such films aimed at creating awareness of the many difficulties that women face in patriarchal societies and demanded equal opportunities, pay, and participation in all areas of society.

Also in West Berlin, Rosa von Praunheim came out with a pioneering film of the gay liberation movement: *Nicht der Homosexuelle ist pervers, sondern die Situation, in der er lebt* ("It Is Not the Homosexual Who Is Perverse, but the Society in Which He Lives") (1971). The film is a militant call to come out of the closet, and it became a much-discussed manifesto of gay liberation. In the United States, films such as the lesbian and gay documentary *Word Is Out: Story of Some of Our Lives* (1977) by the Mariposa Film Collective attempted to counter gay and lesbian shame and served to exchange experiences of living in a heteronormative and homophobic society. This community-oriented approach gained new urgency in the 1980s AIDS pandemic. Documentaries such as *Testing the Limits* (1988) by the Testing the Limits Collective, which was closely linked to ACT UP (the AIDS Coalition to Unleash Power), combined the call for militant action with safer-sex education and the politicization of mourning (Juhasz 1995; Gould 2009). Not all the films mentioned were released as collaborative productions. But they were all characterized by a strong sense of collectivity and community, which repeatedly included conflicts around the homonormative marginalization of queers of color and trans* activists. A testimony to these struggles is the video rediscovered in 2012 under the title *Y'all Better Quiet Down*, which captures the militant speech of trans-of-color activist Sylvia Rivera at the 1973 New York Gay Pride March, and which has been circulating on the web ever since (Tedjasukmana 2018).

The considerable diversity of activist film work and its aesthetic forms accurately reflects the diversity of the social movements themselves—from the civil rights activism of the 1960s to the alter-globalization movement of the late 1990s—and their political agendas. The formal spectrum ranges from explanatory documentaries to agitational films, political satires to experimental aesthetics (Boyle 1997; Harding [1997] 2001; Robé 2017; Adamson 2018). What links many of the various historical strands of political filmmaking is that they rely on collective forms of production and thus other forms of authorship, establish alternative networks for distribution and exhibition, work within local and social communities to help them organize and communicate their issues and demands, and at the same time see themselves as part of an international movement and stand for solidarity. All that can also be found in today's online video activism. In contrast to most of today's activist videos, however, earlier political films more often endorse decidedly anti-commercial aesthetics.

Participation and a Voice of One's Own

In the history of documentary filmmaking, the forms of representing the marginalized were also a recurring point of debate. For example, in the 1980s Brian Winston criticized that politically committed documentary film often remains trapped in the "perspective of the victim" (Winston 1988). He called for it to speak less *about* the people and lament their fate and do more to give them *a voice of their own*, allowing them to assert themselves and express their own concerns, liberating themselves from the position of victims of circumstances to become agents of social change. This is also a central point in video activism on social media, for example, in regard to videos such as *KONY 2012* (Invisible Children and Russell 2012) about a Ugandan warlord—that are videos with an enormous reach and at the same time a paternalist (in this case neo-colonialist and "white savior") stance. The question is, which of the people filmed appear as passive victims or active protagonists? Do they present their cause from their own perspective, or do the filmmakers control how they and their situation are portrayed? Does the film or video just document suffering or injustice, or does it present possible solutions? The question of the "voice of documentary" (Nichols 1983), its origin, its address, its form, and its claim to validity is central to the theoretical and practical debate about representation, communicative power, and the ethics of documentary forms.

In the course of film history, various approaches have been developed in which this relationship has been reconsidered. In "movement films" (German: "Bewegungsfilme," Zutavern 2015), filmmakers explicitly see themselves as part of a social movement, giving them a position from which they can speak with a collective voice, as it were, addressing a public that is presumed to sympathize politically with the movement (see Chapters 5 and 6). The movement forms the point of reference and main site of production, distribution, and reception of the films, which are intended to effect change. Their informational function accompanies their affective one, and their identity and community-building function go with their agitational one.

Filmmakers who involve their subjects in film production in a collaborative, participatory way take a different course. They invite them to become co-producers or teach them to make films of their own about the issues that concern them. This kind of work was central to the first video movement in the 1970s and 1980s with its video workshops in neighborhood or youth centers and its work with women's organizations, renters' initiatives, youth groups, or migrant communities. Empowering the people involved by helping them gain practical skills in "doing media" was part of the movement's didactic and political self-understanding. Approaches of a "shared ethnography" were developed early on in the ethnographic film by filmmakers like Jean Rouch and can be found also in participatory films and later videos. Experts instruct and guide local communities in working with the medium and help them make films to reveal and combat injustice and social problems. The films made in this way are shown to the group and their discussion leads to works that all of them support, which can then be used to address wider audiences and decision-makers to demand solutions (Milne et al. 2012). Nowadays media NGOs like WITNESS provide comparable workshops and tutorial videos to train people on the ground on how to create and disseminate witness videos effectively and safely (Ristovska 2021, 141–75). Interactive webdocs (iDocs) take up such collaborative, multi-voice approaches and link them to the possibilities given by digital, interactive media environments. Other films like the Occupy documentary *Occupy Wall Street: We Are the 99%* (Perlman 2013) or the Black Lives Matter film *Stay Woke* (Grants 2016) involved various people and local chapters who share their video footage with the filmmakers to create a collective, polyphonic work (Aston et al. 2017; Wiehl 2019; Zimmermann and de Michiel 2019; Nash 2022). *Anyone's Child: Mexico* is "a living documentary about families affected by Mexico's drug war" (Brown et al. 2018). The project, which was funded and produced by Bristol University's Brigstow Institute and the Transform Drug Policy Foundation in the United Kingdom, uses a website to collect and present the personal testimonies of Mexican witnesses who lost a child or other family members. Another example of such an approach collecting the experiences of the many who speak with their many voices is *The Quipu Project* (_docubase 2015), an interactive documentary with Peruvian women who were forcibly sterilized as part of a government measure and are fighting for compensation (Court and Lerner 2015; Mitchell 2015). Such films aim not only at changing the viewers' attitudes but also those of the collaborators in the production process, who see themselves drawn together through the joint work, may recognize their own interests more clearly, and be better able to articulate them. The political goal is also to create a counterpublic in the process of making a film, which thus constitutes a kind of self-empowering practice.

Political Aesthetics

Since the 1960s, filmmakers and activists in many countries have engaged in sometimes heated debates about political aesthetics, which are closely linked to questions of representation, participation, and (political and aesthetic) resistance. The so-called "political" and "aesthetic" left in West Germany represented two opposing poles on the question of how art can be politically effective—as a direct, "operative" intervention in reality or indirectly via the artistic confrontation with reality. Proponents of an "operative aesthetic" emphasized the concrete political function of film over its artistic form and called for a simple, easily accessible "art for all." However, the Soviet writer Sergei Tretyakov, who developed this concept in the early 1920s, agreed with the German author Bertolt Brecht and his programmatic demand that workers should not remain consumers, but should themselves become producers of art and active communicators (Brecht [1932] 2003; Tretyakov [1923] 2014). In contrast to such a position of the immediate usefulness of film, the aesthetic left developed a political aesthetic that understood film and art in general not only as a means of protest but also as a form of protest itself. An "aesthetics of resistance" (a term that refers to the novel of the same name by Peter Weiss, 1981) breaks with a simple reproduction of reality, for example, by using alienation effects such as those developed by Brecht for theater. According to this position, the political dimension and potential of films lie less in their content or intentions than in the aesthetic form and the experience it enables or provokes.

Two examples from the West German student movement of the 1960s can illustrate these opposing positions and their different approaches to questions of collectivity, art, accessibility, voice, agency, and counterpublics. Comparable positions with differing accents depending on the political context can be found also in student-activist film production in other countries, but they were particularly clearly defined in divided Germany during the Cold War.

Berlin, 2. Juni '67 (1967) by Hans-Rüdiger Minow and Thomas Giefer was shot on 16 mm black-and-white material and produced by the (notoriously leftist) student government of the Freie Universität Berlin. It demonstrates the use of an operative aesthetic. In the form of a new feature, the film documents the protest against the West Berlin state visit of the autocratic Shah of Persia, Mohammad Reza Pahlavi, who was heavily criticized for the violent suppression of opposition to his regime. The film portrays the events of that day and accuses the local police of first allowing Shah supporters to beat up peacefully demonstrating citizens and then using violence themselves. In the course of the confrontation, the student Benno Ohnesorg was shot by a police officer (who, as became known decades after the film release, was a presumed spy for the East German State Security Service inciting an escalation of the student protest in West Germany). The murder of Ohnesorg was a prelude to the radicalization of larger parts of the student movement.

The film combines turbulent film shots with photos taken by other observers and uses sound recording and text inserts over a black screen where the film ran out. The contrast between sound and silent footage, between still photos and moving pictures is used effectively. The photos document particularly intensive moments and provide visible evidence. The events vividly described later by eyewitnesses are substantiated by photos and film sequences from the location of the events. Furthermore, the film *Berlin, 2. Juni '67* also includes an improvised agitational speech by Rudi Dutschke, the ringleader of the Berlin student movement, confrontational street interviews

FIGURE 2.1: *Berlin, 2. Juni '67*—the filmmakers at work, being controlled by the police. FRG 1967, Hans-Rüdiger Minow/Thomas Giefer, AStA der Freien Universität Berlin.

between the filmmakers and police after the events ("What do you say about this photograph?"; "Where were you on 2 June?"), and commentary by a male voice-over (Figure 2.1). The film concludes with the text: "We have to put up resistance!"

The filmmakers were part of the student movement in the lecture halls and on the streets of Berlin. They were not distant observers, but themselves exposed to repression by the police; they suffered injuries that they provocatively displayed to the camera. In demanding satisfaction, they show themselves as one with their viewers, addressing them as allies in the struggle against the system. The self-understanding of many of today's video activists is similar, particularly regarding documentary and witness videos (see Chapter 5): groups like the Papo Reto Collective in Brazil, Leftvision in Germany, or Reel News in the United Kingdom document action from within a movement or community, in the midst of the events happening on the streets or from nearby. They uncover, educate, agitate, appeal to intellect and emotions, and not least contribute to strengthening the community.

The objectives of the students at the Film Academy in Berlin (Deutsche Film- und Fernsehakademie, DFFB) were emphatically political and anti-aesthetical in

FIGURE 2.2: *Brecht die Macht der Manipulateure* ("Break the Manipulators' Power") (FRG/Finland 1967–68)—the film team (Skip Norman, Helke Sander, Harun Farocki) acting in agitprop style, addressing the camera.

direction. Not aesthetic form, but "use value" was crucial to "operative films" like *Berlin, 2. Juni '67* (Farocki 1969). In the context of the APO, the extra-parliamentary opposition ("Außerparlamentarische Opposition"), the film was seen as a means of mobilization, used to fulfill the function of an audiovisual pamphlet. This understanding of activist work still shapes many documentaries and mobilization videos of protest movements.

At the same time and in the same social environment, other films were produced that aimed in a different direction than the operative and functional approaches. These films critically reflected on the relationship between politics and aesthetics, playfully experimented with it, and displayed an aesthetics of resistance without sacrificing agitation. Helke Sander's film *Brecht die Macht der Manipulateure* ("Break the Manipulators' Power") (1967–68) was made at the DFFB at the same time as *Berlin, 2. Juni '67* and called for an attack on the "apparatus of manipulation" of the influential, right-wing Axel Springer media corporation (which today owns major newspapers in many countries such as *Politico* or *Business Insider* in the United States).[21] Using chalk diagrams to reveal the complex structure of the corporation, the film alludes to school teaching. In addition, it includes ironic scenes with (amateur) actors speaking and acting ostentatiously, scenes of the film team's visit to the Berlin Press Ball filmed with a hidden camera, and appearances of the filmmakers/actors in costumes in scenes reminiscent of agitprop theater. Sander explains the intention of the film to a packed auditorium at the Freie Universität Berlin and includes the feedback from the students in the movie. *Brecht die Macht der Manipulateure* lays bare its means and works with self-reflective distancing effects to avoid being part of the manipulation that it is attacking (Figure 2.2).

Similar pleasure in experimentation and the ironic imitation of familiar forms such as government or corporate PR can be found in today's playful subversive videos with their communication guerrilla tactics made by activist groups like The Yes Men or the Peng! Collective (see Chapter 5). Such collectives carry on the tradition of civil disobedience. Regarding the historical and ongoing conflict about the political aesthetic of activism—whether as artistic resistance or more popular and functional—it seems unlikely that it can be resolved in favor of one or the other of these directions, which are at most ideal types, anyway. Instead, the use of a diversity of forms and strategies is crucial, depending on the topic, goal, target audience, and platform (see Chapters 3 and 4).

The Role of Media Technology in the History of Video Activism

The historical development of film aesthetics, forms of representation, and participation has always been interwoven with developments in media technology and society. The tectonic shifts caused by the combination of digital cameras, smartphones, and social media platforms are only the current phase of a long and ongoing process. Working with 16 mm film was already cheaper than with the large, prohibitively expensive 35 mm professional cameras and film stock, but it was still relatively expensive, difficult, and time-consuming and was therefore only carried out by specialized filmmakers. The new medium of video (VCR, U-matic, VHS) was a much more cost-effective, easier-to-handle alternative, which also made it possible to view what had been filmed immediately. For political work with moving images, this was tantamount to a revolution.

In 1967, Sony introduced its Portapak System, which consisted of a video camera and a recorder connected by a cable. It allowed filmmakers to record 45 minutes of black-and-white images on ½-inch videotape (Hoffmann 2015, 2018). Even though the first-generation video images were of poor quality and the possibilities of editing were limited, many artists and activists greeted the new medium enthusiastically (Boyle 1992; Askanius 2012; Robé 2017). As one West

German activist pragmatically put it at the time: "Better video in your hand than film in your head" (Rettinger 1980).

On this technological basis, a "guerrilla TV" movement grew in the United States around collectives like TVTV or videofreex, in Great Britain TVX, in Italy Videobase, and in Japan Video Hiroba, along with various other initiatives and groups in these and many other countries (Adamson 2018, Chapter 4). In the Federal Republic of Germany around 70 video initiatives, workshops, cooperatives, and alternative media centers were founded between 1969 and 1984 (Köhler 1980). Practical work with media was dedicated to local topics such as affordable housing and the involvement of tenants in decision-making as well as many other issues. Important impulses came from the environmental and anti-nuclear power movements.

Video groups were not just about using the videos to articulate protest and organize resistance but also about larger issues of a different way of living together, of a different society. They became more than just agents of a counterpublic with their own media infrastructure and communicative forums. Like earlier participatory and ethnographic filmmakers, they also tried to empower others to produce videos themselves and thereby create possibilities for action aiming at an alternative society. Community or self-governed media centers were intended to provide anyone interested with access to equipment and practical skills. Early on, the video movement called for media education and critical reflection on mass media in schools to improve what we call media competence or media literacy today. Video activists took care of technical training, conducted courses in schools and youth centers, wrote manuals, and exchanged ideas about technical innovations and ways to solve problems. They set up a distribution service for their own works and political films, provided documentation of their work such as directories of video groups, and wrote about politics and film (Nigg 2017; Beutelschmidt 2018).

The so-called "camcorder revolution" of the 1980s led to new possibilities with the mass availability of analog video cameras with integrated recorders, which in the course of the decade continuously became more compact and provided better pictures (Zimmermann 2009). Various video activist groups such as ACT UP (mentioned above) formed in the United States. One of the most consequential examples of camcorder activism was the witness video in the case of the Rodney King beating trial in 1991/92, which—after the acquittal of the white police officers—led to mass uprisings against racism. Shot spontaneously, the video marked the start of what is now a more common practice: creating political pressure by documenting cases of police violence on videotape. The incident and the events that followed also contributed to the founding of the NGO WITNESS.

In the mid-1990s, analog camcorders were gradually replaced by digital equipment with better image resolution and easier editing options. It was then also possible to produce lossless copies. Digitalization and the "internet for everybody" expanded the possibilities for political communication and, at that time, were celebrated as unleashing a "digital revolution" and cyberspace utopia by many activists (Barlow 1996a). In connection with the protests against the World Trade Organization (WTO) meeting in 1999, leftist activists founded the non-profit online portal Indymedia. From 2004 onward, it enabled video uploads, later also provided streaming applications, and thus the prerequisites for leftist protest groups to further develop their networking in the sense of alternative globalization (de Jong et al. 2005). Repeated security problems, state interventions, the waning of the alter-globalization movement, and above all the rise of commercial social media platforms gradually caused it to lose influence within activist communities (Giraud 2014; Baú 2020). Collective online portals or the websites of individual video groups now primarily serve to provide an overview, networking among activists, and the collection, cataloging, and archiving of videos, which can easily get lost on social media and are often deleted by commercial platforms or state agents.

Citizens' groups have been establishing channels on commercial video-sharing platforms since the mid-2000s, particularly on YouTube, which began in 2005 and was already bought up by Google in 2006. Such initiatives have also set up profiles on social networking sites like Facebook or microblogging services like X/Twitter. Social media have become a fundamental part of activist infrastructures, despite the awareness of state and corporate data surveillance. The introduction of YouTube and its likes, the spread of broadband wireless internet access, the use of smartphones with integrated video cameras, live streaming apps, and easy-to-use video editing and postpro software have made a new kind of DIY video activism possible (Voß 2015).

Today, there are handbooks like *The Video Activist Handbook* (Harding 2002) or *Beautiful Trouble: A Toolbox for Revolution* (Boyd and Mitchell [2012] 2016) and many easily accessed online resources such as the video4change or the WITNESS toolkit that provide technical and practical knowledge about making and using videos (see Chapter 7).[22] In this way, it is much easier to gain media literacy than in the days of the first video movement. In many countries, gaining access to equipment and media infrastructure is much less of a problem nowadays. Knowledge and skills tend to be passed on informally, and it is more often the young, tech-savvy activists who pass their knowledge on to the older ones, rather than the other way around.

In addition to the developments of online video itself, we are currently experiencing new interrelations between moving images on social media and the cinema or television. Occasionally, long documentaries produced by activists are first made for the internet and only later find their way into cinema screenings, such as *Debtocracy* (Kitidi and Chatzistefanou 2011), a film about the brutal pressure exerted by the EU on Greece in the context of the financial and debt crisis around 2010. Conversely, activist groups combine their own video material published online and previously unpublished video material to create feature-length cinema documentaries, such as *Hamburger Gitter* ("Hamburg Grid") (2018) by the Leftvision group, a film about police violence during protests against a G20 meeting. By using the material activists shoot for their regular online reporting as footage that is edited into longer documentary films shown at festivals and in cinemas, the attention of the international publics is directed toward repressed problems. One example is the Oscar-nominated Syrian long-term study *For Sama* (Al-Kateab and Watts 2020) shot in the besieged city of Aleppo. In the past, the established documentary film festivals were skeptical about video, but now films shot with smartphones regularly make their way onto the theater screens, and special "mobile film festivals" like The Mobil Motion Film Festival in Zurich, or Cinephone in Barcelona exhibit political videos, thus increasing their reach.

And now also TV stations are showing interest in films that are based on material taken from inside of a group at risk, for example, the compilation documentaries based on smartphone recordings by refugees documenting their perilous flight across the Mediterranean Sea, such as *#My Escape/Meine Flucht* (Sasse 2016), produced by German public TV, or the BBC documentary series *Exodus: Our Journey to Europe* (2016–present). As a participatory project, this film likewise assembles footage taken by refugees with their smartphone cameras while in dangerous situations (Bennett 2018).

Videos Everywhere: Between Empowerment and Disillusionment

Contemporary video activism operates not only in different media environments but also in different socio-political contexts than earlier committed film practice. The changes since the 1960s include the transitions from colonialism to post-colonialism and from a bipolar to a multipolar world order, and from economy-centered labor movements to the new social movements for civil rights, peace, and the environment. Since the 1980s and 1990s, further upheavals have followed such as the collapse of state socialism in the Eastern Bloc countries and the unleashing of neoliberalist and extractivist capitalism. Since 2000, the world faced a succession of financial and economic crises, austerity measures, the weakening of democracies through populism and authoritarianism, the worsening of the climate crisis, and the increase in refugees fleeing war, hunger, and political repression. More recently, the number of armed conflicts has dramatically grown (see Chapter 7). All these developments have provoked reactions from video activists in various regions of the world.

The interplay of media and social change leads to many differences as well as notable continuities between contemporary video activism and earlier political filmmaking. On the one hand, radical activist groups that are predominantly made up of workers or the poor, as well as filmmakers with an explicitly Marxist or anti-capitalist stance (comparable to Joris Ivens or Fernando Solanas) seem to be less visible in commercial social media today. On the other hand, there are still many video groups that strongly criticize capitalism, such as Reel News in the United Kingdom (Presence 2016), TV Fórum in Brazil, Leftvision in Germany, or Democracy at Work in the United States, a non-profit organization that according to its self-description on YouTube "analyzes capitalism critically as a systemic problem and advocates for democratizing workplaces as part of a systemic solution."[23] And as in earlier times, some activists, such as these groups, still favor a simple, functional "operative aesthetic," whereas others prefer a more elaborate "aesthetic of resistance" in the analytical Brechtian style or in the playful style of communication guerrillas such as Natalie Wynn's ContraPoints or the Peng! Collective (see Chapter 5). At the same time, however, many new aesthetic forms are emerging that are often specifically adapted to their new social media environments (see Chapters 3 and 4). While many earlier political film practices were characterized by collective approaches, today's video activism often seems to favor individual video bloggers and micro-celebrities. However, new forms of collectives and participatory practices are also emerging (see Chapter 5).

Today, video activists operate even more globally than earlier filmmakers. Networks such as the Radical Film Network, EngageMedia, Indigenous Rising Media, or Films for Action link up activist film groups around the world. At the same time, the local political context remains important also for videos on social media. As the documentary filmmaker Hartmut Bitomsky once remarked, it is not primarily a film that is political, but the relationship that it creates between people.[24] The space in which a public is organized around an issue is political (see Chapter 6), no matter whether it is a political arena, a theater, an online forum, or a messenger group. The question is how to develop productive relationships between online and offline publics, between globally circulating videos and locally acting movements. This question is exacerbated by the enormous number of political videos dealing with very different contexts and issues around the world, and the fact that the impact of a single video is rarely direct or strong (see Chapters 3 and 4). Individual videos can be catalysts for political action, but the social impact comes more from the transnational interplay of many videos, the multiplicity of their voices and impulses, which together contribute to strengthening civil society or unleashing collective action (Aguayo 2019; Hamblin and Watson 2019). As the following chapters will show, this impact also depends crucially on the diverse forms and strategies of activist videos, by means of which they succeed in changing attitudes, initiating debates, influencing public opinion, and providing impulses for joint political practice.

A very general continuity between the present and the past is that activist films and videos have always made up only a very small part of total audiovisual production. The cinema era was dominated by entertainment and the camcorder era by family videos. Such a relationship continues to shape the age of digital "mass self-communication," but many activist videos are nevertheless able to make important contributions to "networks of outrage and hope" (Castells 2012) and "connective action" with significant social impact (Bennett and Segerberg 2012). The exchange of information by citizens via social media is especially important in countries with state-controlled media systems. As mentioned before, videos played a relevant role in the protest movements in Iran, in the MENA region, and later in Belarus and Ukraine (see Introduction and Chapter 7).[25] And, of course, they can be effective in democratic states too.

Despite the diversity of contemporary activist videos, our brief overview of the history of committed film and video has also shown that some important insights of the past seem to have been largely forgotten today. Earlier reflections on collective film practice, the politics of representation, the voices of participants, their embodied experience, the communicative authority of filmmakers, the narrative perspective of films, and the political implications of aesthetic forms remain relevant to current video activism and could inform and inspire its future work. Knowledge of earlier political film practices, aesthetics, and ethics is just waiting to be rediscovered, reinterpreted, and utilized.

3

The Impact of Political Videos: Attention, Affect, Action

The discussion about political activity on social media is still haunted by the old but persistent stereotype that it can only lead to lazy, inconsistent slacktivism, disorganized distraction, or hate-filled echo chambers. However, this prejudice has long been refuted by empirical studies from various disciplines that show how social media have effects. Sociologist Tim Highfield, for example, examines how the political mingles with the personal in social media and how this can increase user engagement in "everyday politics" (Highfield 2016; see also Kahne and Bowyer 2018). Communication researcher Zizi Papacharissi (2014) explains how "affective publics" of political discourse form on X/Twitter. Political scientist James Dennis (2019) analyses how "micro-activism" in social media develops in a "continuum of participation" in which online and offline activities merge and citizens take on various new political roles. And cultural and media scholars Henry Jenkins, Sanghita Shresthova, and their colleagues (2016a) study how youth activism fights for its causes by using "any media necessary," especially social media. A Pew Research Center survey of 19 advanced economies indicates that "ordinary citizens see social media as both a constructive and destructive component of political life, and overall most believe it has actually had a positive impact on democracy," and that they "think social media has made it easier to manipulate and divide people, but also say it informs and raises awareness" (Pew Research Center 2022). Another survey shows that high percentages of US social media users (and more people of color than white people) "say these platforms are very or somewhat important to them personally when it comes to finding others who share their views about important issues," "getting involved with political or social issues that are important to them," or "giving them a venue to express their political opinions" (Pew Research Center 2023).

In each of these contexts, videos play crucial roles. Previous chapters have already outlined that activist videos on social media serve important functions by representing marginalized interests, exposing injustices, proposing solutions, and moving people to action, for example, in the context of social movements such as Black Lives Matter,

¡Ni Una Menos!, or Fridays for Future. A fundamental way in which social media and their videos work is that they can contribute to shifting the frames of political thought, speech, and action (see Chapter 1). In the following chapters, the various effects of activist videos and their pathways to political impact are explored in more detail, starting with the crucial question: How do they actually achieve their effects?

Pathways to Impact

Interdisciplinary research shows that media achieve very different kinds of effects—direct and indirect, individual and collective, strong and weak, short-term and long-term (Valkenburg et al. 2016). The main goal of activist videos, however, is to bring about significant and lasting changes in political situations, social practices, and societal structures such as changes in common habits and norms, formal regulations and laws, or political and economic institutions. Such significant effects are often referred to as "social impact" or "transformational change," as is evident in the names of activist communities such as the Video for Change Network or in titles of publications such as *The Impact Field Guide & Toolkit*. Many such strategy guides argue that changes in society can only be achieved in several steps, which can be summarized in the following formula:[26]

> attention → awareness & affect → attitudes → individual behavior & action → expression → connection → communities → collective action → institutions → society

Accordingly, a video must first attract the attention of users in order to make them aware of a problem and influence their political attitudes and affects. These changes in awareness, attitude, and affect must be so profound that they shape behavior and motivate political action, both individually and collectively. Videos frequently influence the attitudes and actions of individual people. For example, the inventor Dave Hakkens stated in an interview that the video *The Story of Stuff* (Fox 2007) inspired him to found a global initiative to upcycle plastic (Kempkes 2019). However, collective effects are even more important. In order to have an effect on the knowledge, affects and actions of communities, advocacy groups, policymakers, and larger segments of the population, a video must reach relevant groups of viewers and set off intensive processes of negotiating and appropriating meaning.[27] For example, the witness videos in the context of the Movement for Black Lives in the United States or the video blogs of Alexei Navalny in Russia or Rezo in Germany had an impact not only on hashtag networks on X or on followers of a YouTube channel, but—via debates in mass media and parliaments—on the general public as well (see Chapters 4 and 6). Especially in the context of "social tipping points," social media and their activist videos can have a significant impact (Juhola et al. 2022). In the run-up to the so-called Arab Spring, for example, drought, failed harvests, and rising food prices exacerbated political dissatisfaction with governments to such an extent that a social tipping point emerged, which was then hit by online and offline protests.

Collective and long-term effects, again, are rarely achieved through one individual video, but more often cumulatively through clusters or sequences of many videos. As Kerstin Schankweiler notes, in the flood of images on the web, the long-lasting iconic images of former times (such as Che Guevera's likeness) are increasingly being replaced by fleeting "image swarms" relating to certain topics (Schankweiler 2019). It should be emphasized, however, that videos by no means just arbitrarily form swarms that emerge quickly via hashtags and by spontaneously sharing. They are often part of strategically developed series, targeted campaigns, and social media channels which take years of painstaking work. The cumulative effects of these efforts can contribute to the lasting transformation of discourses and identities, values and norms, decisions and regulations, institutions and publics.

Four dimensions of the effectiveness of political videos can thus be distinguished:[28]

Mental depth: reaching from awareness about a political topic through intensive feelings and thoughts to influences on lasting political attitudes and group identities, which form the basis of behavior.

Social breadth: from influencing individuals through small communities to larger social formations and entire societies.

Behavioral effort: from quick responses on social media (such as liking or sharing a video) to online engagement that requires more time, money, or effort (commenting on a video, searching for more information, signing a petition, donating, creating content) to more demanding or even outright dangerous actions (protesting in the streets, contacting politicians, volunteering, civil disobedience, becoming an active member of an organization).

Temporal duration: from spontaneous clicks through medium-term practices and discourses that develop in weeks or months to long-lasting movements, organizations, or laws.

These distinctions also make it clearer at what points attempts at social change can fail and why mass media headlines about Facebook or X/Twitter revolutions or TikTok wars are misleading (see also Chapter 7). While such platforms may play a crucial role in connecting and mobilizing people, revolutions or wars are not won through social media, as the so-called Arab Spring, which all too quickly turned into an Arab winter, and many other protests against violent authoritarian regimes have demonstrated. Videos seem to be more suitable for triggering protests and mobilizing people than for organizing sustainable political resistance. Nevertheless, their potential to keep movements going, raise international support, and influence networks of power in the military, administration, economy, law, and workforce should not be underestimated. The impact spectrum of political videos thus ranges from seconds to decades, from individuals to mass movements, from occasional exchanges to the overthrow of a regime. Most videos fall between these extremes, aiming at local, medium-term changes that can nevertheless be crucial for certain groups in society.

Collective effects are most likely to occur when many viewers watch a significant number of related videos and interact with each other—and sometimes also with the content creators, the protagonists, and mass media—before and after watching. One can think of this in terms of dynamic networks interconnecting many local events on social media. The impact of such networks stems not only from a few viral videos but also from countless other videos and posts that attract smaller audiences. Although most videos do not reach large groups of people, there are a great number of them, and they can work together toward the same goals. Their resonance feeds into the network and can have profound and lasting effects. The impact of activist videos is thus mostly cumulative, indirect, social, and transactional.

Nevertheless, the aesthetic form and affective force of individual videos are of great importance (see Chapter 4). Aesthetics and affects drive the very processes social impact is based on: agenda setting, framing, persuasion, observational learning, cultivation, socialization, and participation (Singhal and Rogers 2002). By drawing attention to political problems or to neglected aspects of debates, videos put those issues on the agenda of social action (*agenda setting*). By presenting a particular perspective on a political problem, they shape ideas about its causes and possible solutions, as well as related evaluations (*framing*, see Entman 1993). By embedding individual problems in larger arguments or narratives, for example, about ongoing struggles for human rights, these issues are given a context and meaning that enable observational learning and the development of social identities and lasting bonds within a movement (*narrative persuasion, social learning*; Winskell and Enger 2014, see Chapter 4). By repeating and interweaving narratives, messages, and images, videos contribute to processes of socialization and the cultivation of political beliefs and affect structures (Morgan et al. 2014). Agenda setting, framing, persuasion, and socialization are often described primarily as cognitive processes, but actually they are deeply affective and charged with political emotions that motivate people to participate in political action (see below).

In these ways, activist videos are directed at different groups of people, often simultaneously. Videos can combat "epistemic injustice" (Fricker 2007) by making marginalized people aware of their rights and enabling previously unheard people to raise their own voice. At the same time, they can give sympathizers the feeling that they need to take action and that they are capable of doing so—be it on the web, in the streets, or in the voting booth. Mobilization videos have moved many people to donate or protest, and critical vlogs have cost political parties votes. Video activism also has various effects on the political actors and social movements involved. It might empower them, contribute to their identity and activity, and lead to new forms of protest and self-presentation, to the emergence of outstanding figures and hierarchies in the movement, or to conflicts about its ethical principles. Image events are staged to create powerful visuals to be used in campaigns (DeLuca 2005). The mere presence of witnesses with cameras can influence the behavior of police as well as demonstrators at protests in the streets. In the long run, all these kinds of influence work together to get social movements going, exert pressure on political and economic power networks, and gradually change the norms and structures of social institutions. As expressed in the formula above, however, this dynamic process requires an increasingly scarce resource: attention.

Competing for Attention, Overcoming Obstacles

Some of the most discussed issues in political communication today such as fragmentation, "tribalism," echo chambers, filter bubbles, or filter clashes can be described as characteristic (often dysfunctional) patterns of attention distribution across audiences (Tufekci 2013; Bennett et al. 2018; Vaidhyanathan 2018). We will return to such issues in subsequent chapters. Here, we would like to focus on one basic dilemma of video activism: the economy of attention in the social web (and more generally in today's hybrid media systems) has fundamentally changed the conditions for reaching relevant audiences. On the one hand, it is now possible for activists to gain more viewers than ever before and to micro-target specific groups of social media users. On the other hand, activist videos compete against a massive, ever-growing stream of other moving images that circulate on commercial platforms and follow their logic and economic aims. According to the companies themselves and social marketing agencies, each of the major platforms records billions of views and hundreds or even thousands of hours of new videos every day. The data on that is sparse, not scientifically verifiable, and probably exaggerated to attract advertisers, but it gives a sense of scale (repeatedly stressed by internet trend reports such as Meeker 2019 or Sandvine 2023). In 2015, Mark Zuckerberg told investors that Facebook was already averaging 8 billion video views a day.[29] In 2019, Susan Wojcicki (then CEO of YouTube) claimed that people spent one billion hours watching videos on the platform every day and that over 500 hours of videos were uploaded there every single minute (Stahl 2019). If that is correct, it would take over 82 years to watch the daily video upload on YouTube alone. In this ocean, the individual video does not even count as a drop.

The inflows into this ocean and the large currents within it are regulated and directed by the platforms and their economic interests (see Chapters 1 and 6, Crawford 2016; Gillespie 2018). The affordances and algorithms of commercial social media favor precisely those videos and postings that serve their business models, which means those that are suitable for the ad business, data trading, and shareholder interests. These are posts that increase engagement among existing users, lure new adopters, make the platform grow, and attract additional advertisers. Social media purposefully draw attention to such content, thereby distorting social discourses. Apart from a few spectacular exceptions, activist videos are immensely disadvantaged in this system, and activists struggle to adapt to the algorithms or to trick them as we have seen in the case of *The Most Boring Viral Video*, which was—unsurprisingly—banned from YouTube (Chapter 1).

The logic of commercial platforms interacts with dominant affect structures, value systems, and discourses, creating massive attention streams on the net. Thus, user attention on social media is distributed in extremely uneven ways. It forms clusters and is subject to blockbuster effects. A statistical study found that in 2016 just 3 percent of the most successful channels accounted for about 85 percent of all video views on YouTube (Bärtl 2018). While some of the most popular videos reached billions of views, the median was only 89 views per video—meaning that half of the videos were watched even less. Music and entertainment channels are at the high head of this steep curve, while activist videos are more often found toward the very end of the long tail. Comparable blockbuster effects can also be assumed for other platforms.

Comparing video use across channels reinforces the impression that entertainment, music, and games dominate the web and that news, politics, and activism are facing increasingly hard times. Some typical figures can give an idea of the proportions. In 2021, the then most widely watched YouTuber, PewDiePie, active since 2010 and known primarily for gaming videos but also for some racist provocations, had 110 million subscribers and nearly 28 billion views of his 4,404 videos, each of which averaged more than six million views. Activists come nowhere near such numbers (see also Chapter 5). According to our observations, even the collectives that are most active on YouTube and have uploaded hundreds of videos over the years reach only a few thousand subscribers and a few million views altogether. As of September 2, 2021, for example, the London-based video collective Reel News had uploaded 622 videos that were viewed a total of 1,623,093 times, an average of 2,618 views per video, by 3850 subscribers and other viewers. Even the major international NGOs achieve only rather modest numbers. Amnesty International's main YouTube channel, also active since 2006, had 88,600 subscribers and 422 videos with a total of 13,725,445 views. That corresponds to an average of 32,522 views per video. However, the videos were also available through several national Amnesty channels and on other platforms. With these numbers, Reel News and Amnesty are still far more successful than most activist channels, which average only a few dozen or hundred views per video.[30] Some data also seems to indicate that the situation is becoming increasingly difficult for activists and that average views of NGO videos may have declined over the last decade (possibly due to the growth of competing professional content that is more precisely tailored to the platforms' algorithms).[31] Despite these difficulties, commercial platforms like YouTube are indispensable for most video activists, since the numbers of viewers on their own websites are even lower. That is shown, for example, by Cinemata.org, an open-source site for activist video sharing in the Asia-Pacific region that was set up by the organization EngageMedia. At the time of writing (2022), almost all of the several thousand videos on this site reach only two- or three-digit audiences.

The harsh competitive situation becomes even clearer when one considers *how* political videos are usually viewed: as fleeting bits in the stream of Facebook or Instagram posts, as part of an automated YouTube playlist, coincidentally found while swiping through TikTok, attached to a random tweet or Telegram message, or as one of thousands of items turned up while searching Google. The viral blockbuster effects on such commercial platforms are further strengthened by the fact that attention on the net is quantifiable, serves as a currency, and can be manipulated. It is measured according to various parameters: views, visits, average viewing duration, view-through rate (watching the whole video), user engagement (shares, likes, retweets, and comments), and the conversion rate (follow-up actions such as donations or signing a petition). Commercial agencies monitor these metrics closely and try to improve the reach of their clients' videos appropriately, for instance through search engine optimization, tags, links, and sometimes purchased clicks and followers. Their results and methods are generally not publicly available, or they relate only to specific kinds of videos (mostly advertising). What is known, however, suggests that most videos are only viewed in part and that the average viewing duration is quite short, only seconds on Facebook and a few minutes at best on YouTube.[32] Activists, even well-known NGOs, also struggle with user engagement. The animal rights organization PETA, for example, received an average of 300 user reactions to its posts on its German Facebook and X/Twitter channels in 2019, Extinction Rebellion only 15 (Schneider 2019). In contrast, many commercial video producers develop professional strategies to capture the attention of their target groups as quickly as possible and encourage interaction.

Activist videos not only have to compete with professionally produced advertising and entertainment, but they are also at a disadvantage because of psychological barriers. Audience interest in critical political videos is generally limited by psychosocial obstacles. Some of these have been identified by research on persuasion, especially in the context of climate communication.[33] Environmental videos, for example, usually convey inconvenient truths, cause cognitive dissonance, contradict social identities and cherished habits, or demand personal effort and sacrifice. The problems they depict often seem abstract, over-complex, difficult to solve, or distant in space or time. When videos paint a bleak future, impressions of doom can be chilling or paralyzing. In the case of ongoing, long-term problems such as the climate crisis, the repetition of true but depressing messages can cause weariness, boredom, and compassion fatigue. All this triggers defensive mechanisms in many people such as avoidance, confirmation biases, denial, reactance, and counterarguing as a defense against identity threats.

At the same time, activist videos face increasing difficulties in standing up to political forces that follow anti-democratic goals and use sophisticated media strategies to gain control of public discourse (Earl et al. 2016, see Chapters 1 and 7). Authoritarian regimes have protest videos deleted, block channels, and persecute activists. Political populists, extremists, religious fanatics, and profit-hungry corporations flood the web with their content, disseminate disinformation, use their resources for targeted campaigns, or manipulate attention metrics. Oil companies spend hundreds of millions of dollars per year to influence environmental policy, including many millions on social media (InfluenceMap 2019; Laville 2019). Often veritable image wars emerge over the discourses, frames, and narratives in a political field. When the World Wildlife Fund, for instance, denounced the use of the carcinogenic herbicide glyphosate in Germany with the film *Die Glyphosat-Vergiftung!* ("Poisoning by Glyphosate!") (2019), the producer, chemical giant Bayer, responded with a strategically sophisticated counter-video. When Greta Thunberg called for climate protests in a series of videos, the Heartland Institute and a transnational coalition of climate crisis deniers built up the right-wing influencer Naomi Seibt as an "anti-Greta" in 2019. (Seibt is now banned on YouTube due to harassment and spreading false information.) The question, then, is how civil society activists can be successful under these conditions? How can they hold their own in such confrontations? Let's look at an example.

Image Wars in the Discourse on Migration

Struggles for attention, discourse hegemony, and collective emotions were particularly evident in connection with the EU migration policy around 2015, when hundreds of thousands of people, many of them civil war refugees from Syria, sought asylum in Europe.[34] A massive storm of far-right propaganda then brewed on social media. A striking example is the web doc *With Open Gates*, which circulated across various platforms and extremist forums and with many millions of views became one of the most watched far-right videos. The approximately eight-minute-long film uses incendiary propaganda techniques to evoke as much fear, disgust, hatred, and fury in response to refugees as possible. The fast-paced montage of television and video clips aims to convey the impression that masses of aggressive young men from Africa and West Asia, directed by Islamist preachers and Jewish world conspirators, are flocking to Europe to subjugate the locals. The video strings together shot after shot depicting migrants as brutal, ungrateful, depraved, and animalistic, aiming to dehumanize them and to link physical and social anxieties with fears about purity and sexuality. Its audiovisual form—gloomy music, a nervous handheld camera, and jumpy editing—is meant to intensify the viewers' fears on a preconscious level. Racist statements in the voice-over commentary emphasize the alleged danger. The propaganda film is made to have the appearance of a documentary but contains numerous lies and manipulative falsities, as the journalist Philip Kleinfeld (2015) has demonstrated in detail. For example, several sequences do not show refugees at all, but football hooligans and other violent perpetrators. And when in fact migrants are shown, the video distorts their statements with false subtitles, or it conceals the fact that they were acting in an emergency or in self-defense. Altogether, the video links migration with violence and incites violent reactions.

Distribution of the propaganda video on social media was strategically planned. According to fact checker Dan Evon, a user named Gex uploaded the propaganda file to the /pol/ ("Politically Incorrect") section of the imageboard website 8chan on November 9, 2015, together with detailed instructions for dissemination.[35] Following these instructions, the hate video was subtitled in multiple languages, uploaded to countless channels, shared via a X/Twitter hashtag, and forwarded to right-wing influencers. After radical right-wing US websites such as Breitbart praised the video, the usage curve rose sharply, further boosted by the Islamist attacks in Paris on November 13, 2015. The video was removed from some sites, but only for copyright infringement of the music, and on numerous others it was uploaded again in both the original and new versions. It reached over ten million clicks on just one of the YouTube channels.

Despite its wide reach, *With Open Gates* is just one small bit of the huge number of videos that right-wing extremist groups use to spread threat narratives and incite hatred. They address a broad range of target audiences through a ramified network of channels, supplying them with videos made to fit them. In doing so, they use the dynamics of social media and get others, right up to the then US President Donald Trump and other influential politicians, involved in spreading their messages.

Opposing actors in civil society try to counter such propaganda of hate and resentment with a broad variety of video forms. They present multi-voiced discourses of moving images and try to arouse empathy, compassion, and solidarity with refugees. In Germany, for example, refugees presented their own situation as reporters (e.g., in refugee.tv, active since 2015), left-wing media collectives such as Leftvision reported from refugee camps and demonstrations (see Chapter 5), and organizations such as the NGO Pro Asyl ("Pro Refuge") criticized detention pending deportation. Elsewhere, artists came up with special kinds of protest actions. For instance, the British street artist Banksy linked his London Graffito *Les Mis* (2016) via a QR code to the activist YouTube video *Calais Jungle Police Assaults* (Calais Migrant Solidarity 2016), which transports viewers to an improvised refugee camp on the French coast.

These and many other videos contributed to the empowerment of refugees and activist communities and moved other interested groups and sympathizers. However, they were viewed relatively rarely and apparently did not have a significant impact on decision-makers or the larger publics. In comparison, campaign videos by NGOs attained a far greater reach and were probably more influential in the latter respects. A particularly successful example was the *Most Shocking Second a Day Video* (Save the Children and Stirling 2014) by the children's rights organization Save the Children. The aim of their campaign "Save Syria's Children" was to counteract the increasing numbness of the Western public regarding the war in Syria and to collect donations for emergency aid. The fictional story in the less than two-minute video shifts the Syrian civil war to London. A nine-year-old girl is living a happy life there. She celebrates her birthday with her parents, goes to school, and plays with friends. But in the background, a political conflict is escalating: a bomb hits the house, and the family flees and undergoes increasingly dangerous situations. Eventually, the girl and her mother are separated from her father and seek refuge in an emergency shelter. A year later, the mother asks the girl what she wishes for her birthday, like at the beginning of the film, but the traumatized child just stares blankly into space. The video ends with a message: "Just because it isn't happening here / doesn't mean it isn't happening / #savesyriaschildren."

The story of this fundraising video is based on the experiences of Syrian children, but the setting was moved to Europe in order to evoke more empathy and willingness to donate among Western audiences. Moving the civil war to familiar surroundings was meant to make it easier for the European middle class to relate to

FIGURES 3.1a,b: *Most Shocking Second a Day Video*, UK 2014, Save the Children; production: Don't Panic; Unit9 Films.

the suffering of the Syrian people. The clickbait title, *Most Shocking Second a Day Video*, refers to its special narrative structure—it imitates the *One Second a Day* format on YouTube, whose producers record one second of their lives every day from the selfie perspective and then stitch these shots together (Figures 3.1 and 3.2). This form gives the video an extremely fast narration, as well as an impression of authenticity and closeness. Frontal close-ups of the little girl's face emphasize her emotional expression, the fragmented editing and suddenly changing surroundings make her disorientation palpable. The filmmakers also use tried and tested narrative techniques of eliciting feelings of empathy and care such as personalizing collective problems and stressing the urgent need for help. The plot corresponds to essential aspects of mainstream storytelling: the sympathetic protagonist has to leave her familiar world, her conflict intensifies continuously until reaching a climax, and the ending recalls the beginning, but in stark contrast. Visuals and sound accentuate this development, creating an increasingly dark and dangerous atmosphere. The narrative uses the classic rhetorical devices of persuasion: pathos through empathy, logos through an argument for emergency relief, and ethos through emphasizing the humanitarian identity of the established NGO. Not only does the fundraising video culminate in a specific call to action, but the images are overlaid with links to the NGO's website and to a text-to-donate service while it is running.

On YouTube alone, *Most Shocking Second a Day Vide*o was watched over 21 million times within just five days (in 2022: more than 74 million views). It was widely shared across other platforms and received heavy coverage in mass media as well as several awards from advertising associations. The video's success is due not least to strategies of production, design, and distribution that can now be seen as typical for the work of larger NGOs. Increasingly, they have their more important video campaigns created by professional film companies (in this case, Unit 9) and advertising agencies (McQuater 2014). The agency Don't Panic (n.d.), which conceptualized the campaign, says that the video has been covered more than 150 times in major news media and that it has increased fundraising by over 93 percent. Video campaigners aim to involve journalists, opinion leaders, and celebrities in social media dissemination and interaction to attract viewers. A Facebook post by film star Ashton Kutcher about the video eight months after its release received more than 148,000 likes, 3,000 comments, and 75,000 shares within a few days, boosting the video's reach (Johnson 2014). The many comments on YouTube and other platforms expressing empathy and solidarity indicate that the video strengthened altruistic positions in the discourse on migration.[36] According to Save the Children, the campaign has helped provide tens of thousands of refugee children with basic necessities. While the video has been criticized by some for its forced emotionalization strategies and Eurocentrism, it is questionable whether it would have had a comparably strong impact otherwise—which points to a recurring dilemma of video activism.

Political Emotions and the Different Audiences of Activism

The preceding examples illustrate how crucial the affective impact of videos is when it comes to gaining public attention and influencing social discourses and practices. Politics is by no means driven solely by cool rationality and cost-benefit calculations, but rather by collective affects and emotions: compassion for those in need, outrage at injustice, fear of violence, hope for change, hatred of opponents, contempt for outgroups, pride in the ingroup, feelings of solidarity and countless other conscious emotions, preconscious affects, subliminal moods, biases, and resentments (Nussbaum 2013; Jasper 2018). The layered themes, stories, messages, aesthetic forms, and connections to reality in the videos give them an enormous potential to arouse such affects and emotions (Eder 2018). They can give viewers the impression that the problems depicted concern their own lifeworld, for which they are responsible and in which they can and must act. At the same time, videos on social media also become a means of creating affective relationships and social interactions between creators and users, who, through their videos and comments, convey an image of themselves, express sympathy or antipathy for each other, and show their attachment to values and social groups.

Videos intervene in social conflicts by evoking political emotions in both participants and previously uninvolved viewers. The affective reactions of the latter are largely based on the way the conflicts are framed and perceived, on their attitudes toward the conflict, and their relationship to the people involved. Many videos contain strong affective stimuli. Some are intensely physical: wounded bodies, agitated voices, angry or crying faces. Others are more abstract but also effective such as the clashing interests, values, and moral positions of the conflicting parties. Through their framing and aesthetics, videos can amplify or mitigate aggression, excite or frighten protesters, repress or intensify feelings of guilt, build communities or exclude strangers, and make it easy or hard to feel for them.

This is particularly evident when videos portray the ingroup or outgroups of their target audience—"us" and "them." The previously discussed examples form an extreme contrast in this respect. *With Open Gates* portrays migration as a threatening invasion of aggressive men; the *Most Shocking Second a Day Video* makes us experience the flight of innocent children who call for our compassion and help. Such extreme forms are by no means equal—the crucial question is on what factual ground such frames are based and what practical and ethical consequences they have (see Chapters 2 and 7). Although *With Open Gates* presents itself as a documentary, it contains countless falsifications, whereas the fictional story in *Most Shocking Second a Day Video* is based on actual accounts of refugee children. Given the demonstrable causes and consequences of flight and migration, compassion and solidarity seem ethically imperative, while fear and hatred seem destructive and utterly wrong in this context.

However, the two contrasting examples also have some things in common. Both are highly emotional videos that present their subject matter in a dramatized, intensified way, place it in a polarized frame, and are distributed according to a closely planned strategy. This is typical for political videos aiming at a broad reach and corresponds to the way social media channel attention. That again raises difficult questions about the appropriateness, accuracy, and genuineness of emotion and activism in social videos. There is a danger of simplification, voyeurism, self-righteous one-sidedness, biased aggression, or sentimental pity tourism, especially when videos employ intense feelings or entertainment to reach a large audience and try to overcome the psychological barriers resulting from demands for social change. In his book *Anti-Social Media*, Siva Vaidhyanathan fears that the "cause that makes the catchiest, cutest, or most clever Facebook campaign generates the most financial support," which would indeed be "a terrible way to determine where charitable contributions should go" (2018). He assumes that emotionalization and polarization have comparable consequences on political processes.

It appears that activists face a dilemma: should they try to reach as many viewers as possible with intensely emotional videos, even if that means compromising on ethical principles and on an appropriate presentation of complex political issues? Or should their videos deal with the issue in a differentiated, balanced, sober way, even if that means they only reach a minuscule number of viewers and achieve weak effects? What forms of activism are both adequate and promising on social media? These questions are the subject of bitter debates between "radical" and "reformist" activists, and between supporters of instrumental, observational, or media-reflexive approaches to video work (Eder 2023).

In our view, the dilemma can be resolved—but not so much in terms of individual videos as through the diversity of their complementary, co-existing forms (as the following chapters will show). To achieve social change with videos, different types of activists—from individual citizens to local video collectives to global NGOs—pursue very different strategies, depending on their goals and available options. Large NGOs often devise sophisticated, elaborate campaigns to achieve the broadest possible impact on the widest possible public. Others target more narrowly defined audiences. Video collectives such as Reel News, for example, pursue an ethical stance similar to that of counter-journalists and advocacy documentaries, mostly addressing communities that are already politically engaged. Artivists reach mostly younger, formally educated milieus. Other activists reject strategic impact plans on principle, as they want to involve those affected by their issue as spontaneously, directly, and sincerely as possible. Finally, protesters and witnesses of violence often have no opportunity to act strategically at all. They are forced to react immediately to a given situation or adapt to unpredictable developments quickly and tactically. They often post their videos as a spontaneous outcry or call for solidarity.

While activists work in all these varied ways, and many more, three general approaches, differing in their audiences, strategies, and video forms, seem particularly important: moving large publics, empowering communities, and persuading influential individuals and institutions. The first approach to video activism, which has been at the center of our considerations so far, aims to *move large publics*—ideally the majority of the population or at least significant interest groups or sizable counterpublics. Such videos are used to influence public opinion and convince as many people as possible to donate, sign petitions, demonstrate, boycott goods, or vote in elections, thus putting pressure on governments and corporations. This approach requires attracting maximum attention on social media, which, as we have seen, is quite difficult. As in the case of the *Most Shocking Second a Day Video*, the chances are best if the videos are professionally produced and strategically distributed. This, in turn, requires a high level of craftsmanship, expertise, and resources, which larger NGOs like Save the Children or Greenpeace have at their disposal. From time to time, however, successful vloggers or large networks around very powerful witness videos also reach considerable audiences (see Chapters 4, 5, and 6). According to a tweet by political scientist Marc Owen Jones (@marcowenjones) on October 12, 2022, during the massive protests against the Iranian regime, there were over 274 million tweets with the Persian version of the Mahsa Amini hashtag, referring to the young woman murdered by the so-called Guidance Patrol.[37] Many of those tweets included witness videos of the protests and of police violence. Strategies to reach large audiences also differ in their time frames. In the short term, mobilization videos, witness videos, fundraising films, or strategic impact campaigns draw attention to current events and issues (on equivalent strategies in filmmaking, see Nash and Corner 2016). In the long term, vlogs or explainer videos gain attention using entertainment-education strategies, thereby building a base of followers (on entertainment-education, see Frank and Falzone 2021). More generally, such strategies demonstrate that activism and entertainment are by no means mutually exclusive. On the contrary, entertainment is employed in many ways for political goals. The speakers in the Humane Society's animal rights video *Save Ralph* (The Humane Society of the United States and Susser 2021), a puppet animation mockumentary, are Hollywood stars such as Taika Waititi, Ricky Gervais, and Zac Efron. Moreover, several YouTubers and TikTokers not only run entertaining music or comedy channels with a large fan base but also leverage their established reach for political statements (see Chapters 4 and 7). And some commercial agencies like the German Mesh Collective even specialize in connecting humanitarian foundations with well-known influencers on TikTok, Instagram, and YouTube to introduce young followers to political issues such as racism or climate justice.

A second approach focuses on *community empowerment*. In this case, activist organizers direct their videos primarily toward their own group or to the affected communities they are advocating for. They collaborate with socially marginalized people, their allies, or sympathizers in participatory video production, let them create their own stories and express their political concerns, and train their ability to become politically organized and shoot their own videos (Aguayo 2019). By producing and archiving audiovisual documentation of protest actions, they make it possible for the community to see and recognize itself and thereby contribute to the formation of feelings of group belonging, of shared convictions, memories, and identity. This kind of video work conveys feelings of courage and hope, bolsters up the group, motivates and mobilizes its members, and creates networks among them and their allies. It also often leads to the creation of new kinds of images and artistic forms and strategies that others can use. These forms of empowerment through video usually require relatively little funding (but a lot of time) and are often used by smaller, local video collectives. Examples are the British citizen journalist portal Reel News, the Turkish video archive bak.ma, or on a larger scale, the non-profit organization EngageMedia in the Asia-Pacific region. The main challenge of this approach is to gain access to affected communities and earn their trust and their willingness to participate.

The resulting videos and archives can then also be used in the third approach, which addresses *influential decision-makers and institutions* in politics, law, business, or mass media. The focus here is predominantly on witness videos of human rights violations or environmental degradation. Some essential challenges of this strategy consist of gaining access to the relevant persons and institutions and verifying the videos so that they can serve as meaningful evidence in court, parliaments, or mass media. As Sandra Ristovska (2021) emphasizes, different kinds of non-profit organizations are becoming increasingly professionalized in this regard. Using comprehensive reconstructions of events together with videos, context information, and metadata, counter-forensic verification organizations such as Forensic Architecture and Bellingcat ensure that witness videos can be recognized as evidence in court. The NGO WITNESS provides communities worldwide with training in how to document violence and present their videos to international tribunals such as the International Criminal Court. Amnesty International also aims some of its videos at the UN and national governments. For example, *The Stuff of Life* (Amnesty International UK 2008) about CIA waterboarding torture was screened in the US Congress and in the UK Houses of Parliament.[38]

Of course, these three approaches can be combined to address different audiences with the same videos. To understand the impact of activist videos, we must take into account that they have very different stakeholders and addressees such as the general public, social interest groups, affected communities, political opponents, decision-makers, professional journalists, the videos' protagonists, or other film and video makers. Furthermore, such audiences have diverse and intersecting social identities and cultures, and they often respond very differently to the same video. At the same time, strategic impact campaigns can involve directly affected people, journalists, and political organizations in the production and circulation of a video, as well as making that video interesting to the public through emotional storytelling, encouraging their followers on social media to share it, and organizing special screenings for decision-makers. However, the focus is often on one of these approaches because they can also contradict each other. Emotional videos made for a mass audience often lack credibility and seriousness from the perspective of courts or affected communities, while legally tenable witness videos or amateurishly made empowerment videos are often not particularly attractive to a wide audience.

Not all these approaches depend on reaching many viewers. Participatory videos may even build, empower, and move political communities more effectively if their audiences belong to close-knit interest groups that are of a manageable size and familiar with each other. And a few powerful legislators or lawyers may be enough of an audience for institutional videos to initiate wide-reaching political or legal processes. Nevertheless, in both cases, it may also be beneficial or even necessary to reach a larger public, if it can be brought to support the concerns of communities, witnesses, or political representatives and build up pressure.

The different forms of video work complement one another. Popular, professionally made films such as the *Most Shocking Second a Day Video* can influence the behavior of a considerable part of the population and put public pressure on political decision-makers but may be forced to make compromises in regard to objectivity, ethics, and aesthetics. Approaches that are less willing to make concessions in those regards, again, tend to reach fewer people, but they can serve to establish standards for media ethics, guarantee credibility, and be a source of innovation. There are numerous intermediate forms between these ideal-typical extremes. Nonetheless, activists from the various groups do not always view other approaches as a positive supplement or a potential for collaboration but often distrust each other, even if they aim at achieving similar political goals. In our view, cooperation and networking could provide huge benefits for all of them. Often the reciprocal linking of videos and video creators would already improve their visibility on the internet. In Chapter 7, we will say more about that, and in Chapter 5, we will describe different observable types of video activist practice, ranging from individual influencers to small collectives to large NGOs. Before that, however, we will take a closer look at the specific forms and possibilities of video aesthetics and distribution that are available to activists.

4

Activist Video Strategies: From Creation to Networking

In their struggle for attention on social media, video activists use a variety of strategies. Many of them are well aware of how to improve the reach and impact of their videos, but according to our observations, others still lack sufficient knowledge or skills, despite the increasing availability of manuals, guidelines, and explainer videos. We will now take a closer look at the practitioner and academic literature on strategic social media and video use, and complement this with our own findings. On the most general level, four areas of video activist practices and strategies can be distinguished:

Creative or *design strategies* focus on the rhetorical, narrative, and audiovisual forms and contents of videos, and thus on their potential for evoking attention, understanding, and affects.

Production strategies deal with modes and practices of financing and making vidcos, for instance through crowdsourcing, participatory co-creation, or collaboration with professional agencies or production companies.

Distribution strategies are concerned with planning and implementing effective dissemination of videos, both online across various channels and platforms and offline, for example, through mass media or community screenings.

Networking strategies include many time-consuming forms of interaction, mostly after videos are published, such as monitoring user engagement, managing comments, responding to reaction videos (e.g., with a follow-up video), connecting with other creators, protesting against video deletions, or thanking multipliers who share the video.

In each of these areas, video activists use both strategies in the narrower sense (long-term action plans) and tactics (short-term reactions to changing situations) (de Certeau 1988). Their choice of certain strategies or tactics depends on the nature of their political issue, on their resources and principles, their experience and professionalism, their target audiences, their media environment, their sociocultural situation, and the function of the video in the context of other activist aims (see Chapter 5).

The political topics and intended audiences of a video are of crucial importance in these respects (Doc Society 2019). Relevant factors of topics are, for example, whether the viewers are already familiar with it, whether it is about openly visible violence or less obvious structural injustice, or whether activists expect strong reactions from political opponents or not. Such factors influence the videos' form, production, and distribution. In the case of already well-known issues such as the climate crisis, for instance, it is important to offer fresh perspectives and to counter the distraction strategies of powerful corporate lobbies with emotional messages, for example, in mobilization videos. In contrast, in a case of police violence that is still unknown to the public, it would be more important to document the violent action unequivocally in a witness video. And if the authorities deny the case, one witness video alone will not suffice; it would have to be supported by further evidence, for example, in the form of argumentative documentaries or forensic videos.

Concerning potential audiences, we can ask if a video is primarily aimed at the general public, at powerful decision-makers, or at the impacted communities and their supporters (see Chapter 3). This has significant strategic consequences. For example, if the intention is to empower those affected by an issue, it might be important to involve this group right from the start of production. However, if the intention is to move the general public and win new supporters, activists could look for sponsors to finance professionally made videos and work with film production companies or agencies to prepare an effective campaign. And if the aim is to convince powerful decision-makers or institutions, it might be advantageous to have journalists accompany the video production and to recruit committed scientists, lawyers, politicians, and other experts to the cause.

Strategic practices of video design, production, distribution, and networking are interdependent; they influence each other and ideally should be coordinated. To illustrate this, we can look at the factors that, according to film scholar and producer Caty Borum Chattoo, increase the impact of "social issue documentaries": telling a strong, emotional story well; involving stakeholders and multipliers in production or distribution (e.g., protest groups, NGOs, or experts); developing a temporally sequenced, cross-media distribution campaign; inviting journalists to continue the film's story in mass media news; and encouraging the audience to participate by indicating concrete possibilities for action (Borum Chattoo 2020). Several interrelations are obvious here: a strong story makes it easier to engage stakeholders in production and distribution, develop a successful distribution strategy and marketing campaign, get journalists interested in taking up the story and continuing the narrative, and invite audiences to take action and join together as a community. Conversely, a story is more newsworthy for journalists and more suitable for word-of-mouth campaigns if relevant communities are already involved as protagonists or co-producers. These lessons from committed documentary filmmaking apply to video activism, as well.

The interdependence of the formal qualities, production, and networking of videos is particularly evident in framing political concerns. Here, tensions regularly arise between strategic options. Left-wing video activists could, for example, formulate their concerns about economic justice broadly and soberly in order to sensitize the widest possible audience to the issue, as in the case of *Wealth Inequality in America* (Politizane 2012). Alternatively, they could choose a more specific framing that includes concrete but contested measures (e.g., expropriation) to mobilize their own group. In this chapter and the next, we explore such contexts and tensions, focusing first on the strategies for the creative design of the videos and then on their dissemination and networking. Occasionally, we will also look at production strategies and return to them in more detail later (especially in Chapter 5).

Video Aesthetics and Spreadability: A Variety of Effective Forms

In Chapter 1, we distinguished the most common types of activist videos as witness videos, documentaries, vlogs, mobilization videos, and subversion videos. Beyond these very general types, however, the specific forms of videos require a closer look, because their content-related and formal qualities—their poetics and aesthetics—are decisive for their reach and impact. They are the basis of their power to evoke affects and their spreadability on the web. They are the starting point for videos to attract attention, go viral, become memes, trigger social media cascades, and ultimately serve as catalysts of "affective publics" (Papacharissi 2014, see Chapter 6). Videos move their viewers by steering attention, understanding, and affect on multiple levels: through their audiovisual forms, images, and sounds; their represented worlds, people, and conflicts; their thematic frames, meanings, and messages; and their references to communicative contexts, including the video creators themselves and their political backgrounds (Eder 2018). All these levels interact with one another—harmonious forms can moderate the affective impact of violent events, or strong arguments can be weakened if viewers do not trust the video makers.

What are the most important strategies for shaping video genres and forms? Researchers from various disciplines, including film and communication studies, psychology, social marketing, and behavioral economics, have tried to identify general factors of textual content and form that foster the reach or impact of media messages. The results of their work are condensed in concepts such as "virality," "memes," "spreadability," or "shareability" (e.g., Ford et al. 2013;

Shifman 2014; Harcup and O'Neill 2017) or in models labeled BCOS (Benefits, Costs, Others, and Self-Efficacy) (Andreasen 2002), STEPPS (Social Currency, Triggers, Emotion, Public, Practical Value, and Stories) (Berger 2013), or SHIFT (Social influence, Habit formation, Individual self, Feelings and cognition, and Tangibility) (White et al. 2019). Summarizing such summaries, we can distinguish the following success factors, each of which is mentioned across several approaches:

Emotions: videos tend to spread more easily when they arouse intense emotions and affects, which can be either positive and pleasant (and thus entertaining) or negative and unpleasant (and thus triggering ongoing controversies between users).

Stories: the power of narratives to evoke emotions and persuade audiences is a recurring topic in media psychology and film studies. Stories and emotions are obviously related through moving characters, gripping conflicts, suspense, surprise, and other narrative emotions.

Tangibility: the political theme of a video tends to generate more interest if it is made concrete, simple, specific, local, and vivid (instead of abstract, distant, complex, or ambivalent) and if its closeness and relevance to the audience are stressed. Storytelling can contribute to that.

Topicality: if a video relates to current attention-grabbing stimuli in the users' social environment, such as well-known memes, icons, celebrities, political conflicts, scandals, media events, or other trending topics, it can profit from their attention value.

Identity: a video's impact can be fostered by targeted framing and group-specific appeals to users' social identities and self-concepts, their norms, values, and affiliation with certain communities, organizations, or social movements.

Practical relevance: interest can be increased if a video contains information that is practically useful for viewers such as warnings of imminent dangers or ways to improve cost-benefit ratios in their everyday lives.

Self-efficacy: videos can achieve a stronger impact on viewers' behavior if they include clear, easily implementable proposals for concrete action (including suggestions of how to change one's own habits), thereby eliciting positive feelings of agency, empowerment, and self-efficacy.

Social benefits: a video tends to spread more widely if it can be used for relationship building, self-promotion, or status enhancement on social platforms, for example, if by sharing it you can expect applause from your Facebook friends or TikTok followers.

Several further relevant factors are mentioned less often, such as using positive "gain frames" instead of paralyzing "danger frames," avoiding cultural polarization (when addressing a large, diverse audience), or offering variety and innovation. Some factors are separate from the ones mentioned above, for example, the presence of iconic persons in a video or as multipliers in its social media context. Bishnupriya Ghosh (2011) has studied in detail the central roles played by "global icons" such as Arundhati Roy or Mother Theresa in political conflicts, media events, and everyday appropriation practices, and her observations concerning the multilayered affective-political attachment to such icons can largely be applied to social media. Zeyneb Tufekci has described more recent developments in the concentration of collective attention on public figures online as "networked microcelebrity activism." By this, she means the actions of "politically motivated noninstitutional actors who use affordances of social media to engage in presentation of their political and personal selves to garner public attention to their cause, usually through a combination of testimony, advocacy and citizen journalism" (Tufekci 2013, 850).

Social media consultants propose more concrete rules of thumb for platform-specific video design.[39] Many recommend two patent remedies: the spectacular short form and emotional storytelling. The spectacular short form results from the way most online videos are viewed: as fleetingly passing particles in an infinite stream of content. This is why social media specialists often suggest keeping videos as short as possible (dividing more complex content into a series) and capturing attention right at the beginning with spectacular impressions or "hooks" that act as "thumb stoppers," keeping the viewers from scrolling further down the newsfeed. Strong, striking stimuli at all levels are supposed to make videos stand out in the fierce competition for attention. This could mean using clickbait, eye-catching images, expressive faces, erotic cues, intense conflicts, surprising or comical events, but also sudden sounds, identity-relevant themes, or provocative theses. The second recipe, emotional storytelling, does not refer to narration in general, but to a specific, simple, and strategic narrative form that uses tried-and-tested techniques to get messages across effectively and persuasively by embodying emotions and values in characters and conflicts (Sachs 2012). According to this formula, sympathetic protagonists struggle to achieve well-deserved goals, satisfy urgent needs, or assert fundamental values; they fight for a noble cause against sinister opponents, the obstacles grow, and narrative tension builds to a climax.

The combination of the spectacular short form with storytelling has led to an industry ideal: the spectacular mini-story. An extreme example is *The High Diver* (YouTube Advertisers 2017), a six-second ad that ran on YouTube before the actual videos. It tells a spectacular mini-story: a high diver jumps from a ten-meter board into a pool, but during the jump the years pass almost instantaneously, climate change turns the world into a glowing desert, and the water in the pool evaporates before he reaches the bottom. The diver represents humanity, of course. The brief length of only a few seconds is extreme. More generally, social media videos can be divided into three groups according to their duration, each of which fits different platforms and requires different narrative and aesthetic forms. *Very short videos* like *The High Diver* last from a few seconds to two minutes and are suitable for quick visits on Facebook, Instagram, or TikTok. *Short videos* last two to fifteen minutes (equivalent to classical short films), so you can watch them in between while waiting for the bus. They make up the bulk of the dedicated videos on YouTube and are still possible on Facebook. Finally, *long videos*—that is, anything longer than fifteen minutes—are rarer, but they still include some very successful productions (some of them are discussed in this book). You can find them mostly on YouTube and it takes a longer train ride or an evening at home to watch them. All three lengths have their purposes. While advertising research indicates that most video ads are viewed only in part and the average viewing time is very short (a few minutes on YouTube, a few seconds on Facebook), reliable data on activists or other socially engaged videos does not yet exist to our knowledge.[40] According to an older study from 2011, the hundred most viewed non-profit videos on YouTube were on average five and a half minutes long (Waters and Jones 2011), but the average value says little about the most common lengths, and it can be assumed that both the range of videos and the usage habits have already changed.

Our own observations cast doubt on the common wisdom of social media experts that the spectacular mini-story should be ideal for all online videos, let alone activist ones (see Chapter 5). The limitations of the spectacular mini-story are obvious: it is hardly suitable for doing justice to political realities, conveying complex content, or evoking appropriate, lasting emotions. When it comes to issues like the climate crisis, distributive injustice, or structural racism, mini-stories about starving polar bears, greedy managers, or the experiences of individual discriminated people may sometimes be useful, but they are not enough. Not every subject can be squeezed into a short story. The problems are well known: oversimplification, personalization, neglect of structural injustices, lack of balance, loss of authenticity and credibility, and many further ethical issues (see Chapter 2). Moreover, video creation follows very different aims that depend on the intersecting social identities of diverse audiences—for instance, to reach large publics, mobilize specific interest groups, empower afflicted communities, provoke opponents, convince courts, lobby lawmakers, pressurize corporations, get sympathizers involved or inspire other filmmakers, and all that in different local, social, and cultural situations (see Chapter 3). In some cases, it might be more effective to captivate viewers with short stories, in others to convince them with substantial arguments developed in a longer video. Therefore, a diversity of video genres, styles, and forms is needed to achieve social change. Thus, there are many ways to create activist videos and channel political emotions. Without claiming to be exhaustive, we can distinguish four basic formal structures of activist videos: they can narrate, show, argue, or symbolize.

Narration (schema: protagonists strive for a goal → encounter antagonistic forces → conflict develops → climactic confrontation stays unresolved → viewers are called to action): activist narratives show the development of political conflicts or attempts to solve problems, often with an open ending that urges the audience to join with the protagonists and their helpers online and offline. Greatly simplified, such narratives are usually structured around conflicts between three different positions: a video can either focus on the "perpetrators" responsible for a political injustice, its "victims," or the "heroines and helpers" fighting against it. (Of course, these are only narrative roles; in reality, the people affected should not be reduced to the role of victim, nor are all supporters heroines and all politically responsible people perpetrators.) Each focus is associated with certain evaluations and emotions. Stories about victims, such as climate refugees, mostly appeal to compassion, fear, or sadness. Stories about perpetrators, such as profit-hungry oil companies, are more likely to evoke outrage and moral disgust. And stories about heroines and helpers tend to elicit enthusiasm, admiration, pride, or hope. Viewers can be put in the position of a neutral observer, such as a narrator or journalist who assesses events from a distance, but more often they are invited to share the perspective of (positive) protagonists. A much-discussed example of the strengths and dangers of the mainstream narrative approach is the campaign video *KONY 2012* (Invisible Children and Russell 2012) (Engelhardt and Jansz 2014). Its first-person narrator, activist Jason Russell, describes how he and the NGO Invisible Children (the heroes of the story) take action against the Ugandan warlord Joseph Kony (the perpetrator), who misuses children (the victims) as soldiers or sexually enslaves them. The film is a prime example of strategically emotionalized storytelling and uses every means to maximize pity, suspense, and sympathy. Its climax turns viewers into virtual members of the movement, expected to help and donate. The ending is open, a call to action appeals to the viewers to help solve the problem themselves and to become heroes of the story, linking this directly to possibilities to take action online. In just a few days, *KONY 2012* reached 100 million views, but later many questioned the video's manipulative, simplistic, and even neo-colonial representation of the topic.

Other narrative forms offer other possibilities, for instance by inviting rational deliberation or self-reflection. Several of the examples we already examined also diverge from mainstream storytelling conventions. For instance, *The Most Boring Viral Video* takes a self-reflexive stance and guides the viewers' attention toward their own use of social media. And the *Most Shocking Second a Day Video* has a passive protagonist, an open ending, and subjects its story to the intertextual pattern of the second-a-day format. There is an enormous variety of narrative forms online.

Showing (schema: look at this!): rather than telling a story of several connected events, witness videos are deictic, pointing to one specific event. Presenting visual evidence of injustice, violence, suffering, or protest, they focus on affectively charged incidents that force the audience to take sides. Intensive physical expressions of pain or outrage can inspire empathy, and the sight of injured people may evoke horror or compassion. If the camera reproduces the eyewitnesses' perspective, this can immerse the viewers in the action, for instance, a protesting crowd, and communicate bodily movements of rushing forward, fleeing, and standing frozen. Witness videos do not just claim "that is how it was" but also "I was there taking risks in filming." They vouch for authenticity. Commentaries by a witness's voice-over or vocal expressions of emotion on the soundtrack also suggest an evaluative and affective attitude that the viewers are intended to take toward what is shown. The impact of witness videos is thus also related to which side of the conflict the witnesses are on and whether they appear credible to the audience.

Arguing (schema: information about a problem → deliberation about its causes → suggestion of solutions): this type of video is usually longer and develops an argument by advancing a political thesis and supporting it with evidence, examples, or expert testimony (following the famous Toulmin scheme of argumentation, Hesling 1989; Tseronis 2015). This strategy is particularly common in documentaries and vlogs. In the United States, for example, Natalie Wynn a.k.a. ContraPoints works in this way, in the United Kingdom Owen Jones, and in Germany Rezo (see the example at the end of this chapter). In China, the independent journalist Chai Jing's viral documentary video *Under the Dome* (2015) starts by citing evidence that coal smog is making millions of Chinese citizens sick and concludes that the authorities need to reform the energy system. Various rhetorical techniques are used to support this argument: investigative factory visits, data visualization, the filmmaker's authority as an investigative journalist, and not least emotionalization when the author refers to her own daughter's illness. Images and music create fitting moods, and mini-stories (Jing's personal story, smog cartoons) combine the difficult subject matter with pathos and humor. In this way, *Under the Dome* evokes a dramatic sequence of emotions from initial concern through outrage to hope for change. Other argumentative videos strive more for a tone of distanced objectivity, but they are not free of emotion either. Argumentation videos may unfold political arguments explicitly with all the means of rhetoric, but may also implicitly suggest them in enthymematic (incomplete) form, in which the conclusion must be drawn by the audience itself. Thus, explainer videos such as *Wealth Inequality in America* (Politizane 2012) often begin with a question that arouses curiosity: How is wealth distributed in the United States? This is followed by a surprising explanation (often an animated infographic) that answers the question (the top 1 percent own 40 percent of US wealth, while 80 percent of the population combined own only 8 percent). Such videos keep the explanation short and make it entertaining through the audiovisual form, striking data visualization, satirical humor, or a punchline. They aim at increasing the viewers' knowledge and at the same time at conveying an argument: since the distribution of wealth is so unequal and unfair, a redistribution from top to bottom is urgently needed and the government should implement this through taxes or other measures.

Symbolizing (schema: vivid symbol → condenses → an abstract issue): some videos use predominantly symbolic images and sounds to illustrate abstract meanings. They do not even have to depict concrete events to do so. *Amnesty International: Stop the Show* (2013), a short, animated film made by the artist Max Hattler, accompanied a campaign for global arms trade control. The video unleashes a colorful swirl of geometric shapes reminiscent of the flags of conflicting political parties, rotating kaleidoscopically around the center of the image. The symbols move faster and faster, their collisions are accompanied by an increasingly loud cacophony of military noises. After this reaches a crescendo, abrupt silence is followed by a call to put pressure on governments to regulate the arms trade. In this way, the video drew attention to the campaign that culminated in the UN Arms Trade Treaty in 2013.

Each of the basic video forms moves viewers in different ways and fulfills different functions. Narration reveals subjective experiences, showing makes something visible, argumentation convinces, explaining creates knowledge, and symbolization condenses complex facts. To deal with more complex political issues, narration and argumentation are the most suitable modes; longer videos of these kinds are more likely to be found on video platforms like YouTube than on social networks such as TikTok.

The basic forms can be combined and varied in many ways. For instance, *The High Diver* is an extremely short narrative and at the same time a symbolic condensation of the complex climate crisis. Moreover, many new video forms have developed on social media and experimented with network trends. For example, some videos use parodic *meme-esis*—they tie in with successful memes to increase their own reach. In 2014, the Ice Bucket Challenge went viral: to raise money for research on the neurological disease amyotrophic lateral sclerosis (ALS), thousands of people, including many celebrities, poured ice water over their heads in front of their webcams. Later that year, Palestinian activists used the trend for their cause and invented the Rubble Bucket Challenge (al-Aloul and Yusef 2014) to draw attention to the destruction in the Gaza Strip after an Israeli military operation. In their videos, the student Maysam Yusef and the journalist Ayman al-Aloul stood in ruined landscapes and poured rubble instead of ice over their heads—neither water nor electricity was available on site to produce ice cubes. In this way, the activists tried to evoke the viewers' somatic empathy and vivid imaginations of hot dust entering mouths and noses. The action was widely imitated, shared on the web, and also picked up by Western mass media. Such "challenges" and the *Second a Day* format (mentioned in Chapter 3) are only two among many social media formats that activists adopt for political purposes. On TikTok, young women* smuggle political messages into make-up tutorials. On YouTube, online gaming stars like Destiny hold debates with political opponents on their streams, or they make occasional political statements during *Let's Play* videos, as in the case of the German YouTuber Gronkh. There is hardly an online video genre that has not been adapted to political use. We can find equivalents to almost the entire range of film genres, documentary modes, TV programs, music videos, animation, and experimental films. In addition, there are all kinds of new online forms such as *Second a Day*, *Challenge*, *Haul*, *Unboxing*, *Stitch*, or *Let's Play*. Those forms are often related to narration: they contain narrative elements and activate stories in the viewers' minds (see below). However, they also move the audience in ways that are different from storytelling, and new possibilities for influencing viewers arise as well. Aesthetic innovation, originality, and creativity provide opportunities for activists since network communities are always searching for diversions. The web is hungry for variety, and fortunately, there is indeed a huge diversity of activist videos. Looking through the social media profiles and channels of activist groups or NGOs, we found that some of them—for example, the animal protection organization PETA—focus quite successfully on spectacular mini-stories. More common than storytelling, however, are other video forms such as deictic witness videos, deliberative documentaries, and explainer videos or rhetorical vlogs.

The Dynamics of Distribution: Networked Attention and Emergent Narratives

As the above examples suggest, the forms of videos are adapted to their media environment, including strategies of dissemination across different platforms and in hybrid media systems. It is therefore important to see individual videos in their larger, interactive contexts. The "spreadability" of videos is decisive for their success, or, as Henry Jenkins (2009) put it: "If it doesn't spread, it's dead." But even if the content and form of a video are highly "spreadable," it is not enough to simply upload it and wait. When videos circulate widely, it is usually due to deliberate dissemination and networking strategies that take advantage of the interplay between technical platform dynamics and psychological group dynamics. How people select and use videos is determined on the one hand by platform interfaces and algorithms, and on the other hand by psychological and social motives such as the search for information, entertainment, or connection. The technical affordances of platforms that enable the liking, sharing, or commenting of videos work hand in hand with building and maintaining social relationships that involve feelings of friendship or hatred, self-worth or embarrassment, affirmation or provocation, as well as fears of missing out, public rejection, or humiliation. The engagement rate for a video increases if it can be used for social relations, especially if it makes the person sharing it look good in the eyes of relevant others. And conversely, platform algorithms favor videos that lead to a large number of interactions, whether friendly or hateful.

To understand more precisely why and how activist videos may succeed (or not) in the ecology of attention on social media and in hybrid media systems, we need to take a step back and ask: How can the relevant structures of attention be conceptualized? A helpful starting point is Yves Citton's (2017) distinction between three levels of attention: individual, joint, and collective (or public). Individual attention concerns the relation between one individual person and an object such as a video. Joint attention takes place in social situations, where co-present individuals are not only attentive to the same object but also to their mutual attention to it, following each other's gazes or utterances. Collective attention develops mostly in large, spatially, or temporally dispersed (media) audiences, whose members are not co-present or cannot react directly to each other but are aware that the objects of their attention are perceived by many others.

In the case of social media, a complicated interplay between various layers of individual, joint, and collective attention develops. In addition, *networked attention*—as described by Bennett, Segerberg, and Yang (2018)—comes into play in a complex and media-specific way. Videos flow across various networks of communication with differing gatekeeping processes, human decisions, and distribution algorithms, to different individual social media "friends" and followers, to private or public groups, as well as to larger, dispersed, or fragmented publics. Some of the recipients are in close contact with each other, others in sharp opposition, and still others are linked only by "weak ties" or not at all. Networked attention is thus based on "an iterative mix of selective attention, network interactions, narrative construction, and selective uptake by legacy media," on a "push and pull of information over different communication networks with different gatekeeping processes, content distribution methods, and combinations of human and algorithmic decisions" (Bennett et al. 2018, 680). This means that networked attention emerges from individual attention to specific videos in the context of social situations and interactions on platforms. We are talking about a socio-medial environment, where various factors are interconnected: structures of videos, platforms, minds, user groups, and cultures. On the one hand, video selection and reception are influenced by social relationships, for instance by the fact that the video was made by an adored celebrity, shared by a close friend, or discussed in one's own virtual communities. Videos achieve their impact within a specific social space, which is why video producers often advise communicating on an equal basis, being honest, not preaching, and admitting one's own weaknesses in a funny way. This is particularly important for activist approaches that aim at empowering those involved and strengthening a community's identity. On the other hand, video selection is also strongly influenced by the structures and affordances of social media, for instance, by recommendation algorithms that put a video at the top of one's newsfeed or "For You" page or by a personalized list of "Related Videos" on the YouTube interface.

These socio-medial interactions tend to develop in a nonlinear dynamic with emergent properties that concern various kinds of attentional processes in video selection, reception, and follow-up practices. For instance, interactions on social media are driven by individual self-presentation and impression management. Facebook users who receive more attention are more likely to post more often than users who receive little attention. At the same time, individual users are influenced by ingroup/outgroup dynamics such as social contagion, herding behavior, tribalization, polarization, filter bubbles, or echo chambers. Individual attention shapes socio-medial networks and vice versa.

The temporal spread of attention across social networks is often made visible by diagrams of so-called cyber-cascades, for instance in the case of viral videos. But there are various other kinds of attentional networks and flows through social media, which depend on the specific affordances and networking structures of different social media platforms like X/Twitter or YouTube, on the one hand, and on the kinds of self-selected social formations on those platforms, on the other.

These socio-medial environments and the resulting flows of networked attention also shape new forms of overarching political narratives. In a nutshell, the logic of social media drives a logic of *shared stories*, and networked attention drives *networked narratives* (also called fragmented, emergent, or hashtag narratives) (Georgakopoulou 2007; Kozinets et al. 2010; Page 2013; Dawson 2020; Dawson and Mäkelä 2020; Sadler 2022). By linking countless individual micro-narratives (as well as non-narrative postings), co-constructive macro-narratives emerge. In the context of the MeToo movement, for example, many women shared their personal stories of sexual harassment and violence, usually in the form of short tweets and videos. The hashtag #MeToo, used mostly on X/Twitter and Facebook, connected those personal micro-stories to form an overarching macro-narrative, a shared story of female victims of male aggression finding solidarity and fighting back.[41] A similar pattern of micro- and macro-stories can be observed in other contexts, for instance concerning the shared stories of racist police in the Black Lives Matter movement (see Chapter 6) or of war crimes in Syria, Ukraine, and other countries. In all those cases, individual postings, narrative and non-narrative, fictional and non-fictional, are interconnected by the logic of social media, driven by networked attention. From this emerge collective macro-narratives about conflicts between women and predatory men, Black citizens and racist police, or Syrian freedom fighters and the violent regime. These co-constructed, collective narratives intervene in the larger narrative frames of a culture and its history, critique its ideologies (such as patriarchy or racism), contribute to the formation of users' identities, and sometimes transform the social status quo.

Their building blocks, the individual postings, are connected not only through hashtags but also in various other ways. The interweaving of videos and other online images has often been discussed with a focus on direct intertextuality and intervisuality in the form of imitations, mash-ups, or memes (e.g., Shifman 2014). However, it is far more comprehensive and complex. Videos are also connected, for instance, through playlists, channels, and follower relationships, through platform algorithms and recommendations, through content aggregators and curators, or through the links, shares, and comments of individual users. Networked macro-narratives thus contain a multiplicity of narrators, protagonists, events, places, and times. They are polycentric, polyperspectival, and nonlinear, contain leaps, repetitions, and gaps, and they have neither a closed ending nor a consistent style, but sprawl out with intertextual and transmedial references. This also lends complexity to the individual videos, which become charged with knowledge about their networked contexts and often involve multiple layers of meaning including forms of citation, parody, allegory, or self-reflexivity, as many of our examples show (Sadler 2022).

Interconnected videos form networks, clusters, swarms, or sequences that develop and change over time and can thus also be read as chronologies of political crises, protests, or struggles. The emergence of such video clusters can be more or less contingent or organized, and they have certain macro-structures. One important structure is the category-based collection of posts on related events under a hashtag, for example, of videos on police violence in the case of #BlackLivesMatter (see Chapter 6). Another mostly contingent structure is the chain of imitation that occurs when a viral video is picked up by imitators, as in the case of *10 Hours of Walking in NYC as a Woman* (Bliss 2014), which was posted in 2014 by the anti-street harassment group Hollaback! and subsequently taken up and modified in countless variations. While some memetic chains develop spontaneously in open, unpredictable dynamics, others are deliberately triggered, for instance, in the case of video challenges that invite users to repeat or surpass the action shown (examples are the aforementioned Ice Bucket Challenge or Rubble Bucket Challenge). Finally, some video clusters are based on elaborate planning and guided development. This concerns video campaigns, as in the case of the *Most Shocking Second a Day Video*, or author-created video series, as in the channels, profiles, and playlists of influencers (see below and Chapter 5).

In all these contexts, platform affordances shape how videos are disseminated and interconnected, contributing to the development of specific network structures: for example, is the network fragmented or tightly meshed, is it open or hierarchical, are we dealing with closed groups or opposing camps? In an instructive article, Marc Smith and his co-authors distinguish six common network structures on X/Twitter that can probably also be found on other platforms (Smith et al. 2014; Himelboim et al. 2017). Their terms do not always fit our activist focus but could easily be adapted. Accordingly, users can form a densely networked "tight crowd" by sharing information about a common topic in their own community or (activist) group. In contrast, larger "polarized crowds" may form in a political conflict, or medium-sized "community clusters" around (citizen) journalists with different opinions and followings. In "broadcast networks," many individual users repeat the news from leading media centers. Governments, companies, NGOs, and other large organizations also create "support networks" by responding to individual questions or criticism. Finally, when popular items, celebrities, or brands attract the attention and comments of many unconnected participants (similar to mass media), the authors call that "brand clusters."

With the aim of influencing such emerging networks and their shared stories, video activists often deliberately target the networked attention of users. Guided by practical knowledge, they address the logic of social media by making videos attractive and shareable and by strategically planning their distribution. The following brief overview of the main strategies will be supplemented with more detailed observations on the concrete practices of selected activist groups in the next chapter.

Concerning activist strategies of video distribution and networking, we can broadly distinguish between short-term strategies that aim primarily at achieving a high spread and long-term strategies that aim for more sustainable forms of action and impact. Among the short-term strategies, the planful seeding of a video is crucial for its widespread public distribution. It means selecting the most suitable target groups and addressing them at the right time. Such target groups may include activist communities, political stakeholders, and other relevant groups on social media, but also opinion leaders and celebrities with many followers.

Cross-pollination, in which allies mutually refer to one another and reciprocally link their channels and videos, is also an important technique. Search engine optimization can increase the findability of the video, for instance through appropriate keywords (as in the case of *The Most Boring Viral Video*) or expressive hashtags (like #OccupyWallStreet). Moreover, video creators take the interactions between platforms into account: a popular YouTube video is more likely to be shared on X as well (and this in turn drives up views on YouTube). Finally, some activists use social marketing apps to monitor success.

But even if such short-term strategies are successful and an activist video spreads widely or even goes viral, the question arises of how it can achieve political effects that exceed a mere emotional flurry and network activity. How can it motivate viewers to get involved, to organize, and perhaps to change their ways of living in the long term? When do videos not just lead to short-lived changes of political attitudes, but to protest in the streets and dedicated involvement in activist communities and social movements? Here, long-term strategies of distribution and networking are required. To achieve more significant and sustainable effects, activists embed their videos in larger forms of social practice. They make use of them for transmedia campaigns, combining online videos with various media and events offline such as posters or public performances. In order to raise sustained awareness and keep the topic in the minds of the public, they produce whole video series, for instance in the context of a YouTube channel, a TikTok account, or a cross-platform hashtag relating to a political topic. More work is necessary to groom a target audience actively over a longer period and turn them into loyal followers (audience development and community building), which requires constant maintenance of interactions (community management). Sometimes activists join together to carry out mutual productions, thereby pooling their communities of fans and followers. An example is BreadTube or LeftTube, a loose group of leftist video creators on YouTube, Reddit, and Twitch, who cooperate to combat far-right content, using humor and their expertise with algorithms in doing so.

In addition, political groups utilize their video channels in the context of repeated appropriation and community building, for instance in participative production or crowd production or when watching recorded protest actions together (see Chapters 2 and 5). Social media or their own websites can also serve as collective workshops or archives. For example, according to the activist collective Syrian Archive, their servers currently host more than three million witness videos from the Syrian war; to date, almost 6,000 of them have been verified through elaborate fact-checking procedures. Storing the videos on their own website syrianarchive.org proved to be necessary, since, as we have already mentioned, YouTube repeatedly deleted activist videos without prior warning. To avoid state repression, the Syrian Archive as well as the Turkish activist archive bak.ma, which has over 2,000 videos on political resistance in Turkey, operates from outside their countries (in Berlin). Curated websites such as FilmsForAction, Cinemata, B'tselem, and bak.ma collect witness and other activist videos on specific topics or from specific regions of the world. Organizations like WITNESS provide consultation and advocacy to create favorable conditions for witness videos to have long-lasting impact. Groups such as Bellingcat and Forensic Architecture engage in dedicated video forensics and verify witness videos. Sustained political work also involves activists cooperating in long-term networks such as Video4Change or the Radical Film Network. A combination of such forms of involvement can help activists in civil society succeed in using their videos to effect lasting change in a society's political discourses, frames, narratives, modes of action, and conflict dynamics, including how protest is generally perceived and what is expected of it. Not least, videos have multiple effects on the public sphere, as will be argued in the final chapters of this book.

General Video Strategies in the Climate Crisis Discourse

The many individual strategies that video activists use in designing and distributing their videos are combined into more general strategic approaches that serve overarching purposes. Such approaches can be seen, for example, in the difficult discourse on the climate crisis. Although the terrible consequences of global warming are well known and the window of opportunity to prevent the worst is closing, governments, corporations, and citizens of industrialized countries still seem unwilling to reduce their CO_2 emissions sufficiently and give up some of their usual habits and profits. In this situation, effective climate communication is more important than ever. However, the climate crisis is difficult to communicate. It is an abstract, complex, uncomfortable, and controversial topic. Powerful lobbies constantly sow doubt about it and decades of media warnings have worn out people's willingness to pay attention. Moreover, audiences have diverging opinions about climate issues and are often separated by language and other barriers, but at the same time connected by inter-group conflicts such as over international or intergenerational climate justice. For example, while a majority of citizens in the Vulnerable 20, the most affected countries in the world, are probably acutely aware of the climate crisis, in 2017 more than 60 percent of European citizens were still indifferent or skeptical about it (Metag et al. 2017; Kácha et al. 2022). Among other things, this can be attributed not only to inertia but also to differences in knowledge about the crisis, including forms of "group-based ignorance," which can lead to collective inaction (Schwenkenbecher 2021). A group may be intentionally or unintentionally ignorant about the credibility of climate scientists, the causes of the crisis, ways to mitigate it, or the willingness of others to do so, and all these gaps in knowledge may prevent them from acting. Furthermore, there is the challenge of moving from knowledge to collective action and social change, as mentioned in the previous chapter.

To deal with such difficulties and overcome collective inaction, Bennett (2021) proposes an "idea-flow model" of transformative communication involving

> (1) coordinated development and production of ideas, with illustrations ranging from crowd production to more industrial models utilizing think tanks, strategic communication campaigns, and political organizations, (2) effective packaging of ideas using creative categorization, framing, narration, emotional cuing, and easy breakdown into memes and story elements that travel over different networks, (3) strategies for better network alignment for sharing ideas among diverse stakeholders such as business interests, civil-society organizations, publics, and parties, resulting in (4) unified movements positioning ideas for political uptake by pressurizing political leaders and parties when opportunities arise.
>
> (Bennett 2021, 14–15)

Bennett calls for the coordination of communicative efforts and outlines a general framework within which video activist strategies could operate. This is a plausible approach, but it also raises questions. How could such coordination be arranged? How could the particular interests of different actors (including activists) and the differing logic of various media be aligned? Which communicative strategies are already being pursued and to what extent could they complement each other?

A central concern of "packaging ideas," for example, is how to frame the climate crisis, its causes, and possible solutions. Currently, many researchers are advising against the "loss frames" that have been so widely disseminated through scientists' warnings and doomsday movies such as *The Day After Tomorrow* (Emmerich 2004). The overabundance of media messages focusing on doom and gloom seems to discourage audiences. Instead, "gain frames" about creating a desirable future or about the social benefits of climate-friendly measures are now seen as more promising (Moser 2010; Stoknes 2015; Nagel 2021). Some researchers also believe that instead of "security frames," which address how one's own group can escape climate hazards, "justice frames" should be used, which emphasize the inequitable distribution of responsibility and damage across nations and generations (Roosvall and Tegelberg 2020; Melchior and Rivera 2021). However, danger, loss, gain, security, and justice frames are not mutually exclusive, but rather complementary, and their effectiveness seems to depend on their distribution and interplay in social and media discourses.

Different media—including television journalism, political dossiers, non-fiction books, fictional films, and more—also fulfill complementary functions in climate communication. Activist videos play an essential role in this system of climate media, as they are easy and quick to produce, accessible, vivid, affective, and spreadable, and encourage users to interact. But how exactly do video activists try to influence climate policy? How do they work with strategies of telling, showing, arguing, and symbolizing climate change? How do they consider factors of shareability in video design (including emotion, storytelling, timeliness, tangibility, calls to action, and appeals to social identity)? And how do they distribute their videos, build social networks, and unleash networked attention through video campaigns, challenges, or series?

Our observations suggest that four general approaches are particularly prevalent in climate video activism (and beyond) and complement each other. Each of them addresses different kinds of audiences and favors particular strategies of video design, production, distribution, and networking.

The *(entertainment) education approach* aims primarily at spreading knowledge about the climate crisis and in this way influencing viewers' attitudes and values. The clearest examples of this approach are the countless explainer videos that present facts about the climate crisis and develop arguments relying on expert testimony, data visualizations, and audiovisual symbols (e.g., *Climate Change Explained Simply* by TheDocumentaryChannel 2015). Other educational videos make intensive use of emotional storytelling and vivid imagery to provide narrative persuasion through exemplary stories about affected people or animals (such as polar bears). Typically, videos of this type are (semi-)professionally produced and distributed with the aim of reaching either specific target groups (such as young people) or as many viewers as possible. While this educational approach can have cumulative long-term effects, its impact on individuals often seems to be rather short-term and limited.

Other activists therefore prefer a *participation or empowerment approach* that promotes dialogue and deliberation through collective practices such as participatory filmmaking or collaborative video creation with communities. In this type of shared practice, local groups of intrinsically or extrinsically motivated people (such as students) exchange ideas about the issue with climate activists, scientists, educators, filmmakers, or curators. This can take the form of workshops at schools or universities, as in the case of the Art for Futures Lab at Film University Babelsberg (2020–25). Other video activists involve people interested in climate protection more indirectly by explaining certain ecological practices from urban gardening to entire lifestyles, recommending them for imitation, and giving concrete advice. One example is the New Zealand video project Happen Films, whose aim is "to showcase and demonstrate inspiring solutions to the multiple global crises we're facing today" (Happen Films n.d.).[42] Participatory production and recommending concrete practices have benefits: deep learning and lasting effects are more likely; perspective-taking and exchange between different groups are facilitated. The disadvantages are that such strategies mostly reach relatively few people and only those who are already interested in the topic. Moreover, they usually produce low-budget films of a non-professional or experimental kind that are not very attractive to a wider audience.

The *mobilization approach* is also predominantly aimed at already committed climate protectors, but instead of engaging them in participatory exchange or joint ecological practices, it calls on them to protest climate-damaging projects such as deforestation, coal mining, or new pipelines and motorways. For example, the video *Ende Gelände 19–24.6. 2019 Rheinland* (2019) by the German action alliance Ende Gelände (a wordplay meaning both "time is up" and "end of terrain") urged people to occupy gigantic opencast coal mines in the Rhineland. Such protests were then documented in documentary and witness videos that strengthened the protesters' social identity and community. This approach, also used by activist groups such as Extinction Rebellion or Letzte Generation ("last generation"), is empowering, but again tends to reach only smaller, even more dedicated groups.

In contrast, videos of the *provocation and confrontation approach* address several different publics and stakeholders simultaneously in order to both provoke opponents and mobilize allies and sympathizers. In doing so, they aim to spark a sustained controversy in the media and society, arouse the interest of the disinterested, and convince the doubters through deliberative argumentation. This involves risks of social polarization and resistance but also provides considerable advantages: provocative climate videos can lead to broad reach and deep learning, and they can mobilize concrete action in important political situations. The provocation strategy also seems particularly promising for online videos because it corresponds to the logic of platforms, networked attention, online interactions, discursive macrostructures, and hybrid media systems.

Other strategic approaches could be mentioned, which can also be combined into concrete activist practice (see Chapter 5). The following example, one of the most influential climate videos in Europe to date, is mainly rooted in the provocation approach, but it also illustrates more generally how combined strategies of activist video design, production, distribution, and networking can influence flows of attention in hybrid media systems and thus contribute to changing political power relations.

A Case of Strategic Provocation: Rezo's "Destruction of the CDU"

On May 18, 2019, about a week before the 2019 European elections, the German YouTuber Rezo released his 55-minute video *Die Zerstörung der CDU* ("The

Destruction of the CDU") (Rezo ja lol ey 2019a), which attacks the parties that made up the government in Germany at that time, particularly the conservative CDU, accusing them of political failure on the climate crisis and other issues (Figure 4.1). (The title is a wordplay in reference to a gamer's expression: it can mean that the CDU is being destroyed, should be destroyed, or that it has acted destructively itself.) At the end of the video, Rezo advises his viewers not to vote for the CDU and most other parties, except for the Greens and the Left. Despite its length, the video went viral and topped the YouTube list of most-watched videos in Germany in 2019 (Briese 2019). At the time or writing, in 2023, it had been viewed around twenty million times on the original YouTube channel alone (in a language area of 95 million people) and commented on more than 300,000 times. It has also been shared widely on several other YouTube channels, as well as on Instagram, Facebook, X/Twitter, Twitch, Telegram, and other platforms, where it has led to numerous reaction videos and extensive follow-up communication (Figure 4.2).

Rezo's video sparked heated debates in the German media and political scene far beyond the online sphere. As a cross-platform content creator, Rezo already had a large and loyal subscriber community and was allied with the Fridays for Future movement. However, he was by no means targeting only a young online audience, but various other social groups at the same time: politicians, professionals,

FIGURE 4.1: Rezo's *Die Zerstörung der CDU* ("The Destruction of the CDU"), 2019, screenshot with inserted sources on the climate crisis.

FIGURE 4.2: Rezo on the cover of *Der Spiegel* 23/2019, one of Germany's leading news magazines. The title reads: "The New Extra-Parliamentary Opposition: How the YouTube Generation Is Shaking up Politics."

and the general public, including those who had not previously been interested in politics or climate change. The awkward reactions of the provoked parties CDU, CSU, and SPD triggered a backfire effect with follow-up discussions in all major mass media (Biermann 2019; tagesschau 2019; Wölken 2019). When the CDU questioned the correctness and credibility of the video, many renowned scientists (including the president of the Technical University of Berlin) sided with Rezo and publicly endorsed his statements. For months, a debate on climate change and freedom of expression raged in the main German newspapers, magazines, and broadcast media, and Rezo was invited to several television shows. The governing parties suffered heavy losses in the German EU elections, and the Greens made significant gains, which was attributed in no small part to the video and labeled the "Rezo effect." Later, Rezo was awarded a major journalism prize, and his video is still being used as a basis for discussions in schools and universities today. In the YouTube comments, far-right insults are mixed with calls to make another video for the 2021 federal election and messages of thanks from young fans because his video was exam material at school and they got good grades. At the same time, the example makes clear how strongly the dissemination of online videos is constrained by language barriers and regional conflicts. In German-speaking countries, almost everyone under the age of 50 knows Rezo today; outside Germany, almost no one does. But Rezo's video is also interesting in a broader context because it clearly illustrates crucial strategies of video production, design, dissemination, and networking.

In terms of production strategies, Rezo earns a living and finances his videos in multiple connected ways, similar to other (semi-)professional social media authors. His YouTube channels participate in platform advertising via Google AdSense. In addition, Rezo runs an online shop for merchandise (Rezo Merch), advertises for companies (some with a sustainability focus), and is represented by an influencer agency (until 2019 Tube One, after that All In). His professionalization in social media is also reflected in the fact that he co-developed the analytics tool Nindo, which can be used to monitor user engagement. However, Rezo deliberately excluded his "destruction" video from monetarization, which means that it was ultimately cross-financed by other videos. According to Rezo's own statement, he invested hundreds of hours in the research and production of the long and complex video, supported by his production manager and film editor TJ and to a lesser extent by other friends and family (@rezomusik 2019).

Concerning the design strategies of the video, we can draw on existing analyses of its aesthetic, rhetorical, and affective structures and potentials. According to Jasper Stratil (2019), the thematic chapters of the video connect several strands of political discourse: the second and longest part addresses the climate crisis, others turn to social inequality, political incompetence, war involvement, and the CDU's discrediting of young people. In its audiovisual affect rhetoric, the video aims, as Stratil says, at constituting a "we" group that unites Rezo's mostly young YouTube followers with scientific experts and places both in opposition to the CDU. To achieve this, Rezo combines the rhetorical strategies of logos, ethos, and pathos: the video highlights its numerous arguments and scientific sources (logos), emphasizes the authenticity and credibility of Rezo the rhetor (ethos), and underlines his arguments through the rhythmic expressivity of body and gestures as well as through the affective design of speech, music, camera work, and editing (pathos). This rhetorical analysis can be extended by looking at Rezo's strategies of narration and framing. His video narrates a deep conflict between social groups and activates several related political frames. The narrative conflict focuses on the CDU-led government as the perpetrator causing damage to climate and society (and thus also to the audience). In this way, it emphasizes loss and injustice frames. At the same time, however, Rezo also creates a David-versus-Goliath narrative by making himself the hero and narrator of the story, challenging the established parties. And he is not alone in this: the climate scientists he quotes are his mentors and companions; and he invites his followers, other YouTubers, journalists, activists, and young voters to stand by him as helpers and get involved. This activates a gain frame of better possible futures.

These strategies of video design serve several larger strategic approaches at the same time. The main approaches are provocation and mobilization: Rezo provokes his political opponents into ill-considered reactions in order to initiate a larger social debate and reach a wider public (provocation approach). After luring the otherwise overpowering opponents to the unfamiliar field of social media, he mobilizes his subscribers and sympathizers, as well as climate activist groups, so that they support him in the communicative confrontation (mobilization approach). Moreover, Rezo combines this with an educational approach: footnotes displayed in the video refer to almost 80 academic and journalistic sources, listed in a linked paratext. And finally, he invites the viewers to participate in this communicative struggle by using the affordances of online platforms, which offer opportunities for affective interaction, self-expression, community building, and further attacks on the opponents (participation approach). Rezo's video is therefore linked not only to the infotext and the long list of sources on the YouTube page but also to countless user comments, related videos, and others' channels and websites. In short, Rezo combines the main strategic approaches of video activism in a mutually reinforcing way.

This is also based on smart and effective dissemination and networking strategies. In 2019, Rezo already had two long-standing YouTube channels (rezo and Rezo ya lol ey) and an Instagram account (rezo), and later added two more YouTube channels (Renzo, and Schlumpf) and a Twitch account (Rezo).[43] These channels are used for different purposes and fed with different types of videos. Prior to the release of the destruction video, Rezo had already created a distinctive media persona of himself through hundreds of entertaining videos featuring chat, music, and humor. His striking looks (blue hair, colorful shirts), emphatic friendliness, and witty slang helped him build affective bonds with more than a million subscribers and connect with other YouTube creators. "The Destruction of the CDU" is also a good example of the distribution strategy of an author-created video series. At first, Rezo only posted the video on his second channel, Rezo ja lol ey, so as not to scare away less politically interested fans. Gradually, however, it became part of an extensive video series on political topics that also spread across the Rezo and Renzo channels, as well as other platforms. Among other postings, this political series includes a joint statement by 90+ YouTubers supporting Rezo's election recommendations (*Ein Statement von 90+ YouTubern* [Rezo ja lol ey 2019b]); the video *Die Zerstörung der Presse* ("The Destruction of the Press") (Rezo ja lol ey 2020) about journalistic biases, manipulations, and press reactions to the first "destruction" video; as well as three more recent "destruction" videos castigating political misconduct including incompetence, corruption, and further climate policy failings (*Zerstörung Teil 1: Inkompetenz* [Renzo 2021a]; *Zerstörung Teil 2: Klima-Katastrophe* [Renzo 2021b]; *Zerstörung FINALE: Korruption* [Renzo 2021c]). Again, each of them was watched millions of times. By way of such distribution and networking strategies, Rezo's video series succeeded in forging a new alliance between young voters, climate activists and their allies, scientists, journalists, and educational institutions. Together these groups formed an "ethno-epistemic assembly" (Allgaier 2020) that opposed the ruling parties and called for a more committed climate policy.

The example of Rezo represents a new kind of video activist: political influencers. These charismatic content creators with large followings are active in many countries, often with transnational reach. Their professionalism on social media is often greater than that of other types of activist actors (more on this in Chapter 5). However, Rezo's video shows more generally the potential of combining complementary strategies not only in climate communication but in activism as a whole. By addressing multiple audiences simultaneously, it provoked politicians, informed subscribers, mobilized voters, stimulated participation, triggered public debates, and forged alliances between very different audiences. On the one hand, this demonstrates the importance of the affective and epistemic potentials of individual videos and the strategies of activist video creation, production, distribution, and networking. On the other hand, the example also points to the relevance of social group relations and affective user practices of video reception, interaction, and participation. And finally, it stresses how important it is for activists to join forces and work together (an issue we will take up again in Chapter 7).

5

The Diversity of Video Activists: Practices and Communities

Video activists develop specific strategies and tactics to fight for their causes on social media and beyond, struggling with the logic of commercial platforms and the power of governments, corporations, and political opponents. But which actors actually engage in video activism, and in what ways? What kinds of activists operate on social media, how do they work and how do they relate to each other? And how does all this change the general understanding of activism?

Starting from such questions, this chapter will focus on the activists themselves. The term video activists might often invoke widespread stereotypes of what an activist is, but in fact there is not one kind of activist, but rather a broad spectrum of very diverse actors in civil society. The individuals and organizations that use social videos for political ends differ in their political goals, social identities, ethical principles, and practical strategies. For some, videos are their main tool, while others use them as just one of many means to support their core activities. They draw on different resources and develop their own organizational structures, strategies, and practices. In doing so, they utilize different platforms and engage in specific social contexts—for example, in a social movement, a campaign, a strategic alliance, an identity-based community, or a project-based "community of practice" (Lave and Wenger 1991), all of which address different issues in differing political situations.

In view of these differences, we can distinguish several main types of video activists, ranging from individuals through small organizations to large movements. Much of the research to date has focused on *individual protesters and witnesses*, whose videos spontaneously respond to political events, for instance during the uprisings in the MENA region around 2011 (Andén-Papadopoulos 2013; Mortensen 2015; Schankweiler et al. 2019). Accordingly, citizens become "accidental activists" (Ollis 2008) by documenting political injustice and the protests against it through video practices of "ordinary witnessing" (Chouliaraki 2010) or "citizen camera-witnessing" in acts of "mediated mass self-communication" (Andén-Papadopoulos 2014). The individual videos can then be networked on social media or picked up by professional journalists in mass media, creating connective or participatory forms of political action. This focus on individual social media users and the witnessing of situations of acute violence or protest on the street has shaped the most common notion of what video activism is. At the same time, it is often emphasized that this kind of individual, spontaneous activism has its limitations because effective political work also requires a higher degree of continuity and collective organization.

In line with this, our own observations suggest that several different types of activist organizations and networks operate on social media. Since there is no systematic overview of such activist alliances, we will focus on them in this chapter (whereby the order is roughly based on the size and reach of the groups concerned). The first part focuses on *small, specialized activist media collectives*, including independent citizen journalist groups and news aggregators (Allan 2013; Presence 2016), artivist collectives (Kara 2015; Taylor 2016), and tech-savvy media NGOs (Bach and Stark 2004; Fuller and Weizman 2021; Ristovska 2021). The second part turns to *professional social media influencers and amateur content creators* who form loose online networks of varying size but often considerable reach (Tüfekçi 2013; Liedtke and Marwecki 2019; Kaye et al. 2022). In the third section, we look at *large NGOs* that engage in many other activities besides media work but regularly use videos to promote their causes (Waters and Jones 2011; Arroyo et al. 2013). And finally, we discuss *hashtag movements* (Jackson et al. 2020), in which all these actors can participate to advocate their concerns more effectively. In addition to these most frequent types of contemporary video activism, there are further actors, some of them moving between established professions and part-time activism. For example, many media professionals, artists, scientists, journalists, social entrepreneurs, and celebrities as well as other opinion leaders occasionally create political videos or collaborate with activist organizations. There are also crossovers and interactions among the types of activism mentioned above, which means that political video work in civil society often takes hybrid forms.

In other words, we are dealing with a broad variety of video activists. Their degree of organization ranges from individual witnesses and small groups that regularly intervene tactically, to broader informal networks and large, stable organizations that pursue long-term strategies for social change. These different types of activists sometimes cooperate, but more often ignore each other or even emphatically distance themselves from one another, even when they are pursuing mutual goals. In this regard, we argue that in many cases activists could be more effective politically if they would cooperate—directly or indirectly—and use their complementary strengths. For example, if an accidental witness documents a human rights violation with her smartphone and her video goes viral, this does not seem to require any particular level of organization. In many cases, however, it is only with the help of activist organizations that such witness videos achieve greater reach and political influence. For example, a forensic investigation team might verify the video and build trust, a well-connected citizen journalist collective might provide relevant background information, a specialized media group might present the video to courts or policymakers, an established human rights NGO might launch a broad public mobilization campaign, and together all these intermediaries can engage in a hashtag movement around the case and massively increase political pressure—as it happened, for example, in the #BlackLivesMatter movement (see Chapter 6). As a community of practice, all these different actors are intertwined through complementary action, although they may not even know about each other or share each other's practical goals, aesthetic approaches, or ethical principles.

Our findings on the main types of video activism are based on case studies using varying combinations of methods (including expert interviews, diachronic film analysis, and multimodal website analysis) as the main questions and the possibilities of access to the activists are different in each case. Our studies represent snapshots of a specific spatial, temporal, and political situation. The fieldwork fell within the COVID-19 closure period between 2020 and 2022, a "moment of acute unknowing," as one interviewed activist put it.[44] Thus, this chapter captures the moment of a global pandemic crisis that exacerbated existing social inequalities and changed the terms of activist action. As planned fieldwork trips became impossible, we eventually settled on the idea of conducting the research in our hometown in Berlin, Germany, a city with a rich history and presence of international protest cultures. The focus of this chapter is therefore on activists operating under the conditions of a wealthy, liberal democratic, capitalist state in the Global Northwest. We are aware that activists in authoritarian and dictatorial regimes suffer far more from state repression and often put their own lives at risk, and that activists in countries of the Global South are much more likely to find themselves working under more precarious conditions. Moreover, our interview partners operate in the legal space of the European Union, which in the age of the so-called splinternet (see Chapters 1 and 7) increasingly differs from other internet regions such as China, Russia, or even the United States. Nevertheless, we hope that many of our general findings can also be applied to the work of activists in other political situations, as they often face comparable challenges. In any case, the main types of activist alliances described below—small media collectives, influencer networks, large NGOs, and hashtag movements—can be found worldwide, as our examples will show, and it would be interesting to compare their specific manifestations in different countries and contexts.

Small Media Collectives: Committed and Counterpublic

The first kind of activist alliance consists of media collectives, that is, small groups with shared political goals whose members work together according to principles of equality and equity and without formal hierarchies and rules of sanction. These groups usually organize themselves in simple, flexible units of about a dozen self-taught, semi-professional, or professional video makers and activists, which has proven useful for a wide variety of concerns and purposes. Among other things, such collectives produce and distribute videos of offline protests, monitor the police and other powerful agencies, provide alternative news, gather visual evidence of human rights violations or environmental destruction, or help empower marginalized communities by supporting their self-representation. Usually, these actors work out of civic commitment, continuously and without a hierarchical division of labor, although some specialize in certain practices and increasingly professionalize their work. As small groups with changing memberships, they also have broader supporting networks and join forces with other civil society actors including, for example, artists, researchers, and media professionals, to bring about social change. Often, they are also connected to a specific community, social movement, or counterpublic (see Chapters 2 and 6), but ultimately they act autonomously.

Beyond these broad commonalities, activist media collectives are highly diverse. They differ not only in their political goals but also in their media strategies, personal, technical, and financial resources, their types of videos and their degree of organization, professionalization, and public influence. Some explicitly carry on the historical trajectory of the New Left in today's media environments (see Chapter 2). Others concern themselves more generally with social, humanitarian, or environmental issues and try to refrain from explicit ideological positioning and historical self-identification. In the following, we present the most relevant subtypes of collectives, which we distinguish according to their key practices. These include informing, amplifying, monitoring, training, researching, subverting, and archiving.

As activists repeatedly accuse the established media of ignoring, neglecting, or distorting relevant news and reports, *informing* or rather producing "counter-information" becomes a first crucial practice for media collectives. *Counter-journalist groups and "alternative" news aggregators* inform their respective community or social movement or a specific region by remediating typical television formats such as reports or documentaries. Some members have a background in journalism, film, and media production, while others work autodidactically and are more deeply rooted in social movements. Well-known examples of this subtype are Democracy Now! in the United States, Reel News in the United Kingdom, Leftvision in Germany, or the pro-democratic Belarussian channels Nexta TV and ePramova, which operate from outside the country because of the repressive state apparatus of Belarus.

Another practice is to *amplify and disseminate* the message of a broader protest movement. This work is usually done by small, flexible, and temporary subgroups within a broader movement to which they are accountable. Examples are the short-lived projects OccupyCinema as part of Occupy Wall Street in New York City in 2011; Videoccupy during the Gezi Park protests in Istanbul in 2013–14; and TV Debout, covering the night-time protest assemblies of Nuit Debout in Paris in 2016. Such media units of larger movements usually consist of only a handful of activists with a background or interest in media work. They produce in an ad hoc, DIY/DIT (Do It Yourself/Do It Together) fashion, with little financial resources and formalized organization. Therefore, they often struggle to maintain longer-term operational functions. With the waning of protest movements, the work of these small subdivisions usually also comes to an end.

A third operating practice is *monitoring*, usually conducted by local networks for citizen camera-witnessing and counter-surveillance (or sousveillance). For example, since 2013 Coletivo Papo Reto has recorded witness videos of police and paramilitary assaults in the favelas of Rio de Janeiro and documents these cases in support of local communities. Unlike media NGOs (see below), these site-specific groups are only loosely connected and organized around this issue and need to respond quickly to ever new incidents.

The three practices mentioned so far usually emanate from financially precarious grassroots initiatives that rely on donations and public attention and often use social payment services such as Patreon. But beyond that, there are also increasingly more established groups (or "mini-NGOs") with comparatively more continuous funding. Because of their status as increasingly professional advocates and intermediaries between different stakeholders—e.g., policymakers, legal institutions, journalists, affected communities, and citizens—such groups have been described as a new "proxy profession" (Ristovska 2021, 195) in the struggle for human rights.

Among them are *media NGOs* with a focus on *training, educating, and empowering* vulnerable communities, citizens, and activists in conflict zones. Examples are WITNESS in the United States (founded after the Rodney King trial in 1992) or Engage Media in the Asia-Pacific region (APAC), as well as non-profit technology companies such as Ushahidi in Kenya (Rotich 2017). Such organizations might be smaller and less prominent than large, issue-based NGOs like Greenpeace (see below), but their highly professional and technologically advanced working methods create effective tools for the empowerment of citizens as well as valuable resources for legal institutions, journalists, or activists. In this context, the example of WITNESS is particularly instructive, since the media NGO collaborates with local initiatives like Papo Reto and has also co-founded the global Video4Change Network in 2012 to strengthen collaboration with other media NGOs across continents.

With growing technological possibilities for human rights advocacy, but also increasing dangers of manipulation and misinformation, *activist and non-profit research groups* such as Airwars, Bellingcat, Forensic Architecture, Mnemonic, SITU Research, Tactical Technology Collective, VFrame, and WITNESS Media Lab (a subdivision of WITNESS) exemplify a fifth key practice of activist media collectives: *researching and investigating*. This includes verifying and contextualizing witness material and other documents on the internet as well as "counter-forensics" (Keenan 2014; Fuller and Weizman 2021) based on open-source intelligence (OSINT). Such work often involves big data analysis, architectural modeling, visualizations, and computer simulations to provide visible evidence in cases of human rights violations or environmental destruction. Such projects usually require more funding than other kinds of activist collectives, in part because of the required technology. Some groups publicly document their funding sources, which mainly include public institutions, non-profit organizations, lotteries, their own income, and individual donations. Although video is only one part of a whole range of technical means used by these actors, it plays a central role in the presentation of complex issues.

One of the most prominent counter-forensic investigators is the London-based group Forensic Architecture, founded in 2011, which has investigated, among other things, cases of racist murders, military crimes, and illegal push backs of migrants at the EU borders. The group works at the intersection of activism, research, and art, and has been invited to numerous exhibitions within the global art circuit. Forensic Architecture thus also points to a sixth type of activist media collectives: *video artivist groups* aim at *subverting* a given meaning and the social status quo and navigating between the social systems of art and activism. Artivists can be artists with a strong political stance or activists working within the realm of art. An example of the latter is the Syrian film collective Abounaddara, which has presented its work in many art exhibitions around the world. Since the Syrian uprisings in 2011 and the subsequent war against the Syrian people, they have recorded and released hundreds of short videos and everyday scenes in collaboration with local activists and citizen journalists on Vimeo (a platform particularly relevant to filmmakers and visual artists) to challenge the sensationalist media images of war and terror. From an activist perspective, the art world seems attractive as a point of reference because it allows for more experimental approaches and forms, provides access to broader international audiences and external funding without compromising autonomy, and enjoys legal protection in liberal democratic constitutional states.

The final practice of activist media collectives that should be mentioned in this context is *archiving*. *Video activist archives* can have different functions and serve as a kind of collection point for all the types of collectives mentioned above. They can preserve counter-journalistic reports or video documents of past protest movements. An example is the Turkish website bak.ma, which collects videos around the Gezi

Park movement in Istanbul and other material. Archives also gather witness videos or counter-surveillance that can then be analyzed by counter-forensic research groups. Also, some activist groups have set up their own video portals and infrastructures alongside commercial platforms, often with the central function of archiving videos. Since content on social media is constantly changing and filtered in non-transparent ways, and YouTube and other platforms often delete many relevant witness videos (e.g., from the Syrian war, see Chapters 1 and 4), these archives are becoming important independent sources in investigations of human rights violations and war crimes. For example, the Israeli human rights information centre B'Tselem has been publishing witness videos and extensive recollections of human rights violations committed by Israeli forces in the occupied territories since 1989. Similarly, the Syrian Archive, among other projects, has archived around three million witness videos and footage from thousands of social media channels and accounts related to the war in Syria since 2014 (Della Ratta 2018; Wessels 2019). This project has later been extended to the wars in Sudan, Yemen, and Ukraine on the initiative of Mnemonic, an organization founded in 2017. Both the Syrian Archive and bak.ma are currently working from political exile in Berlin. Whether these collectives are gathering evidence or preserving the images, knowledge, and hopes of past movements, they all function as living archives that ultimately aim at political intervention in current conflicts and social justice for the future.

Against the background of these diverse practices of different kinds of collectives, one can assume that the groups themselves as well as their political and strategic orientations are highly heterogeneous. To clarify what constitutes the variety of activist media collectives, and to ask which political self-understandings and strategic considerations guide their actions and what concrete challenges they face, we will take a closer look at two Berlin-based groups in the following as examples: the counter-journalistic news group Leftvision and the tactical media artivists of the Peng! Collective. This research is based on structured guided interviews, participant observations at workshops and gatherings, as well as analyses of videos, comments, channels and profiles, websites, book publications, and television reports.

Like most activist media collectives, both Leftvision and Peng! are relatively stable groups without a formal organizational structure. Each consists of less than a dozen permanent active members and both have been anchored in the discourses and communities of the political left for many years. But whereas Peng! follows a guerrilla tactical approach, addresses the national public sphere and journalistic mass media, and uses spectacular media stunts to disrupt the political status quo, Leftvision carries out more continuous counter-journalistic work.

Relying on established concepts of counter-reporting and counterpublics (Harding 2001), Leftvision has been a reliable news and information source for the political left in German-speaking countries (the videos usually have German-language soundtracks, intertitles, and subtitles). They report on the activities of social movements and, according to the sections of their website, on issues such as anti-capitalism, racism, feminism, ecology, state and nation, as well as "the right to the city," echoing Henri Lefebvre's egalitarian claim ([1968] 1996). They also aim to mobilize the left for campaigning and action. Since its foundation in 2007, the group has posted over a thousand videos across platforms and on their own website leftvision.de (Figure 5.1).

Although they primarily address the local leftist scene and consider themselves a part of it, they still operate autonomously, setting their own thematic accents, while maintaining a close relationship with other groups and protagonists in the broader community. According to the group, Leftvision enjoys a high level of credibility and trustworthiness in the leftist scene, and the many collaborations with other groups like Extinction Rebellion almost make Leftvision seem like a "service provider for the left scene," as one member ironically remarks. However, the local community is not the only point of reference. They also aim to reach a broader public on social media, which, as we will describe below, is becoming increasingly difficult.

Leftvision began operating shortly after the decline of the leftist web portal Indymedia and deliberately took the step onto the commercial, high-reach

FIGURE 5.1: Leftvision: *Welcome to Hell—Polizei zerschlägt G20-Demo in Hamburg 2017* ("Police Smashes G20 Demonstration in Hamburg"), Germany 2017.

platforms YouTube and Facebook. Today they are also active on X/Twitter, Instagram, and Telegram, while TikTok is only used rudimentarily so far. Their channels feature mostly different kinds of documentaries, i.e., short forms, interviews, and news reports on both national issues as well as mobilization videos for smaller local events that hardly get any attention in the mass media. Some other videos feature playful, satirical content or moderated expert discussion formats. Older videos remain available on their website and their YouTube channel. Occasionally, the group present medium-length video reports such as *Gefangen auf Lesbos* ("Trapped on Lesbos") (2020) about the situation in EU refugee camps, and it even produces longer cinema documentaries, for instance, *Rise Up* (2022) about successful protest movements, or the G20 protest film *Hamburger Gitter* ("Hamburg Grid") (2018). In some cases, these more elaborate films are presented and discussed in public film screenings at protest camps or independent cinemas, comparable to practices of the video movements in the 1980s and 1990s (see Chapter 2). Such onsite events are vital to small collectives since they enable collective experiences in co-presence and connect online and offline audiences.

Thus, the collectively produced videos differ significantly in terms of their genres, the costs and size of the productions, and the aesthetic forms. Interviews and medium-length reports such as *Trapped on Lesbos* have longer sequences and are mostly concerned with having experts and those affected provide insights into complex problems. In contrast, mobilization videos or protest documentation function more like a quick-fire audiovisual leaflet in the ongoing newsfeed. In other words, the group uses different video strategies on different levels such as production and design, distribution, and networking (as introduced in Chapter 4).

A crucial strategic question for the production of a video is funding. In their role as activists, the group members invest considerable time and effort but do not earn any money. Although some members also operate as freelance video producers for NGOs, unions, and other customers, and their videos often look quite professional, their activist work is strictly non-commercial. "As soon as money is involved," a former member emphasizes, "it's not activism anymore"—a rigorous attitude that, as we will see, is rarely shared by political influencers on social media, even those from the left. Generally, Leftvision does not receive any continuous funding beyond occasional project-based support from left-wing newspapers, NGOs, or the Rosa Luxemburg Stiftung, a state-funded political foundation linked to the German Left Party. They do not use the possibilities of monetization that exist on some platforms, because the average reach of their videos is not high enough and left-wing politics is hardly relevant to algorithms. Or to put it bluntly, anti-capitalist activism is not attractive for capitalist platforms. As with many independent online projects, there is only the possibility to support the work via social payment services such as Patreon.

On the level of design strategies, they follow an implicit visual concept that includes, among other things, an ethical imperative of giving voice to affected communities and experts through original soundtracks and interviews, while avoiding material that could be criminally relevant. The way in which many videos are designed can be exemplified (although not representatively) by a short documentary video centering on a witness interview. The six-minute video, prosaically entitled *Prozessauftakt gegen den Attentäter von Halle: Zeugin und Nebenklägerin blickt kritisch zurück* ("Start of Trial Against the Halle Assassin: Witness and Joint Plaintiff Takes a Critical Look Back") (2020), was created ten months after an anti-Semitic terrorist attack in the German city of Halle on October 9, 2019 and received a significantly greater response than the average Leftvision video (around 318,000 views, 1,400 reactions, 130 comments on Facebook, Instagram, and YouTube; plus additional views on the Leftvision website and Telegram channel). It presents a US American activist of Jewish origin who became a survivor-witness of the attack and is appearing as a joint plaintiff in the trial. Throughout the video, she criticizes the victimizing media image of Jews and by pointing to the racist and anti-feminist statements of the perpetrator calls for an intersectional perspective on the case that places the attack in the context of anti-Muslim, trans- and homophobic hate crimes.

The witness appears as an eloquent speaker who, in her role as eyewitness, survivor, and plaintiff, is able to claim authenticity and expert knowledge. But a specific design strategy is also effective here: the video has a lengthy explicative title and a decidedly reduced look; it consists of a single, static, talking head shot with invisible cuts and dispenses with attention-grabbing mood music, voice-over, or intertitles. Only a short original soundtrack at the beginning serves as an intro and is intended to arouse curiosity. However, the fact that the video operates without strong affective cues and storytelling does not mean that it does not follow a design strategy. Rather, it relies on the persuasive explanation of the protagonist and the tradition of documentary "discourses of sobriety" (Nichols 1991, 50). Provided with German subtitles, the English-language video addresses both a national and international audience, and accordingly, many comments come from English-speaking users.

Looking at the aspects of distribution and networking, the video was more widely shared on social media and reached audiences beyond the local leftist community, because, in Germany and beyond, there already was a media discourse on the "attack of Halle" and the anti-Semitic assaults and terrorist attacks that had become a common threat. Another factor is that the videomakers already knew the eyewitness before the attack. This way they were able to shoot the video quickly and provide a crucial perspective that was rarely found in other media. And while the perpetrator's live-streamed video had previously dominated the audiovisual discourse around the case, the activist video now offered an empathetic and empowering counter-perspective.

But only rarely do Leftvision videos reach wider circulation, and the group members self-critically regard distribution strategies as their "weak point." Compared to many other leftist video collectives, who seem simply not to know about seeding strategies and cross-pollination, Leftvision's attitude can rather be described as a reflective hesitation. "YouTube doesn't work so well for us because we don't serve the influencer character. We usually film and upload." They also acknowledge the need to increase their user engagement on Instagram and X/Twitter, but beyond that recognize a general problem:

> There are hardly any opportunities for us to benefit from social media. We had quite a random audience on YouTube in the early years when there was the news and politics section. That doesn't exist anymore. You have to be actively subscribed to us, because the algorithms no longer allow random clicks and we are hidden. It's similar on Facebook: you either must have an extraordinary hit, or you have to pay for the reach. The algorithm only delivers to about ten percent of our subscribers by default. [...] So we have to take care of each video separately and find partners who share it in their network. We can no longer grow on our own.[44]

The collective usually evaluates the metadata of their videos and pays respect to the work of left-wing influencers. At the same time, they emphasize that reach is not their main goal and that producing short, snackable content is not sustainable. "Then rather have a smaller audience and you leave a lasting impression. We don't get so involved in the logic of the platforms." What becomes clear is that some members hardly use social media in their everyday lives and most of them simply do not feel the urge for personal visibility in front of the camera, which is a common prerequisite among social media influencers and other individual content creators (as described below). How far one should adapt to the algorithmic logic of social media remains an unanswered question for the group.

The Leftvision example is typical of a certain kind of counter-journalistic video activism in several respects. From the 1980s until the heyday of Indymedia in the early 2000s, most leftist video collectives tried to build their own alternative news infrastructure (see Chapter 2). Many of them then took the step onto social media, where they hoped for unlimited reach and networking with protest movements worldwide. Despite the difficulties with platform corporations and state surveillance, social media remain indispensable for disseminating their own content, for activist networking, and organizing. However, the "always on" logic and ongoing performance in front of the camera, which influencers and other content creators engage in without any qualms, is seen by left-wing video collectives as at best a strategic necessity, but more often as a burden or an ethical compromise to be avoided.

Parallel to counter-journalist collectives like Leftvision, another interesting type of activist media collective has emerged, which predominantly relies on *communication guerrilla action* and short-term *tactical media interventions* in political discourses. At first glance, such an approach seems to fit better with the networked attention economies of social media. But here, too, activists are confronted with new challenges, as can be exemplified by the second media collective that we focus on in more detail.

The Peng! Collective gained attention in the German-speaking political public with a series of spectacular media actions. Since their founding in 2013, Peng! (translates as "Bang!") have carried out over thirty campaigns with varying participants and can now look back on a broad spectrum of creative interventions. For example, they subverted a greenwashing event of a global oil company and organized their own mock-PR events of corporations or ministries. In one campaign, for example, a major European energy provider allegedly declares that they will completely abandon fossil energy production. In other campaigns, Peng! called on the German public to help refugees enter the EU illegally or to steal food from large supermarket corporations in Robin Hood fashion and transfer the money to exploited local farmers, cooperatives, and unions in the Global South. They also installed Cop Map, a GPS-based online map that monitors police movements via crowdsourcing in real time, thereby ironically mirroring increased police surveillance measures (a list and descriptions of the campaigns can be found on pen.gg). The "Penguins" regard their campaigns as "subversive action art," a tactical definition, since the German constitution guarantees the freedom of art and activists can thus avoid prosecution by defining themselves as artists. Peng!'s transmedial, online-offline campaigns always involve video as a decisive element, although it is merely one of several tactical means used to gain public attention for social change. The videos are either at the center of a campaign or serve to document and subsequently disseminate an offline action. Either way, Peng! tries to "experiment with new visual forms, apart from the boring, increasingly mainstream NGO images," as they see it. The initial question for the collective here is: "What are the aesthetic and narrative forms that have recognition value, that therefore also create trust, but at the same time include moments of irritation?"

Peng! sees itself as a small "network organization" with a core group and an extended sympathizer network to which individual tasks such as legal advice or graphic design can be outsourced. Every campaign is supervised by at least two core members, one of whom is responsible and legally liable; all others determine the degree of their own involvement and have a veto right. In planning, the artivists distinguish between short-term spontaneous actions, long-term strategic campaigns, and projects that arise from personal concern and urgency. Each campaign begins with a basic idea and a subsequent research and exchange phase, in which the desire for joint action also grows. The campaigns are financed by a "relatively small" amount of continuous donations and occasional foundation grants (drawing on Germany's arts funding system). They founded a civil law association (a common legal framework for freelancers, artists, and entrepreneurs) for each campaign and then dissolved again afterward. By these means, the group can ensure that the individual member responsible for a campaign (and thus for the association) is only liable for this particular project and cannot be charged with criminal prosecution for other activities of Peng!

Peng!, of course, is not the first collective of its kind. They follow in the footsteps of older groups such as the Yes Men (since 2000) and the Critical Art Ensemble (since 1987) in the United States, or the ad-critical satirical magazine *Adbusters*. These groups have been developing and applying concepts of "tactical media" (Lovink 2003; Raley 2009), "culture jamming," and "subvertising" (Lasn 2000) since the 1990s. Other historical precedents reach back further to avantgarde movements such as the Viennese "Aktionskunst" ("art for action"), the Parisian "situationists," and the West-Berlin "Spaßguerrilla" ("fun guerilla") of the 1960s as well as the more general tradition of civil disobedience. Using aesthetic tactics of collage and montage, camouflage, reappropriation, and reinterpretation as well as imitation and fakes (Doll 2012), they briefly slip into the role of the powers that be to parody, subvert, and thus expose their practices. They temporarily fool the public in ironic ways to draw attention to serious social grievances. But for Peng! and other emancipatory groups, it is crucial to inform the public of the fake afterward through a surprising, ideally funny, and eye-opening revelation. This strategy of misleading, clarifying afterward, and (potentially) educating the public marks the fundamental difference from "fake news," disinformation, propaganda, and other threats to the democratic public sphere.

But unsurprisingly, the group also reaps criticism for its actions—not only from corporations, right-wing politicians, and media outlets but also from liberal and left-wing sympathizers, some of whom have disapproved of campaigns deliberately crossing the line into illegality. Peng! admits that such actions are provocative, but at the same time emphasizes that they are always the result of a critical analysis. They follow the narrative principle of reversal and mimicry, which can be explained by means of the Cop Map example (the GPS-based project on counter-surveillance of the police). The campaign was a reaction to a recent regional "Police Tasks Act" that according to Peng! assumes a general suspicion of citizens and introduces searches without a judicial warrant (n.d.).

> We turned that around: the police are now under general suspicion [...]. And here's the communicative twist: I learned clowning. The two main strategies of a clown are mirroring and complicity. You mirror your audience and in doing so you are complicit. If

> someone in the audience says, "Hey, asshole," you say, "Hey, I'm an asshole! So are you! Come on, we're friends!" And suddenly you have a dialogue where everybody laughs, you've resolved the conflict, and at the same time you've said what's happening and it becomes transparent. And that's exactly what we did with Cop Map: You are all criminals, the justice system is gone. And we say: police officers are all under general suspicion.

However, Peng! finds that there is sometimes a discrepancy between their initial ideas and their implementation. Sometimes the finished video does not meet expectations, while in other cases a quickly produced video on a topical issue develops an unexpectedly broad impact. The latter was the case with the video *Seebrücke des Bundes* ("Federal Sea Bridge"), which was produced in 2018 in the course of an NGO campaign against European immigration policy, the mass deaths of refugees in the Mediterranean, and the criminalization of sea rescue. Starting from a Telegram chat group, the campaign was launched within just 30 hours (Dorsch 2019). The video was part of an operation using parody in combination with communication guerrilla tactics and demonstrates how to create broad media attention for a political grievance with little means and much humor. Meticulously imitating the style of government advertising videos, it presents a fictitious campaign of the Ministry of the Interior proclaiming the admission of all refugees to Germany. The 75-second video is an anarchic bricolage of generic stock footage representing visual clichés of Germany like Neuschwanstein Castle or the Brandenburg Gate. Randomly assembled glossy images are accompanied by an elevating mood muzak and a reassuring voice-over by a popular German actor. A first hint of the satirical character is given by a discrepancy between the spoken commentary and the image track: while the voice-over invokes the German virtue of loyalty, one sees the friendly handshake between the then Chancellor Angela Merkel and her Interior Minister, whose fractured relationship was widely known to the national public at that time. The video reaches its dramatic peak with the image of a young, white girl in the sunlight biting joyously in an apple, while she candidly gazes at the camera. During this scene, the verbal commentary presents the Seebrücke initiative "out of respect for our own values. For we stay who we are—for we stay who we want to be." The music swells, while a sober insert in black on white states that: "By the end of 2019, Germany will voluntarily take in all people rescued from distress in the Mediterranean Sea." The following insert asks the viewers to: "Convince your city or village to take people in distress." The video closes with a link to the website seebruecke.org and the logo of the fake initiative with a bird symbol and three rising arrows in the national colors black, red, and gold (Figure 5.2).

The video as well as the fake ministry website was soon blocked by YouTube after complaints by the Federal Ministry of Internal Affairs. It was, however, quickly re-uploaded multiple times by supporting viewers, this time with remarks

FIGURE 5.2: Website of the pro-refugee alliance seebruecke.org ("sea bridge"), Germany 2023.

affirming its status as political satire. The comment sections suggest that the video has mostly reinforced pre-existing opinions among users. Left-wing commentators read the narrative as political fantasy and laconically stated that it "would be nice," while right-wing critics were either enraged or proud to expose the (obviously) fake campaign. At the same time, however, Peng!'s tactical media intervention succeeded, at least temporarily, in putting the essential aspect of saving human lives back on the agenda in the ongoing refugee discourse. Tweets and contributions by the well-known satirist Jan Böhmermann on his public television show also contributed to the widespread dissemination. A legal side note in this context is that the lawsuit regarding the mock video took place between the ministry and Google (the owner of YouTube), while Peng! remained untroubled by it. A lasting consequence of the joint mock action, however, is that in the course of this (and separately from Peng!) the broad-based and decentrally organized civil society alliance Seebrücke: Schafft sichere Häfen ("Sea Bridge: Create Safe Havens") was founded. Since then, around 140 major cities and municipalities in Germany have joined their Safe Haven initiative and agreed to accommodate refugees. Thus, the example of the *Federal Sea Bridge* shows how small collectives, integrated into loose networks and supported by popular multipliers, can successfully intervene in political discourse and act as a motor of social change.

How contingent the consequences of their action can be is shown by another campaign from the same year, which Peng! set between civil disobedience and the criminal offence of forgery. Mask ID tested the moral limits of sympathizing participants and asked them to have their own biometric passport photo superimposed on that of an illegalized refugee so that the latter could use the ID document as well. A presumed consequence of the widely received campaign was that a few years later parliament passed a new ID law, according to which passport photos may only be taken by machines provided by the authorities. If one compares Mask ID and Sea Bridge, then—from the group's point of view—the latter was a quick, inexpensive, and ultimately successful intervention in an ongoing discourse and a reaction to the moral and political failure of the EU and the mass deaths of people seeking help in the Mediterranean, while Mask ID was a "much more elaborate action theatre" that backfired and contributed to a tightening of the laws.

It is becoming increasingly difficult for communication guerrilla groups like Peng! to stir up the public with provocative actions through their tactical interventions (n.d.):

> A lot has changed. The [far-right party] AfD ["Alternative for Germany"] has co-opted the concept of provocation and polarization. And words like alternative, democracy and resistance have almost become right-wing. [...] The other thing is: big communication agencies are learning, not only from Peng! but from fakes, lies and manipulations. [...] When we work with fakes, we reveal them afterwards. And we say exactly why, what the motivation is and explain everything. [...] And that is something that is totally frowned upon in the art world, because of this genius-patriarchal thing that says: the artwork speaks for itself.

For Peng!, the subsequent explanation marks the crucial difference between right-wing fakes and the shallow promises of the advertising industry, which the group regards as a kind of fake news agency that created a breeding ground for frustration and cynicism.

A closer look at the specific practices, communities, and strategic or tactical considerations of activist media collectives makes it clear that these groups have many different faces and paths to action. In addition to other types of collectives, citizen-journalist, and alternative video news groups have a longer, more continuous history of grassroots counter-reporting aimed at informing and mobilizing social movements and leftist communities. Artivist collectives are similarly relevant with their spectacular media stunts and communication guerrilla actions. They subvert and intervene in social discourses through creative, humorous, and provocative means to redirect attention to social injustices. For counter-journalistic news projects, video is at the center of their work with documentation and mobilization videos as their most common forms, whereas for artivists video is simply one tool among others, and they act "by any media necessary" (Jenkins et al. 2016) with playful subversion videos as a recurring type.

More generally, activist media collectives are small and relatively stable organizations without formal division of labor. Tasks and members may change throughout the years, but their engagement remains quite continuous, driven by a strong idealist DIY/DIT spirit and what Hannah Arendt once described as "public happiness" or the joy of joint action (Arendt 1963). But as non-commercial actors, the financial situation of such groups remains notoriously precarious, and operations depend on crowdsourcing services, donations, or project-based external funding through media partnerships and independent foundations. In this regard, tactical "action art" collectives as well as artivist researchers have, at least potentially, a clear advantage over citizen-journalist projects by being eligible for funding in the arts and humanities sector. However, artivist collectives hardly cooperate with other actors apart from art institutions and funding agencies that provide financial advantages. This is somewhat less true for counter-journalistic news groups that produce videos for like-minded groups and reports on social movements, for example.

Beyond their general aim of influencing public opinion, both approaches can be regarded more specifically as reactions to and epiphenomena of complex media societies. Citizen-journalist video collectives react to a lack of reliable reporting on issues and aspects relevant to a specific audience, namely the leftist community as their primary target group. Their aim is therefore to not only inform and mobilize but also empower this community. Artivists, as well, react to a certain lack in the existing media system. But their primary addressee is the general public and within this broad realm, they more specifically target and criticize powerful corporations, political decision-makers, and mass media journalists by means of irritation and provocation.

Another crucial difference between the two kinds of collectives in our case studies is their relation to the algorithmic logic of attention on commercial social media platforms. As small actors, activist news collectives find it increasingly difficult to reach their followers and subscribers, let alone the broader public outside their media bubble. In comparison, tactical media artivists have been quite successful in creating spectacular media events, but they as well are struggling more and more to maintain such a high level of public visibility in a rapidly changing media environment. Another difference concerns the impact of their action: tactical media collectives, if they gain public attention, find it difficult to assess the consequences of their actions and to pursue a sustainable strategy, while news collectives have much less reach and direct impact than some more recent types of actors, particularly highly visible social media influencers.

Influencer Networks: Hybrid and Hypervisible

Social media influencers or political content creators are the most recent actors in the history of video activism. Unlike media collectives, they usually work as individuals, but at the same time are often involved in larger informal networks, sometimes with considerable reach. In contrast to older or broader terms such as "blogger," "vlogger," or "video creator," "influencer" refers specifically to the social networks and attention economies on algorithmically managed platform systems. In general, influencers are content creators on social media who have many followers and thus can have an impact on the opinions and decisions of many other users—think of the TikTok entertainer Charli D'Amelio with around 156 million subscribers in 2024 or the video gamer PewDiePie on YouTube and Twitch with over 111 million.

The claim to personal authenticity and the suggested closeness to their community—in other words, the parasocial, public-intimate bond between content creators and followers—form the influencers' capital, which they use strategically on the levels of video aesthetics, production, distribution, and networking. Their videos are mostly short or medium-length vlog formats that they produce and distribute as self-professionalizing autodidacts. They put themselves in front of the camera in a recurring environment (at home, in the studio, or outdoors) and address their viewers directly in a seemingly personal and accessible way. Effective self-presentation and impression management as well as branding and clout on social media are therefore crucial factors, and the boundaries between public and personal communication and between political and non-political content remain constantly blurred. As charismatic personalities and at the same time successful media figures with many followers, influencers sometimes function as role models or idols. They address a wide range of topics, which can be harnessed for commercial and political marketing. Within a short time, a new "influencer industry" has been established as a "complex and far-reaching informational-commercial-personal communication apparatus" (Hund 2023, 157). Its incentive system has created a confusing, unregulated field of economic, social, and political power. In this industry, the influencer emerges as "seller, buyer and commodity" all at the same time (Stoldt et al. 2019, 2). Meanwhile, national and international star systems have arisen among influencers. This tendency repeatedly evokes criticism of the "overly individualistic," superficial attitude, and excessive self-presentation of influencers (Nymoen and Schmitt 2021). At the same time, Jonathan Dean (2023) rightly points out the structural difficulties of being able to detach oneself individually from the imperatives of neoliberal culture and the attention economy on commercial platforms.

Most influencers comment on political issues only sporadically and often without much thought (for instance, PewDiePie was widely criticized for repeated racist remarks). But as influencers are opinion leaders on social media, it comes as no surprise that they can be highly relevant as political actors and video activists. Recent media research defines political influencers as “content creators that endorse a political position, social cause or candidate through media that they produce and/or share on a given social media platform” (Riedl et al. 2023, 2). Videos are key for political influencers like the Brazilian indigenous activists Alice Pataxó (currently 400,000 followers) and Tukumã Pataxó (320,000) who mainly use Instagram and X. The same applies to the entertainer Rezo in Germany (7.8 million) or left-wing activist and journalist Owen Jones from the United Kingdom who has a total of almost two million followers on the main platforms, while the US video gamer and political commentator Hasan Piker has more than two million followers on Twitch alone (Harris et al. 2023; for further insights into the British social media influencer scene, see Dean 2023). YouTube is still highly relevant for longer political content on channels like ContraPoints by the left-wing media celebrity Natalie Wynn (2.8 million) in the United States.[45]

The reach of influencers depends, among other things, on strategies of cross-pollination and thus of being embedded in broader influencer networks to gain access to new and larger audiences. For instance, influencers enter into dialogues with each other (e.g., duets or stitches on TikTok), use comments or videos to refer to one another or create alliances for joint political actions. At the same time, they often try to surpass the reach of political opponents, for example, by rationing (negative comments with high click numbers). Collaborations also develop with NGOs, state institutions, political parties, and companies who bank on an influencer’s popularity among their (usually younger) target groups or voter demographic. In this regard, micro and nano celebrities with stable, parasocial communities of followers are also highly relevant.

Influencers represent a broad political spectrum, in which conservative, liberal, left-wing, and other content creators are present. All influencers develop their own modes of address. They often emphasize opinionated commentary and self-presentation, but in other cases they discuss complex issues in condensed forms, for instance in political tutorials and explainer videos (Sehl and Schützeneder 2023). The direct, affective address of many influencer videos makes them useful tools not only for activism but also for political and commercial advertising as well as authoritarian propaganda, conspiracy narratives, and the right-wing extremist rhetoric of “hate influencers” (Lewis 2018; Stewart et al. 2023). Paying video creators to promote political content has become a common practice. Political parties and their related organizations now hire dubious marketing agencies to have influencers deliver their messages on TikTok (Woolley et al. 2023). As mentioned above, paid influencers in the Philippines have been spreading propaganda in favor of the right-wing extremist former President Rodrigo Duterte, who, among other things, has called for lynchings (Ong and Cabañes 2018; Elemia and Gonzales 2021). Media researchers also argue that influencers are effective in co-opting "non-conforming social groups and counterpublics" for Russian state propaganda (Boichak 2023).

In what follows, we will consider the consequences that the relatively recent phenomenon of social media influencers has had on video activism, emphasizing both new possibilities and more problematic aspects. Our observations are based on field research in influencer networks in Berlin, where we conducted structured guided interviews, participant observation at online and offline workshops and gatherings, as well as analyses of videos, channels and profiles, comment sections, websites, and text publications. In this research, we distinguish between *professional influencers* who seek to finance themselves through content creation and *non-professional influencers* who primarily seek to express their political views as activists and media amateurs. We focus on these two kinds of liberal and left-wing video influencers in Germany that we encountered in two different networks. All participants posted their videos in German and had consistent viewer numbers in the four to six-digit range on at least one of the major platforms for more than a year.

The first group consists of *professional influencers* who have been associated with Funk, the young online content network of German public broadcasters (with a target audience of 14–29-year-olds). Furthermore, they also collaborated with Mesh Collective, a social video education agency that supports young influencers in addressing political topics. Mesh was founded in 2011, and Funk in 2016, and both as a reaction to the migration of young audiences from television to social media. Each in different ways, they gave young content creators a platform and experimented with politically opinionated formats, among other things. Not only were social media influencers invited to enter the public broadcasting circuit in Germany, but these new players also brought along para-activist rhetoric, which made the already porous boundaries between activism and journalism seem even more permeable. Moreover, Mesh Collective is an interesting case because it started as a relatively independent youth education initiative, but then became part of a large media corporation specializing in influencer marketing, where it is intended to cover the area of socio-political engagement.

Our research on professional influencers focuses mainly on three millennial influencers who started as YouTubers in the early and mid-2010s and are now in their mid-30s (a relatively mature age on social media). They have already established their careers and posted several hundred videos throughout the years. Despite their own reluctance to categorize their work, they are primarily self-entrepreneurial commentators and media presenters. What is clear is that they hardly seem to fit the common image of video activists. Yet, it is precisely such in-between positions that are crucial when it comes to tracing the current transformation of activism from its margins and taking into account actors who work across established categories and thus shift their boundaries. Their hybrid positioning between activism, journalism, entertainment, and advertising marks a characteristic tendency that is important for understanding contemporary influencer activism on social media.

An example of this is Louisa Dellert (approximately 570,000 followers in all, mainly on Instagram), who states that she predominantly addresses a female audience (80 percent) in the segment of 21–34-year-olds. Dellert started as a self-taught media amateur in 2013. Beginning with fitness tutorials on YouTube, she then turned to the topics of feminist body positivity, mental health, sustainability, and everyday racism. Labeled a “greenfluencer” by German mass media, she regularly posts short vlog commentaries and documentaries on Instagram and TikTok in accordance with the common formats of these platforms. She combines educational content with occasional calls to action, for instance when she drew attention to the humanitarian catastrophe in EU refugee camps or documented her own rubbish removal action. As a presenter with no formal journalistic education, she also hosts public events where she discusses political issues with decision-makers and, for instance, calls for more decisive action to tackle the climate crisis. In addition to this line of work, she has published two non-fiction books on environmental issues and political communication (Dellert 2018, 2021), runs a regular podcast, a social marketing company, and a zero-waste online shop (Figure 5.3).

Another example of what one could tentatively call a “post-activist stance” is Tarik Tesfu (41,000 followers on Instagram) who earlier had a high number of followers in the six-figure range (Figure 5.4). Tesfu emphasizes that, as a queer person of color, he wants to position himself in-between things. In 2015, he became known to German audiences on YouTube and Facebook with his activist-educational—and often polemical—vlog format “Tariks Genderkrise” (“Tarik’s Gender Crisis”), in which he addressed queer, feminist, and anti-racist issues. After receiving continuous anti-queer and racist threats as well as one-sided journalistic inquiries for several years, he now no longer sees himself as an activist: “I was always addressed as an activist and asked for anti-racist statements. One should, of course, take a stand against racism and sexism. But I didn’t want to make that my profession or purpose in life” (n.d.). In 2020, he deleted all his profiles, channels, and videos. Since then, he only runs an Instagram account with selected professional fashion photos. Fashion, music, and Black/queer culture are also the main topics of his podcast and his late-night show on the platform of a public television broadcaster (target audience: 25–35-year-olds). His current work is political in a more implicit sense by celebrating and potentially empowering Black and queer cultures and communities.

FIGURE 5.3: Louisa Dellert (2023, @louisadellert, Instagram).

FIGURE 5.4: Tarik Tesfu (2015, @dbate, YouTube).

FIGURE 5.5: Rayk Anders (2021, @RaykAnders, YouTube).

While Tesfu and Dellert now locate their media work beyond political activism, Rayk Anders, as a third example, took a different path (Figure 5.5). Since 2013, Anders has been an independent commentator who addresses current German political affairs for the general public in opinionated and sometimes emotional ways. Altogether, he has around 320,000 followers on Facebook, YouTube, and X/Twitter and posts vlogs and occasional documentaries on issues such as the far right and the ongoing threats to democracy. Additionally, he has published two non-fiction books about online hate (Anders 2016, 2021). His strategic advice on how to design, produce, and post videos on social media resembles common marketing literature (setting hooks, including humor, adapting to the platform, producing "authentic content" related to the lived reality of his community, taking care of the community management, etc.). But unlike the other two content creators, he emphasizes that the increasing anti-democratic, right-wing agitation on the net led him to abandon his former more detached stance. "You have no choice but to become politically left. Which I had no intention of doing before. [...] I no longer have any problems positioning myself as an activist" (n.d.).

At the same time, Anders admits that progressive activists could learn from some of the attention-grabbing strategies of far-right videos, which appeal through their "simple, direct visual language." They "seem authentic and trustworthy" while being quickly and easily produced and disseminated. Therefore, he advises other creators to abandon their perfectionism and a certain "leftist arrogance" (n.d.). Dellert, however, sees a decisive difference between right-wing videos and her own approach: "I don't want to impose my opinion on anyone. I want to understand things. And I want to encourage others to form their own opinions, to check the sources and facts, and to question my positions" (n.d.).

Although the three influencers drew different conclusions about their self-definitions and strategies, they agreed on locating their professional work at the intersection of activism, journalism, and entrepreneurism. The tendency toward merging these social roles brings up another issue. Anders (n.d.) describes a permanent "conflict between what you want to say and how you can say it." Not only does he have to respond quickly to current events to gain the attention of users and algorithms in often provocative ways, but there are also financial constraints. To trick the algorithms, political content must appear as apolitical as possible: "Politics doesn't sell." Platforms demonetize some political videos, such as Anders's comments on cases of police violence, and for professional influencers, this means a loss of income. However, he does not regard this as censorship, since the content remains visible, but rather as a kind of subtle self-restraint. Similarly, Tesfu remembers his previous frustration as a political influencer. There was "no way to make money," and his turn toward fashion culture later allowed brand collaboration that had previously been out of reach. Whereas Anders cooperates mainly with political actors from the non-profit sector, including fellow influencers (e.g., Volksverpetzer ["People's Snitch"] or Goldener Aluhut ["Gold Aluminium Hat"]), or organizations such as Mesh Collective or the activist campaign network Campact, Dellert's partners form a broader spectrum. This includes ministries,

NGOs, green energy providers, and sustainable fashion labels. Dellert's and Tesfu's collaborations with state institutions and companies also brought criticism. For example, Dellert was described as "pseudo-political" by a journalist and competing YouTuber (Schmitt 2021), while Tesfu recalls that after a certain brand collaboration, around 400 users unfollowed his account. In short, professional social media influencers are confronted with the dual problem of earning money with well-researched political content on the one hand and losing followers and influence through certain collaborations on the other. The work of a professional influencer is a full-time job that usually cannot be mastered continuously without financial gain. The changing nature of political influencers' often self-entrepreneurial activities, however, indicates that the common and strict distinction between paid labor and unpaid activism (which still holds for many small media collectives) seems increasingly inadequate in this context.

Moreover, posting political content generally leads to several risks for influencers. Criticism, in general, is readily available on social media, and politics, by nature, is conflictual and easily scares off followers, which, in turn, results in losing reach, influence, and money. More specifically, when authenticity is one's capital, then monetizing political content is walking a tightrope (de Gregorio and Goanta 2022). Rezo, for instance, who uses several channels per platform, initially posted his political videos only on the smaller secondary channel so as not to alienate his fans. Other influencers like RobBubble remark that political videos are basically a losing proposition, with influencers being put under pressure to take a stand in polarized debates (Hund 2023, 145). Because influencers are constantly visible in front of the camera and because they often perform from their home and use their real name, they can quickly become the target of criticism, agitation, and harassment. Anders, Dellert, and Tesfu—who have used their real names from the beginning—have continuously received hate comments and threats. They responded with humorous reaction videos at first, but then largely tried to ignore the problem as far as possible. In 2017, Tesfu's account was hacked, but reporting it to the police proved to be useless. Anders received death threats against his family, but he has no confidence in the police. "Death threats are a part of my life today," Dellert laconically remarks.

However, professional influencers like Anders, Dellert, and Tesfu and their strategic networking with broadcasters and agencies are only one part of the story. Other relevant actors in this context are amateur content creators who primarily want to express their political views and often still aspire to become influencers. In our field research, we encountered a network of non-professional left-wing content creators that was founded in 2020 as part of an initiative of the Rosa Luxemburg Foundation (which, as mentioned above, is linked to the German Left Party).[46] At the initial workshop for "leftist influencers," approximately 100 participants in the age group of 20–35 and with project names ranging from Sozialistisches

Videokollektiv ("Socialist Video Collective") to Schminken mit Linken ("Makeup with Lefties") gathered and discussed strategies to end right-wing hegemony on social media, as they saw it. They also assembled video collections (subreddits and YouTube playlists) as well as an internal but easily accessible Telegram group where they share insights, video links, and experiences. Antifa vlogs, documentaries on the housing crisis, mobilization videos for climate action, and playful subversion videos mocking the powers that all circulate through these channels. Anglophone left-wing influencers like ContraPoints, Lindsay Ellis, Three Arrows, or PhilosophyTube functioned as role models in the beginning, and most activists seem to follow the subcultural strategies of these well-known creators. The primary addressee therefore seems less the German public in general than a certain subcultural, left-leaning part of the web.

Among the many projects introduced at the meeting, there were also two German-language political education vlogs that serve as brief examples here to point out the structural challenges that this kind of activism faces on social media. The channel Systemrelevant ("Systemically Relevant" with 3,400 subscriptions on Facebook, YouTube, and X) is a small, yet interesting project dedicated to everyday labor struggles from the perspectives of the workers. The COVID-19 pandemic gave rise to the title "Systemrelevant," a contested term in Germany for front-line workers during that time. Unlike most influencers, who work individually, Systemrelevant consists of four people with a background in trade unions, social work, and journalism. Although there is a group behind Systemrelevant, they refer to the common influencer format rather than videos of counter-journalistic media collectives. For example, the videos often feature a single presenter named Clemens, posting from his kitchen table and represented by thumbnails on YouTube. The videos are simple vlogs that not only address and inform the general public but also serve to empower workers' communities. They are usually about 45 minutes long and depict conversations between the group and interview partners, or Clemens alone addresses the audience directly from his home in a portrait shot. In most cases, the videos are simple recordings of Zoom meetings and remain static and rough. The target group is users over 30, which is why Facebook and YouTube are the central platforms, while X and Discord serve as secondary sites for further comments and distribution.

Another example of applying influencer strategies for left-wing political education is Linke Sau ("Leftist Pig," 2,500 subscriptions on YouTube and X/Twitter). The title is the pseudonym of an activist YouTuber who uses debunking vlogs to refute and discursively contextualize far-right content and to problematize distorted representations of the left in established mass media. While network colleagues such as Unruly July or Emily Laquer appear in front of the camera, Linke Sau (like his English-language role model Three Arrows) gives no hints as to his identity. The debunking genre allows him to remain invisible, being present only through the voice-over, and to rely visually entirely on found footage from the political opponent. In the process, he exposes racist modes of argumentation, but in doing that, he also has to visually reproduce the original racist content. While the right-wing extremist videos that he deconstructs are often produced quickly and entail unsubstantiated allegations, Linke Sau deals intensively with his opponent's argumentation. In his 30–60-minute videos, he analyses and points out contradictions in a reflective and technically adept way. He states that he has a humanities background and compares his video production to writing academic papers. He makes his videos in his spare time alongside his job in a video production company, and each takes him about three months. The effort he puts into his work seems due more to a desire for political argumentation than for attention and influence. By using appropriate keywords, he tries to penetrate right-wing filter bubbles to burst them with sharp arguments.

Both Linke Sau and Systemrelevant work autodidactically and operate purely non-commercial channels without external funding. Their focus is on the elaborate discursive problematization of social grievances. They pay less attention to questions of strategic communication or audiovisual design, production, distribution, and social networking, partly because the effort involved is simply too great in addition to their paid work. Hence, they have a significantly smaller reach than professional influencers or non-activist everyday content creators.

Nevertheless, we can conclude that influencers and other individual content creators are decisive players in video activism. While older video collectives and NGOs had to adapt to social media, these more recent actors are children of the current commercialized platform ecology. They epitomize a new form of everyday activism, in which parts of one's everyday life are staged for the camera and become visible on social media. Melanie and Viktoria, two Austrian TikTokers in their early twenties, are symptomatic of this. They recounted how, out of boredom during the COVID-19 lockdown, they began posting videos on their channels @zoffnix and @vik.talk and commented on the state measures and their everyday lives during those times, which brought them an increase in attention.[47] Far from being petty clicktivism, this development represents a tendency toward an *increasing everydayness of video activism*, which is conditioned by social media and can indeed be politically impactful (Highfield 2016), as our analysis of the German influencer Rezo in Chapter 4 also demonstrates.

While the appearance, self-understanding, and practices of activism are changing in the face of new actors, it is important to distinguish between professional influencers and the significant number of individual amateur creators. *Professional influencers*—political and other—are the poster child of a new industry within the neoliberal political economy and, as freelancers, have developed a strong sense of personal independence and self-determination, while rejecting traditional occupational titles. Sometimes they take on the role of activists or citizen journalists, sometimes of self-entrepreneurs, and sometimes all at the same time. However, by monetizing political speech on social media, they become increasingly dependent on platform algorithms as well as lucrative collaborations with companies, NGOs, or other powerful stakeholders. While financial independence was a crucial aspect of their political self-understanding for most video activists of earlier generations and media environments, and for some it still is, this is much less true today for many of these new kinds of actors. On the one hand, this has to do with the low-threshold everyday media that have made it easy for countless new voices to be heard and have given rise to the more recent phenomena of occasional or accidental activists. On the other hand, this media environment has produced a fiercely competitive attention economy in which professional influencers have also specialized in political issues as part of their brand. These actors obviously do not see financial considerations as contradicting their political work and their personal independence. Another, much more problematic characteristic of professional influencers is that by using their real names and being hypervisible media figures, they often face ongoing threats. This is especially true for people of color as well as female, Jewish, and LGBTQIA+ content creators and those with disabilities. While far-right influencers and conspiracy demagogues had long been supported by platform algorithms due to the many user reactions they provoked (some are, however, banned from the major platforms), many professional influencers conclude that specializing in political content is not feasible. Such content might be popular among users, but it is often polarizing as well and demonetized by platforms in many cases. As our case studies suggest, activist influencers on social media seem to follow other paths in the long run: to focus on other topics, to be present in other media, or to pursue entirely different careers.

Non-professional individual content creators are comparably freer to choose their formats and approaches, but have fewer resources, funding opportunities, and practical skills in developing attention strategies and thus mostly achieve only limited reach and influence. For instance, the disproportionately high amount of work put into production combined with low response was ultimately the reason why Linke Sau now only posts very few videos at irregular intervals. At some point, the effort became too great for him to continue in this way without financial incentives or at least symbolic recognition. Interestingly, many influencers at the workshop hosted by the Rosa Luxemburg Foundation asked for financial and technical support. But that might compromise their independence, and the appearance of institutional names and logos in videos or in the channel info section can also create mistrust and criticism among users who long for personal, authentic content with no interference from established political institutions.

In general, there is little interaction between the two networks of professional and non-professional content creators. While smaller activist creators usually do not consider professional influencers as part of their community, the latter seem hardly to notice amateurs with a small reach. Ultimately, it remains to be seen how far activist influencers will be influential in the long term. Professional influencers with their often glossy and streamlined performances are currently being challenged not only by successful far-right and conspiracy influencers with their rough and seemingly authentic appeal. The occasional, playful activities of younger TikTokers with their casual political commentaries, who are not aiming at professionalization or complex explanations, are also gaining popularity. After the heated initial phase of the influencer industry, there might perhaps be a period of normalization and convergence of influencers with other content creators.

Large NGOs: Established and Evolving

Another type of video activists with specific practices are nongovernmental organizations. NGOs fighting for human or civil rights, for peace, or for the protection of the environment use video on social media in a variety of ways, mostly as part of larger political campaigns online and offline. International nongovernmental organizations (INGOs) such as Amnesty International, Attac, Care, Food Watch, Greenpeace, Human Rights Watch, Médecins Sans Frontières (Doctors Without Borders), Oxfam, Save the Children, Terre des Hommes, or World Wide Fund for Nature (WWF) rely, amongst other media, on the power of videos to pursue their political goals, recruit supporters, and shape a brand name that also stands for a group identity (Kavada 2012). By professing to work independently of government support, the organizations rely predominantly on donations and membership fees to fund their advocacy campaigns, as well as their concrete relief actions and their continuous support for the vulnerable. Compared to the types of activist alliances described above, large NGOs consist of many more people, have many more resources, and are structured in much more stable, complex, formal, and hierarchical ways.

The activities of NGOs are multifaceted. Much of their essential practical work consists of offline activities, and their political campaigning ranges from organizing demonstrations or acts of civil disobedience to so-called "e-tactics—collective actions that involve varying degrees of online components" (Katz-Kimchi and Manosevitch 2015, 250). Some NGOs commission journalistic or scientific research in their field or even run their own publications (such as book series, annual scientific reports, or journals for members). Data and arguments gathered in these publications can be used not only in their campaigns but also in exchanges with policymakers or business executives, or as evidence in court, for example, when they file lawsuits against corporations (Ristovska 2021). With their social media strategies, NGOs aim at raising awareness in a wider public or mobilizing like-minded people. An important part of the work of NGOs—political lobbying in back rooms or at summits—remains mostly unseen by the public, but it is often also done with the help of video.

NGOs are important actors within the field of video activism. They are a powerful force in terms of outreach and social impact, not least because they have considerable financial resources at their disposal, which they are able to spend on systematic, long-term media work, often in cooperation with professional media and PR consultants. Because they usually employ their own specialists, such as media analysts, online journalists, storytelling experts, and video editors, they can react quickly to current events with short-term video tactics and are also able to develop and pursue long-term video strategies on recurring topics (Fahlenbrach 2020).

Independent political actors sometimes question the activist credibility and legitimacy of NGOs for various reasons: first, because their activities often involve political lobbying (Krebber et al. 2015; Köhler 2018). Second, critics have repeatedly raised doubts concerning the large amounts of money (from donations and membership fees) that international NGOs use not only for their political activities and for campaigning but also to pay for their considerable administrative apparatuses, employees, and infrastructures. Third, the videos produced by NGOs often have promotional aspects and aim at increasing membership rates and donations, and they offer, as some left-wing critics notice, a contemporary kind of sale of indulgences to provide for the donor's good conscience. Finally, further objections concern the fact that the massive media presence of some environmental NGOs is in itself extremely energy-consuming and unsustainable (Koch 2007).

The situation becomes even more complicated by the fact that the term NGO in general is only vaguely outlined and serves as an umbrella covering a wide variety of organizations with different goals and political orientations, which in some cases fulfill quasi-governmental or corporate tasks (Lang 2013, 2015). Additionally, under this umbrella, numerous fake NGOs, so-called GONGOs, PANGOs, and BINGOs, run by governments, parties, or business organizations, pursue their own hidden agendas through greenwashing, astroturfing, or sock puppeting (Götz 2008, see Chapter 1). In our study, however, we focus on actual, generally recognized NGOs with civil society, not-for-profit objectives. Such NGOs have come under increasing pressure from authoritarian and totalitarian states such as Russia, Afghanistan, and Iran, where they are banned (such as Greenpeace in Russia after 30 years of political work in the country) and their employees and volunteer activists have been persecuted as "terrorists," "criminals," or "Western agents."

Their use of videos, the aesthetic forms of these videos, and their dissemination via different platforms are as diverse as the goals of the NGOs. In addition to their own websites, most of the large NGOs make use of large social media to distribute their videos. The form of the videos is usually adapted to the respective platform, its specific features, affordances, and the target audience. The production values also depend on the specific NGO's image and its ethical guidelines in dealing with campaigns, donations, and grants. Some organizations like Care or Doctors Without Borders have qualms about investing larger portions of their budgets in video production and social media marketing rather than in concrete relief efforts and therefore tend to produce cheap, DIY videos as a kind of side activity. In contrast, other NGOs such as Greenpeace, Amnesty International, or Save the Children see social media campaigning with video as a central means of information and mobilizing and an important tool for achieving social impact. Therefore, they consider it an indispensable part of their work and invest more effort and resources in it.

In the following, we will focus on the video work of Greenpeace, one of the largest global peace and environmental protection organizations worldwide with over three million members and sites in 55 countries. The organization deals with a wide range of issues, including climate change and energy supply, nuclear plants and nuclear weapons, toxins and pollutants, genetically modified organisms, oceans, forests, and sustainable agriculture. Greenpeace has been relying on the power of images since very early on and constantly spends considerable resources on video production and media activities. We will give a brief glimpse into Greenpeace's use of campaign videos and look at some characteristic aesthetic and rhetorical strategies used to win people for the NGO's causes. As we will see, Greenpeace's video strategies have changed significantly since the NGO was founded. Its early DIY aesthetics have given way to professionalization and a more coherent brand design. The look of the videos has become more opulent and the communication more strategic and uniform since the initially small organization grew into a powerful global institution. In 1971, a group of young peace activists in Vancouver, Canada, protested against American nuclear weapons testing on the Amchitka Island in Alaska. The group used a former fishing vessel later renamed Greenpeace for their protest actions (Brown and May 1989; Weyler 2004). From then on, the NGO successively grew into "an international, strong and independent professional organization with an internal and functional structure that can be compared with other world market organizations" (Chartier 2015, 502, our translation). As this comparatively long-term development also reflects the changing history of social movements, we offer a diachronic analysis of Greenpeace's ongoing work with film and video.

"Casting light on action"—this phrase coined in a photographic record of the first 30 years of Greenpeace (Boettger and Hamdan 2001, 12)—concisely outlines the NGO's media strategy. Greenpeace has always been waging its struggle for peace, human rights, and environmental protection with the help of photos, films, and videos, relying on the stirring and emotional effects of spectacular, visually documented actions against nuclear power plants, whalers, oil rigs on the high seas, or dumping radioactive waste. The daring actions can at the same time be characterized as "dramatic image events," as a form of communication, and as proof of the urgency of interventionist practices as the activists put themselves at high risk. Photographs and videos serve as documents and visible evidence of the activists' commitment against environmental crimes (Boettger 2001, 14). As these action documentaries and witness films depict a courageous fight against an overpowering opponent, they were widely distributed to newspapers and TV stations—letting the world know and calling for fighting for the cause. To pursue their goals, the NGO has effectively cooperated with established mass media from the very beginning and provided compelling footage with high news value.

Peace activist and ecologist Bob Hunter, one of the founders of Greenpeace, described the specific function of these spectacular, highly symbolic images:

> My idea was: if you took an image and you passed it through the media into the mass mind, you could essentially blow the mass mind [...]. And the images of small whales against great whaling machines was a mind bomb.[48]

As "mind bombs," the images are not only meant to inform and educate, but first and foremost to shake up, to outrage the public, mobilize people for political action, and invite them to join the movement, that is to evoke political emotions and actions (Eder 2018). The concept of the "mind bomb" was later taken up by other NGOs and became a common instrument of PR campaigners and advertisers (Hofmann 2008).

So, from early on the organization produced action documentaries, or "battle footage," that provided key visuals, highly symbolic images, like those shown here. The image from the 1970s *Soviet Whaling Action* (American Masters PBS 2014), one of the first short films depicting disruptive actions against Russian whalers,[49] depicts a Greenpeace activist standing upright in a small, swaying boat, filming the action while confronting the enormous Russian ship (Figure 5.6).[50] Two film cameras were used to shoot the organized, dangerous effort on the sea. One of them took care to document not only the risky action itself but also the work of the camera person collecting visible evidence. Thus, there was a second witness filming and in doing so trying to protect the first cameraperson from assaults by the whalers while the activists were trying to prevent them from slaughtering the endangered sea mammals. Such a double safeguard of camera presence is commonplace at demonstrations today.

FIGURE 5.6: *Soviet Whaling Action* (1975): an early Greenpeace campaign video, or "action documentary" of a risky action against a Russian whaling ship on the high seas.

This early Greenpeace film already fulfills all four functions of activist videos described above (see Chapter 1): the video informs (epistemic function), arouses emotions (affective function), appeals to primary and secondary audiences like policymakers and Greenpeace supporters to act to prevent such events (appellative function), and it has a performative function in that filming protects the activists themselves from assault.

Greenpeace's images invite the public symbolically and emotionally to join David in its rebellious provocation of Goliath and thus become part of a bigger community with specific ethical principles. The NGO's fight for the good cause always has self-promotional aspects as well, because ultimately it is about strengthening the movement through public attention and increasing membership numbers. Greenpeace insists on its unconditional financial and political independence and therefore does not accept government grants or donations from political parties or commercial companies; and as trade in merchandising products also plays only a minor role, donations and membership fees are the central source of funding. From the beginning the group aimed at growing from a small grassroots movement to a powerful force that governments and the industry cannot ignore and have to cope with.

Greenpeace still follows this tradition of carrying out spectacular actions, well documented by cameras, against overpowering opponents (oil companies, nuclear

FIGURE 5.7: A spectacular image of a Greenpeace campaign fighting for biodiversity by hoisting a banner on the Christ the Redeemer statue in Rio de Janeiro in 2006.

and coal-fired power plants, etc.). Some actions are aimed less at preventing injustice against nature than at providing symbolic images, such as activists hoisting an enormous banner on the Christ the Redeemer statue in Rio de Janeiro in 2006, while the Convention of Biological Diversity with representatives of 188 nations took place in Brazil (see Figure 5.7).

Because it has valued the mobilizing quality of images as "mind-bombs" so highly, Greenpeace has always devoted a significant portion of its funding to media analysis, image production, communication, and outreach (DeLuca 2009). For example, Greenpeace Germany's annual report for 2020 (Greenpeace 2021) breaks down the use of membership dues and donations (a total of 80.3 million Euros): the costs for video production in total are not shown separately, but can be allocated to the categories "communication" (11.5 million Euros), "advertising" (7.2 million Euros), and maybe also to "implementation of campaigns" (47.3 million Euros), in so far as some campaigns take place exclusively online. Due to its financial strength, Greenpeace Germany also takes on a large share of the financing of international campaigns (Schicha 2001).

Greenpeace Germany, located in the city of Hamburg, is the largest national group with 620,000 sustaining members and local groups in almost all German cities and districts. It runs cinema and TV commercials to distribute its campaign videos, and its website greenpeace.de also contains videos on various topics. Above all, however, Greenpeace Germany is represented on various social media platforms. It has maintained a YouTube channel since 2007, only two years after YouTube was founded. This channel also serves as an extensive video archive users are invited to browse through, although only a fraction of all the Greenpeace videos can be found there. Greenpeace Germany is especially active on Facebook and Instagram, but also on Snapchat and TikTok, aiming at the platform's younger users to become supporters or members. The videos found on the website and the Greenpeace channel on YouTube show an astonishing variety of forms and at the same time a high recognition value, not only because of the use of the Greenpeace logo at the end of each video but also because of the mode of address and a balanced connection between delivering bad news and giving people a sense of hope at the end. This leads to a call for action that is easy to understand and aims at changing affects like fear, melancholy, or distress into moral emotions and a sense of empowerment, a political consciousness that makes people feel they can actually make a difference. A closer look at a few examples produced by Greenpeace Germany or Greenpeace International may show this and illustrate how Greenpeace's video activism has changed over the last decades, as well.

In addition to videos documenting their actions, Greenpeace began to use humor and satire early on as a means of communication, agitation, and community building. The oldest video presented by Greenpeace Germany on its YouTube channel is an antinuclear spot directed against the electricity giant Vattenfall, one of the dominant suppliers in the German market. The clip *Bei Vattenfall: Neulich in Krümmel* ("At Vattenfall: The Other Day in Kruemmel") (Greenpeace Germany 2007, nearly 89,000 views since then) was produced as a direct answer to a serious incident that took place shortly before when a transformer fire broke out in the nuclear plant south of Hamburg. The fire was caused by "a communicative misunderstanding," as Vattenfall evasively announced to the public. The fictional clip is shot in apparently semi-professional DIY mode and with its poor quality in style and acting is reminiscent of an amateur theater performance. In its stereotypical representation, the incident at the power plant is attributed to the individual failure of a lone, irresponsible worker in a seemingly run-down and untrustworthy control room, who simply ignores the flashing emergency signals while building a house of cards and eating doughnuts. Reluctantly he answers the emergency call on the phone, and, in the regional working-class dialect, insists on his worker's rights. Finally, he has had enough and leaves the control room for good, not without putting on a gas mask for the sake of his personal safety. "Just switch off" is the request at the end of the video. Due to its DIY aesthetics and its omission of the real responsibilities for the incident, the humorously intended video is likely to be limited in its social impact and presumably preaches to the choir, reaching only those who are already supporters of the anti-nuclear movement instead of appealing to a wider public.

The gradual professionalization of Greenpeace's video activism is shown in clips that more convincingly follow the tradition of agitprop, using strategies of subversion or communication guerrilla familiar to artivist collectives. Greenpeace posted several elaborately produced satirical clips that parody the language of advertising or TV commercials. A well-known example is the (in)famous spot *Give the Orangutan a Break: Nestle KitKat Spoof Video* (Greenpeace Int. 2010), "featuring a bored office worker taking a break to enjoy a KitKat, but instead bites into an orangutan's finger," as the Greenpeace website describes its content. The video served as part of a strategically planned, multifaceted advocacy campaign attacking Nestlé. The Swiss food and beverage corporation, by using palm oil with their products, exploits the rain forests and thus contributes to the destruction of the last orangutans' habitat. The advertising parody relies on shock effects and evokes diverging emotions like disgust and black humor. The subversion video caused a PR debacle for Nestlé on the web. After the corporation had a British version of the video deleted from YouTube, it spread like an avalanche on the internet—a tactical victory for Greenpeace, as the video achieved worldwide attention, triggered a great media echo, and put pressure on the all-powerful opponent (Harrild 2010). Greenpeace produced numerous other types of videos in an artivist style such as the short, poetic mash-up *A Song of Oil, Ice and Fire* (Greenpeace Int. 2015), which pays tribute to the popular series *Game of Thrones* by depicting a wasteland created by the evil forces of Shell's drilling practices at sea.

After the early, rather raw, and quickly produced live-action footage of Greenpeace interventions, the communicative strategy of working with carefully scripted narrative short films also gained ground. Greenpeace campaign videos are characterized by strong storytelling (Reinsborough and Canning 2010, 88f.), catchy style, symbolic images, attention-grabbing effects, intense emotions, and thus memorability. This mode of video activism that has left a lasting mark on the Greenpeace brand is based on high-value, costly productions created with the help of well-known advertising companies.[51] Such videos were produced in English original versions and then dubbed or subtitled for distribution in various countries.

An important variety of such videos are animated shorts that seemingly address children but in fact mainly appeal to adults with sometimes funny, sometimes sad, but always emotional stories. An influential example is the cute *Facebook: Unfriend Coal* (Greenpeace Int.) short from 2010, which was released when campaigning with the help of web videos was a rather new and exciting way of reaching out to a huge audience all over the world. *Unfriend Coal* promoted the carefully planned and organized worldwide campaign against Facebook's use of dirty fossil energy, especially for cloud computing with its enormous CO_2 emissions (Katz-Kimchi and Manosevitch 2015). The funny cartoon, drawn in a child-like style, tells the story of the rise (and then beginning downfall) of Facebook in a parodic mode, filtering it through a child's voice that in disarmingly childlike logic asks Mark Zuckerberg to unfriend dirty, angry coal (the story's monster) and befriend a white and peaceful cloud instead. The video was released on YouTube very shortly before the premiere of the Zuckerberg biopic *The Social Network* (USA 2010, David Fincher) and went viral: it was watched nearly 624,000 times on the Greenpeace YouTube channel alone (Figure 5.8).

The "*Unfriend Coal*" campaign was one of the first that systematically used not only the Greenpeace website but Facebook as well to target an international audience beyond the Greenpeace members and supporters who regularly visit the website or the YouTube channel. Katz-Kimchi and Manosevitch highlight the importance of this campaign: "the *Unfriend Coal* campaign [...] is the first Greenpeace campaign implemented via a Facebook fan page" (2015, 255). So Greenpeace effectively campaigns against Facebook with the help of Facebook. In their analysis of the campaign, Katz-Kimchi and Manosevitch describe how Facebook users in different countries created their own *Unfriend Coal* related Facebook groups to disseminate the clip that Greenpeace had dubbed in various

FIGURE 5.8: *Facebook: Unfriend Coal* (Greenpeace International, 2010).

languages. In the end, 500,000 Facebook users worldwide were involved (2015, 256). The campaign works like a parasite that eats its host from within by appealing to Facebook users to articulate their protest against the platform—and to leave if Zuckerberg does not change Facebook's energy policy. As this example shows, Greenpeace developed platform-specific mobilizing strategies early on; in this case, Facebook's "like," "share," and "comment" features were used to achieve a sense of empowerment or the joy of joint action among users who became active supporters of the NGO and their causes by participating.

Because the campaign work with animation clips in a child-like mode proved successful, it was continued in the following years, for example, with the widely spread campaign video *There's a Rang-tan in My Bedroom* (Greenpeace Int. 2018), which continues the fight for the rainforests, the orangutan's habitat. It tells the story of a little girl who finds a little orangutan in her home because the animal lost its mother and has been forced from its home because Indonesian rainforests are destroyed to grow fields for the palm oil used to make our everyday products. The children's story is narrated in rhyme by the well-known British actress Emma Thompson, and additional dubbed versions of the poem were produced to make the clip more accessible to international audiences. The clip focuses on mixed emotions such as terror, sympathy, and fighting spirit and depicts the little girl acting heroically to help her orangutan friend. When these mobilization videos are compared, their common elements stand out. Both clips (and others following in this direction) put children in the role of courageous actors who challenge global corporations and governments with seemingly naive, but irresistible logic: if children can understand the connections between the consumption of fossil energy and climate change or the consequences of deforestation, then adults must also understand this and fight alongside their children so that the next generations have a future.

This strategy to evoke empathy for an individual animal as a representative of an endangered species, to make people feel responsible and act as advocates for those who cannot is also clear in the more recent campaign videos to save the Arctic, a central Greenpeace issue since the early days of the movement. These works differ from earlier "Save the Arctic" campaign videos in that they avoid images of supposedly untouched ice landscapes and sublime nature, for those could too easily override the message of the severe endangerment of the Arctic by global warming (Doyle 2007, 2011; Abbamonte 2021).[52]

A Homeless Polar Bear in London (Greenpeace Int. 2012) is different from those earlier clips and relies on emotional storytelling and the symbolic power of surprising, defamiliarizing images. Like *There's a Rang-tan in My Bedroom*, which benefits from Emma Thompson's voice and popularity, this Greenpeace campaign also worked in close cooperation with social celebrities to spread the video and its political message and so increase its social impact.

Collaboration with well-known pop or film stars as supporters can be identified as a Greenpeace strategy since the early days of the movement when rock musicians gave a free concert in 1971 to help finance the anti-nuclear weapons campaign on Amchitka Island. In 2012, more than 40 years later, Greenpeace International commissioned the high-quality, expensive, and very successful call-for-action music video *A Homeless Polar Bear in London* as part of the "Save the Arctic" campaign. It features Radiohead on the soundtrack and the British actor Jude Law as narrator, using celebrities and their fan communities to generate attention and increase dissemination. Both Jude Law and Radiohead's Thom Yorke had—just like Emma Thompson—previously campaigned for environmental protection and thus enjoyed credibility as spokespersons and patrons (Figure 5.9).

The campaign video with its cinematic quality and style relocates the polar bear's desperate search for food from the Arctic to the streets of London. Accompanied by the minimal, loop-like song *Everything in Its Right Place* (which the polar bear obviously isn't) by Radiohead, melancholically sung by Yorke, we see a distraught polar bear roaming through desolate London areas, digging through the rubbish and waste on the streets, homeless, tired, and hungry. Nowhere does the animal find shelter, and food only in the form of surrogates such as advertising signs in front of a fish and chips shop. No human beings seem to notice the huge white bear that doesn't belong here, only children trapped behind car windows look silently

FIGURE 5.9: *A Homeless Polar Bear in London—Ft. Jude Law and Radiohead* (Greenpeace International, 2012).

at the sad beast sniffing car exhaust fumes in dense traffic. The video closes with Law's calm but insisting voice-over commentary calling for action: "As the Arctic melts the rush to exploit its resources is starting." And while the polar bear finally lays down to die under a London park tree, Law continues: "Nobody will listen to her, but I listen to you. Join the movement: Save the Arctic." The last image, as always, is the Greenpeace logo and the link to its "Save the Arctic" campaign.

Throughout its history, Greenpeace has released many professionally produced and widely disseminated mobilization videos like the *Homeless Polar Bear* which received more than 1.1 million views in total and is thus one of the most prominent productions of the NGO ever. Besides such prestige campaign videos under the responsibility of Greenpeace International, there is also a huge number of simpler and presumably cheaper shorts produced by various Greenpeace national groups. These videos respond to specific requirements in the respective states, cities, and counties and focus on local issues. On the one hand, the short videos denounce local grievances, for instance, supermarkets offering meat from non-species-appropriate animal husbandry. On the other hand, Greenpeace Germany, for example, provides numerous videos that can be described as consumer advice or as educational advertising, for example, on how to preserve resources in our daily lives by saving electricity or buying clothes second hand. Consumer work is in general another important area for Greenpeace (DeLuca 2009, 264).

What all the different formats Greenpeace has been using over five decades of its activist work have in common is, primarily, that they effectively aim to elicit attention and attract interest by using strong storytelling and an eye-catching style. Second, the videos rely on calculated provocations to shake things up and stimulate debate. To this end, they merge their informative content and educational stance with environment-related empathy and a strong emotional appeal.[53] This seems to combine the three basic strategies of provocation, education, and participation described in Chapters 3 and 4. Third, the campaign videos evoke moods and become affectively charged in various ways, leading for instance to shock, disgust and humor, anger and sympathy, fear and hope, melancholy or sadness, as well as joy or feelings of empowerment and agency. They use these feelings to engage viewers and appeal to an affective public as an imaginary movement, or as an encompassing "we" that shares environment-related values and moral emotions. In this regard, humor is also an effective and widely used tool, as it addresses those in the know, who are supposedly in advance of the rest of society. This knowledgeable audience might experience a sense of empowerment, which is important if passive viewers are to become active supporters. The delicate balance between frightening images of climate change ("danger frames") and those depicting a better, possible future seems crucial to avoid paralyzing the viewers and instead setting specific impulses for action ("gain frames", see Chapter 4). This seems to be a reason for Greenpeace to rely on a large number of consumer advice videos that identify concrete ways to become a "climate fighter" in your daily life and, in doing so, become part of a greater movement for a better world.

This strategic approach also becomes evident when we shift our focus away from the videos on the Greenpeace YouTube channel and look at how the NGO has recently been adapting its video strategies to new platforms and their requirements and audiences. The strategy of addressing users as climate fighters and part of a community taking responsibility for the planet is central to the NGO's recent activities on TikTok. While the Greenpeace videos on YouTube seem to address a broader, more heterogeneous audience, its TikTok channels currently target younger users with an affinity for the Fridays for Future movement. The TikToks make use of the app's green screen or stitch function, for example, to pick up on media coverage of environmental issues or comment on the consumer behavior of fashion influencers. They pick up trending sounds on the app to be noticed by Gen Z users who before did not actively follow Greenpeace. The short TikToks use uplifting music, images to prove the power of the many, and they offer the opportunity to participate easily by liking, leaving a comment, or sharing the video.

Greenpeace Germany, for example, posted approximately 300 videos on TikTok (two clips per week on average) within the first three years since it opened its account in 2021. The content creators rely on constant production to feed the maw of the TikTok algorithm and in doing so increase the channel's visibility. On TikTok (and, to some degree, on other platforms), it's much less the individual clip that counts, but the steady stream of video content that carries the message over time and in ever new facets.

The Greenpeace TikToks use the common vertical format with likable anchor figures, relatively young creators who work for the NGO and are close to the Gen Z target audience, addressing it directly. From early on, Greenpeace Germany sought cooperation with activist influencers and other content creators who already had a large number of followers and a wide network in the TikTok ecosphere and who identified with Greenpeace-related issues like climate justice, animal welfare, or even the reworking of used clothing to save resources. These activist TikToks follow the usual connection with a "sound," i.e., a song or spoken phrase currently trending on the app and used by many. They work with memes popular on TikTok or aim to produce memes themselves to be shared by others to emphasize the message: Greenpeace belongs to your generation, shares your swag, is part of an ecological, peace-loving, and sustainable youth culture. Greenpeace's video activism on TikTok thus corresponds to what John Hartley has described as "playful activism" (Hartley 2010; see also Kaye et al. 2022, 120–37)—starting from the proposition that fighting for the climate can also be fun.

A closer look at Greenpeace's video work from a diachronic perspective reveals the changing strategies and modalities through which the NGO has attempted to reach different audiences as well as its transformation from a grassroots movement in the 1970s to today's largest and most influential environmental NGO in the world, along with WWF. Anchoring video content in popular practices of internet culture is a crucial strategy for generating attention and reaching a wider public, and this applies to large NGOs, as well. Greenpeace, with remarkable strategic consistency, has adapted its political campaign work and videos to the everchanging affordances of commercial social media. It aims to address and activate different audiences in different ways and to use networking with other activist organizations, independent activist content creators on diverse social media platforms, as well as with journalists across different media.

Programmatically, Greenpeace is committed to interaction with its members and supporters. The NGO, regardless of its institutional size, tries to address and involve its supporters directly, encourages them to share suggestions, and thus presents itself as accessible and its activities as transparent. Occasional live events like presentations with Greenpeace staff on YouTube, where the audience can join in the discussion and contribute ideas, also serve this purpose. And the TikTok channel in particular presents itself as open to all; direct address and dialogue with the users are of central importance here. Even though Greenpeace uses all these strategies to reach out to the public, the staff are aware that the possibilities of mobilizing people are limited. Concrete offline actions are therefore mostly carried out by professional activists or local Greenpeace members. The larger public targeted by the videos is more likely to be addressed as donors or possible members.

Greenpeace is a globally active NGO that nevertheless relies heavily on financially more potent supporters from countries in the Global Northwest. In addressing this affluent base, which is at the same time responsible for much of the environmental destruction, Greenpeace recognizably shapes and promotes alternative lifestyles beyond consumerism, resource consumption, and extractivism. The NGO tries to do this by envisioning a more solidary society and linking the struggle for a better world with feelings of agency and pleasure. The addressees do not have to risk their lives or health for their support (as some of the core activists do), but they can already make a difference by sharing a video, signing an online petition, turning down the heating, and at best getting rid of the family car. Some critics accuse Greenpeace of having developed into a feel-good organization for people in the affluent Global Northwest, which emphasizes the "green" in its name more than the global fight for peace, as one participant in our activism research workshop remarked. In contrast to this position, Greenpeace's self-image is that it is a strong fighting community with moral integrity ready to take a stand against industry, governments, and extractivist capitalism as a whole. At the same time, this self-image is combined with the conviction that networked media strategies are necessary for knowledge transfer and mobilization and that the NGO must therefore constantly produce images and information that have an impact both on social and mass media.

Hashtag Movements: Polyphonic and Unpredictable

Hashtag protest movements are arguably the most visible and at the same time elusive phenomenon of video activism (see case study in Chapter 6). On several of the most widely used social media, videos are posted in seconds with a series of hashtags. Algorithms then assess the relevance of a hashtag or trend and help the video in question to gain visibility (according to criteria that hardly correspond to those of activism)—or lose it again. Hashtag movements are thus essentially ephemerous phenomena; they focus on specific topics or events and emerge, grow, and decline in a limited timeframe, often in sudden, short- or medium-term waves. Hashtags can be written in any language, but influential transnational movements of this kind such as #ArabSpring and #Occupy (with heydays in 2011) or #FridaysForFuture (since 2018) are usually based on a hashtag written in English. However, there are also popular activist hashtags in other global languages such as #NiUnaMenos (since 2015) that galvanized protests against femicides from Argentina throughout South America and across the world. As the cases of #MeToo (since 2017) and #BlackLivesMatter (since 2013) demonstrate, hashtags are often used to assemble individual cases and personal experiences (here: of sexual harassment and abuse or, respectively, anti-Black racism and police violence) by connecting many individual videos and other posts, thereby denouncing widespread structural problems such as sexism and racism (see Chapter 4). Local initiatives also benefit from the public attention given to transnational hashtag movements, for example, when they link well-known hashtags to more specific ones such as #BlackTransLivesMatter (#BTLM) or #Asians4BlackLives.

Obviously, hashtag movements should not be imagined as collectives with clear organizational structures that carry out actions according to predetermined strategies. Although they are political forces in their own right, they ultimately emerge from the dynamically changing networked attention of many different actors including average users and accidental witnesses, influencers, activist collectives, and small and large NGOs. Distributed in a generally contingent manner via a multitude of user nodes across various platforms, such movements can be described more accurately as loose, multipolar assemblages of "connective action" (Bennett and Segerberg 2012). They connect, collect, and circulate all kinds of videos, for instance, witness videos and vlog comments on issues related to the hashtag, mobilization videos and calls to action, as well as community documentaries attempting to cultivate the identity of the loose movements. Hashtag movements are linked to public figures and offline events, and their videos and texts can spread via mass media and thus circulate in wider spheres and in the longer term. Hashtags also have a basic archival collecting and ordering function that enables users to find related content on a protest movement.

Every hashtag movement has a beginning, and the users creating a hashtag might be seen as its authors. But whether and how a hashtag is picked up and becomes a political movement depends primarily on the online and offline networks these original users are involved in. The phrase "Black Lives Matter," for instance, was presumably first written in 2013 among anti-racist feminist activists in a Facebook comment on the murder of Trayvon Martin, then was quickly picked up and used heavily as a X/Twitter hashtag, before it became a global social movement and was tagged on witness videos documenting anti-Black police violence (Khan-Cullors and bandele 2018). Within the largely horizontal networks of a hashtag movement, vertical structures, such as informal organizers, microcelebrities, and more established groups that form the temporary "hard core" of activists, also play a decisive role. These opinion leaders give strategic impulses in open forums or closed groups on Facebook, X/Twitter, Telegram, and other services, but as the case of the so-called "Twitter pashas" during the "Arab Spring" has proven, their political influence outside their communities or media bubbles remains limited (Gerbaudo 2012). Even though protest movements thrive on interlocking online and offline action –"tweets and the streets" (ibid.)—opinion leaders on social media are not necessarily charismatic leaders on the streets. This seemingly paradoxical character of hashtag movements can also be described as the "organization of the organizationless" (Nunes 2014).

Importantly, a hashtag movement is only one particular force within broader "hashtag publics" with a multiplicity of diverging and often conflicting opinions (Rambukkana 2015; Burgess et al. 2015). Thus using the same hashtag that is connected to an activist video and participating in a public discourse does not necessarily mean that the user supports the demands of the original activist creators and their allies. For instance, in reaction to the Movement for Black Lives, its opponents and racist agitators, including a secret Russian troll army with the cover name Blacktivists, also heavily used #BlackLivesMatter (Levin 2017). This battle *over* hashtags and their meanings is often also accompanied by a battle *of* hashtags. In the case of #BlackLivesMatter, counter-movements were formed primarily via counter-hashtags such as the relativist #AllLivesMatter, the pro-police #BlueLivesMatter, and the neo-Nazi #WhiteLivesMatter.

Such hashtag battles can be seen as a new way of forming public opinion. In this context, hashtag movements can be powerful and effective actors in social discourses due to their easy accessibility through everyday social media, the multitude of users participating, and the medial snowball effects. They have the potential to empower their specific communities and at the same time involve broader publics. However, they are also rather volatile assemblages of heterogeneous and often diverging actors, and they strongly depend on conflicting goals, contingent offline events, and non-transparent platform algorithms. The open structure of hashtag movements makes them ultimately uncontrollable not only for platforms and opponents but also for the different kinds of activists themselves. The question remains, especially for smaller initiatives and their local and less spectacular issues, which hashtags, cases, and videos ultimately trend, which ones stay invisible or are actively suppressed by algorithms, and which ones are shifted in their meanings or taken over by powerful opponents. It, therefore, seems important from a critical perspective to look not only at the abstract meta-level of volatile hashtag assemblages but also be attentive to the specific and concrete activist individuals, collectives, and NGOs that contribute to and ultimately form them.

Embracing the Diversity of Video Activism

Hashtag movements epitomize the enormous diversity of video activist practices and communities that can be found more generally on social media and the internet as a whole. Such diversity extends beyond the prevailing images and clichés of video activists as lone, heroic fighters, spontaneous masses, or inert clicktivists. These images not only contradict each other but also neglect the fact that many activists coordinate with others and operate in an organized or strategic way. As we have pointed out in this chapter, there are recurring types of activist groups and networks, each with a different focus: the news coverage of a rally documented by a small media collective, for example, stands next to glossy entertaining influencer content and polished campaign videos by a large NGO. Such a diversity of actors who produce and disseminate different kinds of videos engage with equally varying user groups: the general public, affected communities, supporters, opponents, decision-makers, and other stakeholders. In doing that, they all are confronted with the challenge of using the problematic structures of social media without compromising their own political goals and integrity (see Chapter 1). Different types of activists deal with this challenge in different ways. Influencers within the attention ecology of social media seek to build up reach with virtuoso performances, but in doing so they submit to the commercial platform logic. In contrast, video collectives are more independent, but usually lack the resources or skills to reach a larger audience. NGOs also have considerable difficulty operating the competitive platform logic and adapting to their ever-changing trends and affordances.

Funding is another issue that activist alliances face in different ways. Almost all of them rely on donations, but NGOs in particular have to launch large fundraising campaigns regularly to finance their activities and staff. Small media collectives may work either with short-term, project-based funds or no additional resources at all and mostly remain in a precarious state of implicit self-exploitation. Professional influencers, in turn, can monetize their content and choose to collaborate with brands, broadcasters, or established institutions, but this may involve compromising their political independence and community credibility.

When activist groups work together, it is often on unequal terms. For example, some NGOs try to gain popularity by cooperating with young influencers, while the influencers tap into additional income by doing so. Often, however, cooperation is avoided altogether because of the considerable discrepancies among activist groups' political, ethical, and aesthetic stances. It might be, for example, that left-wing media collectives find the political demands of NGOs or influencers not far-reaching enough; or that artivists consider the videos of NGOs or news collectives not original enough. In this context, Christina Neumayer and Jakob Svensson differentiate activist types according to their attitude toward the political opponent and their willingness to engage in civil disobedience (Neumayer and Svensson 2014). To them, "law-abiding activists" are those who respect their political opponents and act only within the framework of existing laws, while "Gandhian activists" also respect their opponents but are willing to cross legal boundaries in their actions and face harsh consequences. "Contentious activists" also engage in civil disobedience but are irreconcilable with their political enemies. Similar radicalism exists among "salon activists," but their actions remain in a low-risk comfort zone. Although these distinctions are not free of simplifications, they are useful in pointing out that behind the diversity of activist groups and networks, there are also different sociotypes of activists who are attracted to certain forms of organization to different degrees.

In any case, it seems important to distinguish between the above-mentioned types of activism to better understand what activists intend, in what ways they proceed, how they reflect on their actions, and why they are more or less successful in reaching their strategic and substantive goals. This knowledge is relevant for further research, but, hopefully, also for activist practice. Our observation was that the different groups and networks of activists hardly cooperated with each other, even though they often worked on similar political issues and pursued very similar goals (climate justice, support for refugees, and more), used the same practices and platform strategies, produced similar video forms, and addressed the same target groups. Nor did they recognize their actions as complementary. But such complementarity can be a strategic advantage in the contested space of social media platforms. It might even be possible to imagine a kind of implicit division of labor in which different kinds of activists fulfill different functions in the struggle for social change. For example, counter-journalists could uncover a political grievance, research groups could verify witness videos and provide evidence, video archives could store and contextualize this evidence and make it accessible, professionalized media groups could use it to approach courts and decision-makers, artivist collectives could rouse allies, opponents, and publics through a provocative media spectacle, and NGOs could use their established professional networks and strategic campaigns to reach sympathizers and the general public.

Such loose, flexible complementarity would correspond to a political approach that could be called *diversity in solidarity* (a concept that we develop further in Chapter 7). The diversity of video activism could also be solidary in that activists pay closer attention to those in other political systems and regions. Activists located in the Global Northwest often have limited knowledge of the pressing issues and activist struggles in the Global South or of the concrete situation in authoritarian regimes, despite global hashtag movements, internationally operating NGOs with national and local chapters, and media initiatives such as the Video4Change Network. Thus, the guiding principle of diversity in solidarity could also mean listening to and supporting activists who are censored, threatened, and persecuted or have to work from exile. Furthermore, this principle could invite stronger transnational networking and joining forces, as the global movement for climate justice demonstrates. Hashtag movements play an important role in this and form a convergence point of diversity in solidarity where activist collectives, influencer networks, and NGOs gather and jointly create counterpublics, as the following chapter will point out.

6

Video Activism and the Public Sphere: Creating Counterpublics

With the rise of social media at the beginning of the twenty-first century, new protest movements emerged worldwide, organizing on platforms and combining online and offline actions—or as Paolo Gerbaudo (2012) put it—"Tweets and the Streets." The number and relevance of activist videos accompanying these protests have been constantly increasing since the uprisings in the MENA region, Occupy, the Indignados, and other movements of the early 2010s. Countless videos on social media have also documented the subsequent pro-democracy activism in Belarus, Hong Kong, Iran, Myanmar, Turkey, and many other countries, as well as the widespread movements such as Black Lives Matter, Extinction Rebellion, Fridays for Future, or ¡ Ni Una Menos! But as we have seen, the images and practices of video activism are more diverse and go beyond the spontaneous mobile phone video recordings from locally gathered crowds. Video activism is not a homogeneous field but consists of a variety of different actors and organizations, including individual citizens, media collectives, influencer networks, and NGOs. They use diverse strategies of video production, creation, distribution, and networking to contribute to social change. A prerequisite for achieving this is that activists shape societal discourses and through them ultimately the collective practices and institutions of a society. Discourses and their associated practices develop within a network of interacting forums of communication that include personal encounters, assemblies, mass media, and, perhaps most notably, social and other online media. This assemblage of communication forums is the basis of the collective negotiation of common concerns, or in short, of the public sphere.

According to the relevant political theories, the public sphere as a normative ideal is a freely accessible space of communication in which everyone has equal rights to participate and in which discussion ensures that a better argument prevails in the dispute of opinions. In reality, however, this ideal is confronted with unequal power relations, commercial interests, collective psychodynamics, and dysfunctional media logic, so that neither free access to the public sphere nor the deliberative weighing of arguments is guaranteed. Distorted publics lead to an unquestioned dominance of hegemonic discourses and practices that exclude or disadvantage social groups and can cause enormous inequalities and suffering. They can also lead to fragmentation and polarization of society, to a bitter, paralyzing struggle between opposing parties with different legitimate partial interests. Both tendencies are reflected on social media. Furthermore, platform algorithms accelerate them, and the problems are increasing significantly. The question is how video activists can act in this difficult environment and confront and change hegemonic discourses.

This chapter therefore focuses on the relationship between video activism and the public sphere in today's complex media environments. It aims at a better understanding of the dynamics of this relationship, its problems and potentials, and how video activists can achieve social impact. Based on a case analysis in the context of the Black Lives Matter movement, we argue that video activists may be better able to overcome obstacles and give voice to their concerns by reframing the historical concept of counterpublics in contemporary hybrid media systems.

Publics and Counterpublics

The public sphere is the focal point of any political video on social media. And no activist video is posted online without an explicit or implicit understanding of what it means to "go public," of publicizing or addressing a public. Thus, reflecting on the underlying concepts of the public sphere is highly relevant to the practices (and the success) of video activism. According to the most influential strand of political theory in this field, the public sphere is a political realm distinct from the logic and purpose of the state and its administration as well as from the economy. Some conceptualize it as a material or virtual space where citizens gather to discuss public affairs, while others regard it more as a mode of address in which citizens make "public use of their reason" (Kant [1784] 1999) to deliberate on common concerns.[54] By setting aside differences in social status and identity, as well as political and economic power, the "non-coercive force of the better argument" (Habermas 1984, 144, our translation) is supposed to become decisive for the participants. Moreover, the public sphere is understood as the common ground on which differences on political issues can be negotiated, taking into account the "variety of aspects" (Arendt 1958, 57). Despite the conceptual differences between these approaches, they all suggest that the public sphere is a central prerequisite for vibrant, plural democracies and civil society action. Such considerations become the political model for many citizens in liberal democracies as well as in authoritarian countries.

Although some of these theories strike a notably idealistic and sometimes nostalgic tone, they also consider the fact that their ideals are far removed from social reality. Their normative notions of the public sphere are conceived as critical demands, recalling the radically democratic promise that everyone can equally appear, speak, and be heard—a potential that had been lost in "modern mass society" (Arendt 1958, 57) after "the fall of public man" (Sennett 1974). According to Jürgen Habermas (1962), the spread of mass media in the twentieth century led to a "structural transformation of the public sphere," in the course of which spaces of discourse were increasingly determined by power structures that distorted the process of public opinion formation. This development (which Habermas, according to his critics, explains only inadequately) was driven in particular by media corporations that select their content according to sensationalism and entertainment value, established routines, or the interests of investors, advertisers, or political decision-makers. Later authors also speak of this as "manufacturing consent" (Herman and Chomsky 1988). Public opinion is thus influenced by the logic of the media and its orientation toward news values and interest groups, the influence of collective affects and prejudices, the flooding with irrelevant messages, the undermining of factuality, and the staging of media events. Agenda setting, framing, and gatekeeping limit the perspective on issues, actors, and arguments. The boundaries between information, entertainment, advertising, PR, and propaganda are blurred. Furthermore, politics is personalized, emotionalized, and adapted to the demands of the media, while the media distribution of public opinion restrains the expression of dissenting views. Many of these critical factors influence public discourse and activism, which must take them into account when developing strategies to make its concerns heard.

In addition to media distortions, there are major differences in status and power between social groups that are historically based, still operative, often maintained by force, and cannot simply be set aside. These differences undermine the ideal of equal access to the public sphere. For a long time, the voices and concerns of colonized or enslaved people, indigenous peoples, immigrants, workers, women, LGBTQIA+, disabled people, and other marginalized groups were hardly or not at all listened to, and this is still the case in many contexts. Furthermore, there are structural barriers that make it difficult for them to access the public sphere or make their voices heard, for example, unequal educational opportunities, economic resources, or social privilege. Demographic trends can lead to the underrepresentation of younger generations in political decision-making. In many countries, policymakers are not only predominantly male, but also on average older than the general population, and they tend to pay less attention to the media platforms that younger people use to raise their concerns.

The logic of media, differences in social power, collective affects, and forms of exclusion and deception continue to strongly influence public discourse in today's post-digital media environment, albeit in new ways and with different effects. In line with other media and communication scholars, Habermas himself now diagnoses a "new structural transformation of the public sphere" in the twenty-first century, the dominant feature of which is the rise of social media corporations (Habermas 2021). Others have pointed to the increasing blurring of conventional oppositions such as public and private, virtual and real, synchronous and asynchronous, online and offline communication in "networked publics" (boyd 2010; Yuan 2020). These recent developments do not make the conditions of activism unequivocally better or worse, but definitely more complicated. Knowledge about the everchanging media logics is spreading only gradually, while at the same time new inequalities are emerging, for example, to the disadvantage of the older generation and materially poorer sections of the population. As we outlined in Chapter 1, the transformation of the media public sphere brings with it an "ambivalent promise" (Schäfer 2016): on the one hand, social media platforms offer a "wealth of information" (Benkler 2006), many new voices and positions, more open and direct channels of communication with fewer restrictions on content, and means of dissemination, opening up access to areas of discourse that were previously inaccessible (boyd 2010). Activists and users can now bypass the gatekeepers of mass media, build their own networks, achieve wide reach, and inform the broader publics.

On the other hand, platforms are by no means neutral spaces for user-generated content. Instead, they stimulate users' activity so as to exploit their data and act as gatekeepers themselves. Instead of news editors, it is now algorithms, overworked content managers, and so-called cleaners who make crucial decisions about visibility and censorship in partially "automated" and "calculated" publics (Gillespie 2018; Pasquale 2018). Opportunities to access the public sphere remain unequal on social media, for example, when companies or marketing agencies buy space for their promotional videos on the platforms. Public opinion is partly shaped by short-term waves of outrage and cascading effects of "affective publics" (Papacharissi 2015). Moreover, social media sometimes foster the development of "echo chambers" (Sunstein 2001) that tend to close themselves off to outsiders. They often spread disinformation or hate campaigns, reinforcing them through algorithmically generated recommendations. The already existing dangers of bias, fragmentation, and polarization now threaten to become even more serious and cause lasting damage to the democratic polity in new ways. Christian Fuchs (2021b), for example, summarizes the problems of digital public spheres and argues that they are distorted by the concentration of power in platform monopolies, the continuous surveillance by corporations and states, and the unnoticed manipulation through algorithmically controlled, automated decision making (ADM or AI; Alfter et al. 2019, 9). Additional factors are the superficial acceleration of political communication, the diversion of attention to influencers, advertising, consumption, fake news, and ideological messages, as well as a growth of fragmentation, "tribalization," and anti-democratic tendencies such as authoritarianism, nationalism, racism, or fascism (Fuchs 2021b).

In short, social media are a highly ambiguous terrain for video activism. They expand its sphere of action, providing greater visibility and effective tools for internal organizing. At the same time, however, they also lead to greater insecurity among users, create new dependencies, increase extractivism and exploitation, and often make unwanted content disappear. In the face of these numerous problems, some have highlighted the role of every day "civic cultures" (Dahlgren 2005) that may increase political online participation. Others emphasize the "agonistic" (Mouffe 2005), "disrupted" (Bennett and Pfetsch 2018), and "dissonant" (Koc-Michalska et al. 2023) aspects of the public sphere and focus on (overt and covert) conflict dynamics, asymmetrical power relations, extreme distortions of issues, and struggles for hegemony, without neglecting the basic value of discussion.

As pro-democracy movements in authoritarian states make clear, activism is not simply about articulating demands *in* the public sphere, but always involves a claim *to* the public sphere and a struggle to participate in it. Activists face numerous obstacles when they demand the right to appear and speak in public (Butler 2015). This is true even in liberal democratic states with constitutional rights of assembly. For example, the G20 summit in Hamburg in 2017 was accompanied by many videos that captured the conflicts between police and demonstrators, and their material and symbolic struggles over public space. On social media, such conflicts increasingly manifest themselves in the form of comments, reaction videos, "likes," and "dislikes." Online activism often takes place on the threshold of what Arendt calls the "space of appearance" (Arendt 1958) and manifests itself as a form of "everyday politics" (Highfield 2016) that crosses the influential metaphorical distinction of the classical theatrical public sphere in ancient Greece between the actor on the well-lit center stage and the indistinct spectators in the dark auditorium.

A central concept that we have previously mentioned and that emphasizes the power imbalances and conflicts of the public sphere is that of "counterpublics." Originally stemming from the context of the New Social Movements of the 1960s and 1970s (Negt and Kluge 1993, see Chapter 2), this concept has been developed further during later waves of protest and is experiencing renewed interest with the rise of social media (Celikates 2015; Wimmer 2015). Counterpublics give voice to pressing concerns that have long gone unrecognized or have been ignored in hegemonic discourses (e.g., trans persons' rights to define their sex and gender). Counterpublics are communicative spaces in which alternative discourses and practices are developed in a dialectical relationship to the hegemonic public sphere, which they both oppose and engage with. Nancy Fraser's concept of "subaltern counterpublics" specifies this relationship and describes the modalities in which socially marginalized groups "formulate oppositional interpretations of their identities, interests and needs" and develop their own forms of expression (Fraser 1990). Although Jeffrey Wimmer (2015) argues that counterpublics often emerge from the context of social movements and stand for democratic ideals of enlightenment, authentic reporting, and audience emancipation, it is important to note that they are not identical with such movements or political activism, since they do not have an organized form. As Michael Warner (2002) emphasizes, counterpublics are more deeply rooted in specific everyday cultures and lifeworlds with collective practices of worldmaking. Following Catherine Squires (2002) and others, we can point out that "Black counterpublics," for instance, have historically constituted themselves less on the central city square and rather in community places such as barbershops, churches, jazz clubs, etc. However, the more informal character of counterpublics and their united oppositional stance toward the hegemonic public sphere does not mean that they are non-coercive safe spaces. Rather they are often carried by privileged actors such as intellectuals, religious leaders, or students who have access to higher education and cultural and social capital. This is especially true for communicative spaces on social media (e.g., what used to be called "Black Twitter"), where opinion leadership and spheres of influence quickly emerge apart from formalized organizational structures. At the same time, the sensitivity of socially marginalized groups to power relationships enables them to better reflect and criticize internal informal hierarchies, as the history of Black feminists in their struggle against patriarchal *and* white structures has shown, for example.

Looking at the second-wave feminist, environmental, LGBTQIA+, and civil rights movements since the 1960s, it is evident that their issues and demands were articulated through counterpublics and had a lasting impact on society. The creation of counterpublics has thus been a crucial strategy for activism in its attempts to challenge the status quo of society, for example, through new impulses from collective and alternative ways of living. However, this renewal and pluralization of the public sphere can also be accompanied by the countervailing tendencies of fragmentation and polarization, driven both by state- and corporation-controlled mass media and by social media platforms that massively disseminate rabble-rousing commentary and extremist content. The following case analysis illustrates how video activists contribute to the creation of counterpublics in contested media environments. It outlines how video activists address the public through social media and beyond, how they face numerous conflicts in doing so, and how they can still achieve social impact.

Creating Counterpublics: The Case of Black Lives Matter

In 2020, a viral video documented the murder of the Black American citizen George Floyd by a white policeman. Filmed by the witness Darnella Frazier, the video depicts Floyd lying on the ground while officer Derek Chauvin presses his knee to his throat for almost nine minutes until Floyd finally suffocates in agony. The eyewitness video was posted on Facebook and Instagram and later shared billions of times on other media. It sparked the Black Lives Matter movement's largest-ever international protests against racism and police violence, which did not end when Chauvin was sentenced to 22 years in prison for murder.

The murder of George Floyd is only one of over a thousand similar incidents of deadly police violence in the United States per year, most of them hardly noticed by the public. According to the data analysis project MappingPoliceViolence.org, by the time of Floyd's murder, Black Americans were nearly three times more likely to be victims of fatal police violence than white Americans, with hardly any convictions or even charges resulting. (Since then, Black Americans are still more than twice as likely to be killed by police as white Americans.) The guilty verdict against Floyd's murderer and his accomplices might indicate a change in the long history of structural marginalization and violence against Black bodies that stretches from slavery through segregation and the Jim Crow era, the Tulsa and Rosewood pogroms, to the 1965 Watts Riot, the 1992 LA Riots in the aftermath of the Rodney King trial, and the 2014 Ferguson protests (Daniels 2023). That the cases of Trayvon Martin, Sandra Bland, Breonna Taylor, and many other victims of deadly police violence became public knowledge at all is due in no small part to the Movement for Black Lives—and often to related witness, documentary, and mobilization videos, as well as vlogs and mash-ups on social media. Black Lives Matter, as the movement is also called, started in 2013 as a comment and then viral hashtag on Facebook and X/Twitter after the acquittal of Martin's murderer (Khan-Cullors and bandele 2018). This means that there was already heightened attention and awareness among the Black community and the US American public when the following case from 2014, which contributed significantly to the growth of the movement, took place. By looking at this case more closely, we would like to illustrate the ways in which a video, in this case a witness video, contributes to creating a counterpublic that, in turn, challenges the hegemonic discourse of the dominant public sphere.

In 2014, in Staten Island, New York, the witness Ramsey Orta used his cell phone to film how his acquaintance, the African American Eric Garner, was attacked and thrown to the ground by several white police officers during a routine check. The video shows one of the attackers, officer Daniel Pantaleo, using a chokehold, which by that time was already prohibited in the police department there (Fisher 1993). Several times, Garner shouts "I can't breathe" before losing consciousness. A second eyewitness video, recorded by Taisha Allen, shows that Garner's motionless body remains lying on the ground without first aid being administered, despite the pressing demands of bystanders. Only after seven

FIGURE 6.1: The Eric Garner case—eyewitness video by Ramsay Orta (distributed via @dailynews, YouTube), 2014.

minutes—the officers had made a low-priority emergency call—did medical service arrive. Shortly thereafter, Garner died (Figure 6.1).

Orta's eyewitness video was viewed millions of times online within a short period and had the immediate effect that the medical report, which diagnosed heart failure due to asthma and obesity as the cause of death, had to be corrected (Baker et al. 2015). It was not until 2019 that the officer who used the fatal chokehold was dismissed from the police in the wake of the Garner case, but no criminal prosecution was initiated.

Against the background of existing forensic case analyses and following critical perspectives on "Black witnessing" (Richardson 2020), Black "hashtag activism" (Jackson et al. 2020), and "Black liberation" (Alexander 2010; Taylor 2021), we will focus on the dynamics of social video to illuminate the social and media conditions under which counterpublics emerge. A relevant factor that explains why the Garner/Orta video went viral is not only *what* the recording captures, but also *how* it documents the event—that is, the *content* it depicts and at the same time the *form* of its depiction. Visually, the three-minute-long video is made up of slightly shaky, intense raw footage that was taken from a close distance in full shots with a vertical aspect ratio, all of this marking it as authentic. The audio track comprises Garner's calls for help and the filmmaker's off-screen comments that convey his stunned sense of urgency, desperation, and powerlessness. This form of depicting the event evokes sympathy for the victim and at the same time a sense of outrage at the failure of the system, as several YouTube comments reveal. Such reactions between empathy and outrage within affective publics are characteristic of the mode of address of many eyewitness videos (this, however, does not exclude divergent modes of emotional reaction).

Eyewitness videos generally follow the activist strategy of showing (see Chapter 4) and address their viewers in a testimonial mode of documentary. They make the claim that what is shown in fact happened just like that before the camera. Viewers respond emotionally to the audiovisual event, but they are not able to intervene in the action shown. This invites alternative actions such as sharing the video and commenting on social media, as well as moving from online to offline action, like protesting on the streets. However, an individual case shown in a single video will only create public outrage if it is seen as representative or as a symptom of a widespread social problem. This symptomatic character of a video usually results from the fact that it is part of a series of videos addressing similar incidents. A series of witness videos of the Black Lives Matter movement showed, among many others, the murders of Freddie Gray, Walter Scott, Alton Sterling, Philando Castile, and George Floyd, whose last words were like those of Eric Garner: "I can't breathe." The symptomatic character of the Garner and Floyd videos, but also the visible and stark difference in power between the armed police and an individual, unarmed and nonviolent Black American reinforces the outrage felt about the individual case and the general problem.

Along with the characteristic effects of such videos and their audiovisual forms, media circulation is another crucial factor in explaining the dynamics of creating counterpublics, as the example illustrates. Orta passed his video on to a daily newspaper, from which various versions of it made their way onto YouTube and other online platforms. Further print media and TV stations picked it up from there, and their reports in turn circulated online. Video activists, influencers, and celebrities (such as the New Black Cinema director Spike Lee), in turn, used the circulating footage and incorporated it into countless vlog comments, documentaries, and mobilization videos (Kaap 2016). This kind of dynamic interplay between social and mass media, as well as among different platforms, video versions, and intertextual references is characteristic of the "hybrid media system" (Chadwick 2013) and underlines the power of dispersed witnessing, everyday politics, and affective publics today. Altogether, such witness videos and their circulation dynamics form networked narratives (see Chapter 4). They put the individual events in context, offer a shared political frame, and channel collective feelings such as sorrow and outrage. Garner's and Floyd's desperate words "I can't breathe" became a testimony about the repression of Black lives and then turned into the collective, self-empowering battle cry "We Can't Breathe," called out by demonstrators, put on protest signs and proclaimed in further videos (Figure 6.2). Here,

FIGURE 6.2: Black Lives Matter: "We Can't Breathe" (Google search results). Partly from Brandon E. Patterson's now deleted X/Twitter account @myblackmindd, 2018.

the remediation of the witness material is accompanied by the activist reinterpretation of the event depicted. Such collective self-empowerment also contributes to the formation and strengthening of the subaltern group identity that can have a mobilizing effect for further action. This is also expressed, for example, in the Black Lives Matter documentary *Stay Woke* (Grant 2016), which was in part produced collectively "by the movement for the movement."

However, the case of Black Lives Matter also illustrates the enormous challenges that video activism faces in today's automated and polarized public sphere. The mechanisms of selecting news on personalized social media feeds have repeatedly proven to be non-transparent and misleading (Tufekci 2017, 154ff.). This becomes a problem particularly when people use a platform like Facebook, X, or TikTok as their central news source or when activist videos are intentionally "demoted" or "shadowbanned." Witness videos are shared and edited in different versions, and their modes of dissemination and commentary can also lead to confusion and make the images seem unreliable. Various other dynamics and network actors cause further problems. Among them are conspiracy narratives that use pseudo-forensic analyses and discrediting claims to cast doubt on the authenticity of a witness video. As mentioned in Chapter 5, Black Lives Matter came under pressure from right-wing counter-networks with the misleading slogan "All Lives Matter," from the police countermovement "Blue Lives Matter," and from white supremacists with comments spread under the hashtag "White Lives Matter." In addition, after the 2016 presidential election, the former X/Twitter group Blacktivists was exposed as the product of a Russian troll army designed to further polarize the American public (Levin 2017). Governmental agencies have also long been operating as political network actors, such as when police departments evaluate and use protest and surveillance videos strategically. Police body cameras, introduced after the protests against police violence, were intended to provide greater transparency, but they also shift interpretive power to the side of potential perpetrators. Another issue is that witness videos can make it easier for the state to identify protesters—which in authoritarian states can lead not only to their imprisonment but also to their torture and murder.

The cases around Black Lives Matter also demonstrate that being brought to public attention is not always voluntary, both for the victims who were filmed and for the passers-by who happened to become witnesses of the events. Orta, for example, who filmed the video of Garner, complained of repeated police harassment and intimidation in the weeks following the incident. Putting the blame on witnesses and victims, which often is done in the case of socially marginalized groups (Moody-Ramirez and Cole 2018), usually aims at silencing their voices and portraying structural violence—in this case racism—as just individual wrongdoing in order to exclude the problem from the public realm. All these dangers persist and are difficult for activists and affected citizens to navigate. Therefore, a considerable degree of media literacy and a broader knowledge of the problematic mechanisms of audiovisual witnessing on social media are required for attempts to raise awareness (see Chapter 7).

Despite these persistent problems, our case analysis has also pointed out that videos can succeed in contributing decisively to the formation of a counterpublic that challenges and changes the hegemonic discourse in the dominant public sphere. In the Garner case and beyond, several factors have contributed to this process: pre-existing activist communication networks (e.g., around #BlackLivesMatter) that enable oppositional discourse and, ideally, transnational reach; the audiovisual form and mode of address of the video; the depiction of a tangible imbalance of power (here: between brutal police officers and a defenseless citizen); the symptomatic character of the case or video, which points to an ongoing structural problem; and finally, the remediation and reinterpretation of the individual case and its fitting into the framework of activist struggle. These factors contributed decisively to the transformation of a cruel local case to a global, diversified counterpublic.

Retrospectively, it is evident that the Black Lives Movement succeeded in establishing long-term counterpublics and oppositional narratives in numerous countries after decades of hegemonic "tough on crime" and "zero tolerance" discourses, and in contributing to a change of opinion in the dominant public sphere. By creating counterpublics, the movement was able to establish its agenda as a decisive issue in local elections for leadership positions in city governments, district attorney offices, and local police forces, particularly in the United States. The protests also generated a heightened sense of alarm in the everyday lives of Black Americans and led to the establishment of informal, community-based security networks. Here, as in many other protest movements around the world, the gesture of the raised smartphone became an empowering symbol of citizens' vigilance against arbitrary state power.

Expanding the Democratic Public Sphere

The example of Black Lives Matter underlines the importance of understanding contemporary media public spheres for video activism. But of course, this analysis does not point out all the possible ways in which activist videos can reach public attention. And obviously, not every witness video goes viral. On the contrary, most of them disappear almost unseen, and success or failure often depends on coincidences and timing. But it is precisely because of the media logic and structural power imbalances mentioned above that video activism relies on the creation of counterpublics. Like the historical attempts with "politically committed documentaries" in the 1960s–80s (outlined in Chapter 2), the issue here is to make problems visible that have not been adequately represented publicly, and to change the dominant perspective on those problems, that is to reframe the issues and tell other stories with other meanings. If this succeeds, activists then try to go beyond the specific event and solidify the counterpublic by building up their own infrastructure with local groups, social media groups, and channels and loose informal networks on social media, messenger services, independent websites, and, of course, offline.

The fact that "counterpublics" are an essentially democratic concept that emphasizes the plurality of perspectives does not mean, of course, that it is only relevant in liberal democracies. On the contrary, it is precisely in authoritarian states and war zones that the arduous and dangerous creation of counterpublics is of utmost importance. This is the case, for example, when video witnesses and activists expose propaganda lies or uncover potential war crimes in the Russian war of aggression against Ukraine or when the state-terrorist murders of Neda Agha-Soltan in 2009 and Mahsa Amini in 2022 in Iran provoke international hashtag movements and the circulation of protest videos.

However, counterpublics can be generated not only through individual witnesses and hashtag movements but also through all kinds of videos and actors, through vlogs, documentaries, campaigns, or playful subversion videos produced and distributed by activist media collectives, influencer networks, or NGOs. For instance, activists also produce videos for strategically oriented lobbying campaigns (targeted advocacy tools) aimed at stakeholders, decision-makers, supporting celebrities, and other segments of the public. This strategy provides a way for activists to respond to the existence of highly differentiated public spheres and the power that some networks hold (Bennett 2020).

It is obvious that different types of issues require different approaches and strategies. More than that, such practical distinctions ultimately reflect the inherent diversity of democratic public spheres that reject "one-size-fits-all" notions when it comes to issues of political participation and access to this sphere. It is precisely this diversity that is currently threatened by the rise of authoritarian rule, new and escalating wars, repeated terrorist attacks, discrete global chains of exploitation, ubiquitous surveillance, group-focused enmity, and structural discrimination and exclusion. Moreover, activists of the far-right often also claim that their videos are part of a counterpublic sphere. However, this can be regarded as misleading for at least two reasons. First, right-wing extremists and conspiracy ideologues often reject established knowledge and scientifically proven facts (Fielitz and Thurston 2019), while public discourse implies and presupposes the "right to unmanipulated factual information" (Arendt 1972, 45) and stresses the importance of argumentative discussion. Second, as Wimmer convincingly argues, far-right communication strategies include "alternative and movement media" that can structurally be regarded as counterpublic; however, they do not correspond to "the normative context of counterpublic spheres in the sense of emancipatory communication that serves to strengthen democracy" (Wimmer 2015, n.pag.). Right-wing extremists have no desire to include the perspectives of marginalized groups in public debates. In blatant contrast to normative ideals of the public sphere and free access to it, they try to restrict the public to their own in-group and replace it with a homogenized ethnic or nationalist community isolated from the outside world. The concept of counterpublics, however, aims precisely at widening this sphere, making it more inclusive, and holds to its radically democratic core, which is incompatible with the concept and reality of the extreme right's logic of the "infowar" (Wimmer 2015; see Chapter 7).

However, one-sided portrayals, offensive formulations, insults, and smear campaigns often prove to be effective ways to gain public attention among pro-democratic actors, as well. This makes it even more important to distinguish clearly between argumentative exaggeration or satire and deliberate deception, between justified outrage and sheer hatred, between democratic persuasion and authoritarian propaganda, and between political action and warmongering, as we will argue more closely in the following chapter. In this respect, it is useful for video activists to consider their own storytelling and affective rhetoric self-critically and make changes where necessary. It requires practical judgment, based among other things on media literacy and an ethical self-understanding.

Here, another way for activist videos to have effects on the public sphere becomes noticeable: beyond their specific demands, they also contribute to structurally strengthening the public sphere as a whole by drawing ethical and political lines between activism, on the one hand, and disinformation, manipulation, and propaganda, on the other. Against the fragmentation and polarization of the public sphere through "filter bubbles," "infowars," and what Habermas (1992, 451) describes as "generalized particularism"—the domination by powerful interest groups—the creation of counterpublics aims at expanding discursive and democratic spaces. In this way, video activism pursues the fundamental promise of equal participation outlined in the classical theories of public space, which has so far remained unfulfilled.

7

Video Activism in Times of Upheaval: Toward Diversity in Solidarity

What is the state of video activism today? In many countries of the world, the political influence of activists reached a peak between 2010 and 2015. By discovering the potential of social media, they temporarily managed to outsmart the discourse machinery of political institutions and big business and to give more weight to their causes. Since then, however, much has changed. Currently, video activism is involved in profound upheavals in media and politics, the outcomes of which are uncertain. Established centers of power are reclaiming their discursive dominance and new aggressive actors are exploiting the logic of platforms. Entire media systems are being transformed under political and economic pressure. In many places, activists are sidelined, repressed, persecuted, or instrumentalized even more than before. The operating environment of video activists as well as the counterpublics to which they contribute is undergoing rapid and profound changes. Consequently, activists are altering their practices, strategies, and alliances, and one could even say that the whole concept of video activism is currently shifting.

In this chapter, we will first look at activist and other political videos in the Russian war of aggression against Ukraine as a particularly drastic example that illustrates some of the main developments of activism in contemporary wars and crises. Many other countries have been affected by this war, whether through military strategies, economic hardship, famine, or flight. Obviously, it is not the only recent war or violent conflict that involves horrific suffering and geopolitical shifts (think of the military coups in the Sahel region since 2020 or the 2023 Israel–Hamas war). However, the Russian invasion of Ukraine affected us as scholars located in Germany—with its history of imperialism, world wars, and Nazism—in particular ways. In 2022, our home city of Berlin became a hub where nearly 400,000 Ukrainian war refugees, mostly women, children, and senior citizens, arrived and received initial care. Some young refugees were also accepted as students at our universities. It was not only because of these encounters that we take the Ukraine war as an example but also because this war brings into sharp focus many relevant developments that affect video activism elsewhere as well.

Such developments raise wider questions about the future: how can video activism promoting values such as equality, human rights, and democracy sustain itself in difficult environments? How can activists respond to the growing challenges of information wars, authoritarian power, and political polarization online and offline? Considering these pressing questions, at the end of our book we will further develop the idea of *diversity in solidarity* that we briefly outlined above (see Chapters 5 and 6). In doing so, we by no means claim to provide conclusive answers, but would like to emphasize a crucial prerequisite for video activism on social media to remain a crucial counterforce to abuses of power and a catalyst of democratic counterpublics.

Video Activism at War: Changing Contexts, Shifting Roles

Our reflections so far have focused mainly on video activism in peacetime. Even if this peace might be fragile or marked by ongoing injustice, violence, and suffering, video activism plays a relatively consistent role: it denounces injustice primarily within its own society, criticizes its hegemonic public sphere, and protests against its power blocs. This role of criticizing one's own society or state remains structurally similar in civil wars such as in Syria and even intensifies in them. However, in the context of contemporary interstate wars, the role of video activism shifts fundamentally, as we will see. Moreover, such wars lead to other profound changes that affect activism in a variety of ways. These include the upheaval of entire media systems, the splitting of information environments, increased propaganda and disinformation, censorship, and persecution, but also new activist alliances, practices, and video forms.

Such developments are particularly striking in the context of Russia's current war against Ukraine. Western journalists soon called it "The World's First TikTok War" (Chayka 2022) and were apparently surprised that an entertainment platform for young people, of all things, spread countless images of war and brought international attention to the suffering of Ukrainians. However, this labeling is, of course, as inadequate as in the case of the so-called "Twitter revolutions" or "Facebook revolutions" around 2011. In contrast, war studies rather consider videos on TikTok and other platforms as open-source intelligence (OSINT), as part of a "cyberwar" (Dyer-Witheford and Matviyenko 2019), or of strategic informational and psychological operations (INFOPS and PSYOPs). Accordingly, a war of images accompanies the ongoing killing and wounding of thousands of people and the devastation of cities, landscapes, and infrastructure.

Both views are complementary: the first emphasizes the everyday politics and experiences of individual media users, and the second focuses on the strategic deployment of videos for information and propaganda by the warring parties. The coexistence of these perspectives also points to the fact that videos are used in war by very different actors in the context of specific "information theatres" (Tucker 2022). When Russia invaded Ukraine in February 2022 in violation of international law and launched its war of imperialist aggression, this led to global shocks and the tearing open of geopolitical rifts between countries that supported Ukraine (such as the United States, the EU, Australia, or Japan), the few states that sided with Russia (these are Belarus, Syria, North Korea, Nicaragua, Mali, and Eritrea), and those that tried to navigate between these positions, often according to their political advantage (such as China, India, Indonesia, Iran, Pakistan, South Africa, and other countries in the Global South). Such divisions had a huge impact on the political agendas, publics, information environments, and media discourses in these countries.

Against the background of such frictions in the realm of international politics, we will look at the consequences of video activism and explore the ways in which videos are used by activists in the context of the war against Ukraine and how they compete with and relate to videos by state and military actors from both warring parties. Our observations do not rely on in-depth academic study, but only on a tentative exploration from the external perspective of media researchers in an EU member state. We focus only on a limited selection of videos from the first months of the war, and—due to media and language barriers—videos without spoken language, or with subtitles or explanations. We are also writing at a particular point in time: the war is in its second winter and fierce fighting on barely moving front lines has been going on for months, while Russia is also constantly attacking Ukraine's cities and energy supply.

According to our observations, there are three key developments influencing video activism in war. First, not only does the video content differ in Ukraine and Russia, but so do their whole hybrid media systems and platform ecologies. This was already the case before the war, but now this split has become more drastic and both systems are being further transformed. In the two countries, video activism operates under highly different conditions and tries to adapt to them continuously. Second, the separation of media systems creates distinct information environments and discourse streams with only a few points of contact with each other. Some activists, however, are deliberately trying to use these points of connection. Third, the very roles of activists, as well as their relationships with state and military institutions, shifted due to the war. In some cases, the boundaries of activism begin to blur.

Throughout this book, we have pointed out that video activism operates in the context of hybrid media systems in which social media interact with mass media. In war, it becomes abundantly clear how different these hybrid systems are and how rapidly and profoundly they change under political pressure. Most of the earlier chapters have focused on the media systems of the United States and Western Europe. Their liberal democratic frameworks emphasize freedom of the press and freedom of speech, and their citizens predominantly use the major US platforms and TikTok alongside largely free, if mostly commercial, mass media. Elsewhere, however, media systems can be quite different (Makhortykh and Bastian 2022). In Russia, all media are nowadays tightly controlled by the government and its agency Roskomnadzor. Most people watch state television, which manipulates its audience with propaganda (Edel 2023). Social media is dominated by country-specific platforms like VKontakte (international name: VK), an equivalent of Facebook. Since 2022, Western platforms such as Facebook itself or Instagram have been banned, their parent company Meta has been declared a terrorist and extremist organization, and X/Twitter has been severely throttled. Only YouTube is still available, and the popular channels of critical YouTubers arguably form Russia's most important counterpublic (Kaltseis 2023). However, activist influencers like Irina Shikhman or Yuri Dud as well as independent journalists like those of Doshd have to work from exile. And the state persecutes and imprisons oppositional leaders like Alexei Navalny, who died in custody under unclear circumstances, and brands human rights advocates and other NGOs as "foreign agents," while it is running massive disinformation campaigns on foreign social and mass media (Bösch 2023).

Ukraine also tries to control the media system, albeit far less strictly and brutally than Russia (according to the World Press Freedom Index, Ukraine currently ranks 79th and Russia 164th among 180 countries) (Reporters Without Borders 2023). Until recently, the largest TV channels represented the interests of the oligarchs who owned them, there were many pro-Russian programs, and Russian social media like VK were at least as popular as Western ones. Since the Russian annexation of Crimea in 2014 and under martial law, the Ukrainian television system is now largely state-controlled (Feng 2022). Russian social media were banned in 2017 and US platforms like Facebook increasingly filled the gap.

This brief outline already indicates how media transformations in different countries are interrelated and how antagonistic media systems emerge, where video activists are working under highly different conditions. Moreover, these media systems are further reshaped by significant changes within the platform landscape. Established platforms are restructured, new platforms emerge, and the whole landscape of social media, their interconnections, and their relative importance can change. One notable example is Twitter. In 2022, billionaire Elon Musk bought the microblogging service, renamed it X, restructured it, and opened its floodgates to disinformation. One consequence is that X is now throttled in Russia while spreading Russian propaganda abroad. At the same time, many operations by the Ukrainian military—as well as by Ukrainian activists—are only possible because Musk's StarLink company provides internet access in war-torn regions. This means that not only states but also powerful individual actors can exert a huge influence on media systems.

In other cases, the war causes certain social media to gain importance because they fulfill indispensable functions for users. In the war against Ukraine, this is particularly true of Telegram and TikTok. The messenger service Telegram, originally founded in Russia and designed for private communication, has so far managed to escape state control and censorship in both warring countries. This makes it one of the essential sources of both news and propaganda (for example, follower numbers suggest that it is arguably the most important distribution channel for President Zelenskyy's regular videos). In Russia, the number of Telegram users has more than doubled in one year (Reporters Without Borders 2023). Telegram transcends the boundaries between the national media systems, enabling both friendly and hostile encounters between activists and other users. In this way, Telegram takes on an ambivalent role in the media system, which varies depending on the geopolitical context. For example, while the app allows users in Russia to watch Ukrainian witness videos, Zelenskyy's video messages, or Western news, it is also an international gateway for disinformation, military propaganda, and spectacles of violence and war crimes.

While Telegram seems to be particularly important for the dissemination of uncensored information *within and between* the Russian and Ukrainian media systems, TikTok's importance seems to lie more in the *international* dissemination of a huge number of videos from both countries to the outside world. Thus, the entertainment app also became an informational battleground. Even though the label "TikTok war" is inadequate, it reflects the increasing importance of everyday media for political action. While Western politicians and journalists in February 2022 still assumed that Russia would not dare to attack Ukraine, Russian TikTokers were already documenting the movement of tanks toward the border and expressing their concerns. Shortly after the invasion, countless, mostly young TikTokers from both Ukraine and Russia flooded the platform with videos about the war. And in the first days of the war, when Western mass media were still only reporting from Kiev, the world could see via TikTok how Russian tanks rolled into Ukrainian villages and opened fire on soldiers and civilians alike (Bösch 2022, 5). For people around the world, TikToks provide a glimpse into the lives of civilians at war as well as soldiers on the frontlines. They point out the difficult living conditions in the war zones or solicit sympathy for the fighting troops. Furthermore, professional war reporting increasingly depends on such videos, and legal institutions need them to document war crimes. Individual video makers have therefore become even more influential in how we see and understand war.

More generally, these developments show that the media systems in which video activists operate differ significantly from one region to another and change dynamically. These specific, mutable media systems then determine which platforms activists use, which audiences they reach, how freely they can work and interact, and which mass media re-distribute their videos. Moreover, the divergence of media ecologies in war draws attention to the fissures in the global "splinternet" (see Chapter 1). While the major US platforms dominate overall globally, they do not play a central role in countries like Russia, and other apps such as TikTok or Telegram are gaining ground. Moreover, the same platforms can take on different meanings and functions regionally. Today, in the EU, Telegram may be mostly seen as a propaganda swamp, in Ukraine as a major news source, or in Russia as a nest of resistance. Or TikTok may be considered to be a mere entertainment app for some, an indispensable window to the outside world for others. Anyone who wants to understand video activism must take into account the specificity and malleability of platforms, media systems, and usage patterns.

The difference and antagonism of regional media systems give rise to a second crucial development exemplified by the Ukraine war: the geopolitical separation of attention ecologies and image streams. The logic of opposing media systems contribute decisively to the fact that people in Ukraine, Russia, and their allied countries literally *see* and understand the war differently (Milmo and Sauer 2022; Perez and Nair 2022; Shestopalova et al. 2022). In Ukraine, the war is presented as a heroic defensive struggle against cruel occupation, imperialist oppression, and for political sovereignty. In Russia, however, the same event is framed as a "special operation" to "liberate" the Russian people of Donetsk and Luhansk from fascist oppressors and to defend the greater Russian world against Western decadence, an operation in which—as in the Second World War (in Russia referred to as the Great Patriotic War)—one's own losses must be accepted (Urman and Makhortykh 2022). Unsurprisingly, there is a strong antagonism of "Us" against "Them." The differences concern both the regional media systems as a whole and the individual media within them. For example, an explorative study by a Norwegian broadcaster has pointed out the striking difference between the Russian and Ukrainian TikTok worlds: in Ukrainian TikTok, war-related content is eminently present, while Russian TikTok favors the usual entertainment videos, hiding the war and barring Western content (Bøe and Bjørke 2022; Milmo 2022).

The attention ecologies in national media systems are, one could say, characterized both by a coexistence of mainstreams, sidestreams, and counterstreams of images and by certain recurring topics, political frames, and visual forms. Mainstreams of related images (such as certain frames of war) are fed largely by television broadcasters, who also influence social media trends through their celebrities. Sidestreams are generated, for example, by bloggers and other content creators who serve state-tolerated image flows (Gilbert 2022), for instance, extremist pro-war channels in Russia. Counterstreams emerge from both the local and international opposition. In times of war, all these visual streams are under strong state influence. In its own country, the state may control the mainstreams, tolerate sidestreams to a certain extent, and try to suppress counterstreams. At the same time, it may try to strengthen counterstreams in opposing countries and to influence information streams in allied or neutral countries.

The audiovisual discourses of individual countries are largely separated by languages, laws, and media systems. For example, relatively few videos from Russia, directed at Russian audiences, gain attention in the West (and vice versa). However, some streams cross the borders between the separate worlds, mostly in attempts to influence the other side. For example, Ukrainian and Russian actors each try to reach the other country as well as further countries through their media work. But they do so in significantly different ways. Ukrainian users often address their own population and Western allies at the same time; they therefore produce a strikingly large number of videos in English or with English subtitles. Russian creators, on the other hand, choose different platforms depending on whether they want to address their own population, Russia's allies, or its enemies abroad, and most of their videos are either exclusively in Russian or in the languages of the target countries. All this contributes to a very heterogeneous visibility of war or other conflicts in different geopolitical spaces.

But how are video activists situated in this context of antagonistic media systems? This question leads us to a third crucial development in video activism in times of war: the shifting of activist roles and the blurring of boundaries between activism and other political practices. Typically, activism is seen as part of a civil society that negotiates societal concerns independently of the state and the market, often criticizing both and thus producing counter-discourses and counterpublics (see Chapter 6). In war, however, two strong tendencies affect activism: civil society tends to align itself with the state against the external enemy, and the state tends to suppress counter-positions in civil society more rigorously. Both tendencies narrow the space for critical activism considerably. Under the severe conditions of war with its extreme national media control, the work of video activists who disagree with their own government becomes extremely difficult and even dangerous. At the same time, state or military actors sometimes present themselves like activists, as we can see, for example, in the appearance of President Zelenskyy on social media.

In Russia and Ukraine, these tendencies manifest themselves in quite different ways. In the neo-imperialist authoritarian state of Russia, critical video activism is almost impossible today. At the beginning of the war, some Russian activists documented anti-war protests to show their criticism of the Putin regime, their fear of being sent to the front, or their solidarity with the suffering people in Ukraine. But now the leading critical voices are in prison or in exile. In Ukraine, pro-Russian bloggers are also likely to be suppressed, while some Ukrainian content creators also voluntarily join forces with their government in attempts to defend their nation under attack. Such associations are difficult to assess from the outside, and it is not always clear whether the videos are part of independent activism or state propaganda. At the beginning of the war, countless images spread on social media: witness videos documented the invasion and the courageous resistance of the people against the occupying army. Vloggers reported on their daily life in bombed buildings or bunkers, or they asked for humanitarian aid and the supply of weapons. And the horrific images of the Bucha massacre led to an even stronger international condemnation of Russian war crimes.

Particularly in times of war, however, such civilian and activist videos documenting resistance can hardly be viewed in isolation from the videos of other, often more powerful actors. Instead, activist videos are in a complex interplay with other political videos. We can distinguish four major groups of particularly common non-activist videos according to their sources, functions, contents, and aesthetics: videos by governments, the military, journalists, and lifestyle influencers. Within each group, one can observe certain image mainstreams, sidestreams, and counter-streams, certain relations to video activism, specific shifts in activist roles, as well as a blurring of boundaries between professional and non-professional, activists and other video creators. In this context, Russian and Ukrainian videos again show significant differences because of their political contexts, cultures, and media systems.[55]

The first group forms around government videos featuring iconic national leaders who demonstrate strength and determination, aiming to mobilize internal support from their own people and external support from other countries. Russia and Ukraine pursue very different strategies for that. In Russia, there seem to be no videos posted by President Putin himself, but many videos about him, mostly footage from state television or other controlled sources. They show Putin as a stern statesman in a tailored suit intended to express powerful superiority. In contrast, President Zelenskyy posts videos almost daily on Telegram and other platforms, dressed in his signature olive green military T-shirt with the Ukrainian national emblem on it. While Putin presents himself as an intangible and untouchable leader, Zelenskyy appears as an approachable, hands-on commander-in-chief expressing sociability, determination, and integrity. One could also say that he presents himself as Ukraine's leading influencer. These official images of both presidents are picked up and supported by countless videos of individual citizens. For example, Zelenskyy fans create funny mash-ups from the former actor's television appearances, sometimes erotically charged, but always celebrating him as a national hero or as a cool guy with swag (Otto 2023). In contrast to such affirmative videos, both Zelenskyy and Putin are often satirized, even in drastic ways.

Sometimes it is hard to determine whether these mock videos originate from critics at home, from international activists, or whether they were commissioned by the adversarial side.

A comparable interplay of official and unofficial, pro-Ukrainian and pro-Russian videos can be found in a second group: military videos that focus on events on the battlefield. Here, institutions such as the Ukrainian Defense Ministry with their official channel Defense of Ukraine, as well as many Russian and Ukrainian brigades, are very actively spreading videos that aim at strengthening the morale of their own troops and undermining the morale of the enemy. They celebrate their own successes and portray the enemy as weak and outmatched. At the time of writing this, many Ukrainian videos show destroyed Russian weapons, demoralized Russian troops (Harwell 2022), or heroic Ukrainian fighters. In a frequent type of video, soldiers at the front sing and dance cheerfully, accompanied by Western pop songs and using TikTok dance routines to evoke sympathy and solidarity.[56] Other soldiers present themselves with cute kittens and other animals in front of the smartphone camera. And others again show off their weapons or share instructions on how to destroy enemy tanks. Both warring parties also disseminate videos that re-edit enemy footage to denigrate the other side. For example, several Russian propaganda videos on VK use re-edited material and compare Ukrainian soldiers to pigs (Dellar 2023).

Such videos are apparently produced by individual soldiers, by activists, and by professional military units alike, and circulate fluidly between their channels. A video genre that is especially difficult to classify is made up of the war blogs of either activists or military personnel with many followers.[57] This includes mercenaries who pose as military influencers, such as Karl Balderson, a Danish volunteer known as the "Viking," who fought in the Ukrainian military. On Telegram, radical Russian warmongers such as Igor Girkin, Ramzan Kadyrov, or, until his death, Yevgeny Prigoshin have agitated against Ukraine, shared extremely violent content, or taken on the Russian military leadership, which they accuse of being too timid. In many of these cases, the borders between professional strategic communication, shared experiences by individual vloggers, activism, and propaganda are increasingly blurred, especially as sock puppets of the state disguise themselves as ordinary soldiers or independent activists.

A third group of videos is dedicated to journalistic news in the wider sense, purporting to provide evidence and information about the war to the national and international public. While state control over journalistic content increases in times of war, the lines between journalism and activism are blurred in many ways as well. Some Ukrainian citizens document war atrocities so regularly and professionally that they de facto become citizen journalists or activist journalists. Conversely, critical Russian journalists from professional broadcasters such as Meduza, OVD

Info, or Doshd have been driven into exile, have largely lost their domestic audience, and therefore work on a precarious donation basis, comparable to activists. Another messy field concerns video fakes and subsequent fact-checking. Many video channels spread disinformation to mislead the opposing side or their own population. The war began already with Russian deep fake videos of Zelenskyy allegedly surrendering (*The Telegraph* 2022). There are fake combat videos created from computer game images and sock puppet vloggers spreading mainly Russian propaganda (Agency France Press 2023). But there are also fact-checkers and OSINT researchers who try to verify the sources of videos and analyze the depictions forensically to find out the truth about events.[58] Some of them are activists, others are linked to state institutions such as the Ukrainian Centre for Combating Disinformation. In another twist, there are even fake fact-checkers: the Russian TV program *AntiFejk* claims to debunk Ukrainian fake videos, but in fact these videos were not produced and disseminated by the Ukrainian side or their allies (Sasse 2022).

A fourth group comprises videos by influencers or celebrities who came from an entertainment background but then turned activists, often achieving a huge number of views and strong user involvement. Internationally, this includes videos by stars from film or the art world like Arnold Schwarzenegger or Banksy, who took a stance for Ukraine on Western platforms. Even more importantly, Ukrainian influencers on TikTok or Instagram, mostly young women who had previously only posted on topics such as beauty and lifestyle, now became witnesses and activists who reported on their experiences of war. The most famous is probably Valeria Shashenok, or @valerisssh on TikTok (Figure 7.1). One of her videos about everyday life in Ukraine under the conditions of war has been watched nearly 60 million times to date (Sato 2022).[59] She reports with black humor about her daily routines in emergency shelters, later about her experiences as a refugee, and in every post invites her followers to respond. On the Russian side, in video protests against alleged "Russophobia," fashion influencers like model Victoria Bonya cut up handbags of Western luxury brands that had withdrawn from the Russian market because of the war.

These different kinds of videos flow within the main, side, and counter visual streams of the national media systems of the warring parties, their allies, and other countries. At the same time, these video streams are present in different ways in the various information theaters. Russia and Ukraine are dominated by their own government, military, and journalistic videos and those of their own state-affiliated celebrities and influencers. Numerous Ukrainian activists, journalists, soldiers, and politicians post videos from inside the country via TikTok and the US platforms, reaching audiences in the Global Northwest. However, Russian media audiences rarely see war videos from Ukraine; the desperate calls

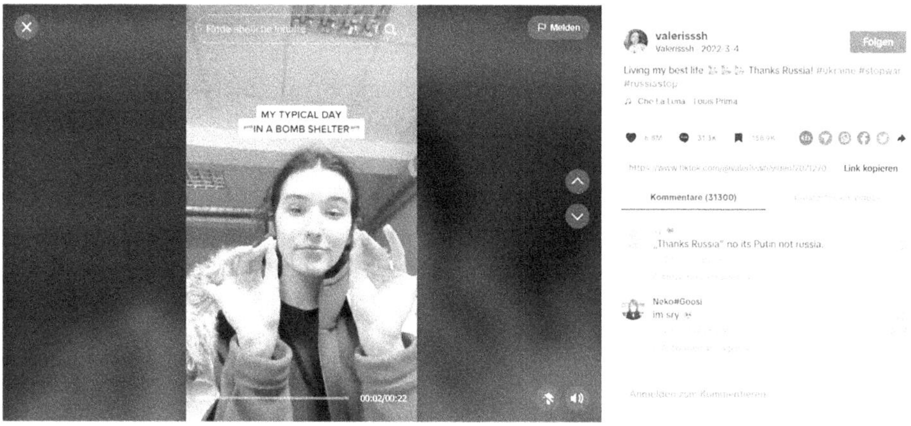

FIGURE 7.1: @valerisssh (Valeria Shashenok) using her TikTok channel to report on her daily life during the Russian war against Ukraine, 2022.

of Ukrainian content creators are invisible to them or become the subject of mocking videos from Russian pro-war users. To be clear, Ukrainian and Western videos are certainly available in Russia; one can quite easily access them via Telegram and YouTube. But this is where the specificity of these two platforms comes into play: their videos are only automatically recommended to a very limited extent; users would first have to deliberately and actively search for them. Platforms that function more via recommendation algorithms and news feeds, such as Instagram, are accessible by using a VPN, but this requires a degree of technical effort that only the more media-savvy users take on. State television and national platforms remain the most important sources of information, especially for the older and formally less educated sections of the Russian population. For observers from the West, this also means that the communication strategies of Russia (or other authoritarian states), which primarily focus on established mass media, should not be underestimated, even if currently the state actors in Ukraine appear to be more adept at communicating on social media and are therefore more strongly represented in the Western media system.

During war, the complex networks of relations between activisms and state apparatuses are transformed. The space of video activism is constricted by state repression, persecution, and expulsion on the one hand, and challenged by its convergence, cooperation, or even complicity with state positions on the other. Within all four groups of videos (by governments, the military, journalists, and lifestyle influencers), one can observe that the boundaries of video activism, previously already fragile, are beginning to blur further. In the case of government videos, this involves, for instance, the voluntary alignment of state and activist positions, the use of paid pseudo-activists, and the self-presentation of state actors as accessible, authentic activists. In the case of military videos from the front, former activists and ordinary users become soldiers and war bloggers, and their videos are picked up and circulated by official military bodies such as the Ministry of Defence, which produces similar videos itself. In the group of news videos, many Russian professional journalists have become de facto activists in exile after losing their jobs and homes; conversely, citizen journalist vloggers (who usually lack journalistic education in researching and checking sources) professionalize and provide the public with reliable up-to-date information. And even glamorous lifestyle influencers gradually become desperate war witnesses or political activists in front of the camera. In all these cases, the boundaries between video activism and other forms of communication seem to dissolve, or at least they appear extremely variable. This ultimately raises the question of what actually characterizes an activist today. While in many practical cases, the answer is clear—for example, when content creators provide concrete help to war victims[60]—the previously discussed video groups show how difficult it can be to decide whether one is dealing with activism at all. Although the fundamental differences between state and civil society, between propaganda and activism are still valid, it is necessary—for activists, scholars, social media users, and the general public—to take a closer look at such blurred border regions.

Video Activism Under Pressure

Going beyond the Ukraine war as an example, some more general conclusions can be drawn about the current situation of video activism worldwide. Video activists are confronted with a whole range of challenges: the regional fragmentation of platform and media systems, increasing persecution of activists, hate speech, propaganda, disinformation and fakes, ubiquitous surveillance and capitalist data extractivism, the need to understand the complexities of political issues and, ultimately, of activism itself.

First, there is an increasing tendency toward a global splinternet with separate or even antagonistic media systems and platform ecologies (see Chapter 1). These regional media systems become more divergent in times of war or other interstate conflicts, leading to increasingly discrepant perceptions of political events in the countries concerned. However, social media also continues to open avenues for visual countercurrents that especially reach younger parts of the population. In this context, non-US platforms are gaining influence, a development that could change the power structure of the global platform system.

At the same time, governments have understood the logic of social media and are increasingly bringing them under their control (Tufekci 2017, 223–60), even building their own internet ecosystems. In this context, activists and other civil society actors are suppressed and persecuted more brutally and effectively, most severely in authoritarian states such as Belarus, China, Egypt, Iran, Russia, or Saudi Arabia (Earl et al. 2022). Direct strategies of repression and coercion include physical violence, harassment, legal prosecution, and permanent surveillance. As a result, a growing number of video activists are being forced to leave their country and work from exile. As Jennifer Earl and colleagues point out, information and activist practices are also "channeled" more indirectly through national laws restricting free expression, social credit systems, corporate and institutional policies (e.g., regarding employee app use), or platform community standards. Moreover, authorities can restrict internet connectivity, impose internet blocks, filter content, or ban certain platforms. They can force platforms to "moderate" activist content, demote it in search results, throttle it in the news, block or "shadow ban" users, and delete their accounts. In addition, they can flood social media with disinformation or distracting and irrelevant material to drown out activists' voices and confuse the public. Some of these activities are done overtly, others covertly and through intermediaries, some by local or national authorities, law enforcement agencies, or the military, and others by private agencies, law firms, paid hackers, troll farms, or the platforms themselves (Earl et al. 2022).

More generally, social media platforms distort and polarize public debates due to their data-extractivist business models, and accelerate the spread of hate, lies, and conspiracy myths through proactive suggestion algorithms—often with devastating consequences, even including genocide (see Chapter 1). For example, since 2016, tens of thousands of members of the Rohingya minority in Myanmar have been murdered after calls for lynching circulated on Facebook (Amnesty International 2022). The spread of disinformation and propaganda, that is deliberately false, misleading, or manipulative political content by powerful social groups (Tuttle Ross 2019), remains one of the biggest challenges for video activism. With the growing influence of authoritarian states, as well as right-wing populist and extremist networks, on social media, the volume and reach of their propaganda have massively grown, often directly targeting activists, undermining their testimony, advocacy, and information, and inciting the population against them. Another danger is that activists themselves can be instrumentalized for propaganda without being aware of it. Especially in interstate conflicts, a tendency can develop for activists to solidarize with the leading actors of their own country. This may be politically justified, as, for instance, many Ukrainian activists demonstrate. However, caution is always advised, as shown, among other things, by pseudo-activist Russian influencers paid by the Kremlin, but also Ukrainian war propaganda bloggers (Gilbert 2022). Particularly in war and other violent conflicts, activists' video discourses tend to be closely intertwined with discourses of propaganda, and it is important to be aware of their practices and their relationships with authorities. The longer the conflict lasts and the more destruction grows, the more difficult it becomes for activists to maintain an independent position. Nationalist propaganda videos are by no means spread exclusively by official institutions, but also by influencers and ordinary users. Some of them may be paid or indoctrinated, others act on their own in support of their country, which they might perceive as surrounded by enemies. In any case, given the media logic and state interference described above, video activists should reflect carefully on their own actions and draw clear boundaries against getting involved in disinformation and propaganda. A test for this consists of validating and comparing various sources of information.

The situation is further complicated by the successive implementation of increasingly sophisticated systems of artificial intelligence (AI) or "algorithmically controlled, automated decision making (ADM)" (Alfter et al. 2019, 9). This embedding takes place in many different places and is not sufficiently noticed by the public, and accordingly causes various political problems. One striking effect is the dissemination of deep fakes (which, for instance, deceptively imitate the appearance and language of political actors).[61] At the same time, cheap fakes, i.e., videos taken out of context with lying captions, are still proving to be easier and just as effective (and have been used extensively in the wars in Ukraine and Gaza, for example). The influence of AI or machine learning systems is further evident in facial recognition software that extends state surveillance, making it possible to identify protesters on videos (Gregory 2022). China, for example, is supplying Iran with sophisticated facial recognition software (Ryan-Mosley 2021). AI tools are also used by authoritarian and some democratic governments via opaque contract service providers to automatically censor critical content and influence or manipulate public opinion (Funk et al. 2023).

To uncover such practices and develop one's own approaches, certain forms of activist knowledge are required—knowledge about political issues and discourses as well as the logic of the media online and offline, at home and abroad. In many cases of personal experience, it will first and foremost be important to document abuses and atrocities, to bear witness and express outrage. Other situations of activism cannot be done without careful analysis and specific expertise on complex political problems.

Most of the aforementioned challenges also affect video activism in peacetime and within the framework of liberal democratic capitalist states, albeit to a lesser extent than in contexts of war and authoritarian regimes. In Chapter 6, we outlined some distortions of liberal public spheres, which Christian Fuchs (2021b) pointedly describes as "pseudo-publics of digital capitalism." According to Fuchs, the platform logics of monopolization, commercialization, accumulation, surveillance, automation, acceleration, individualism, and ideological "tribalism" transform the digital sphere into a mere pseudo-public characterized by huge economic, political, and cultural asymmetries of power. Billionaires like Elon Musk, for example, have the power to buy entire platforms and restructure them as they see fit, according to their political and commercial interests. The high speed of online information flows makes concentrated political discussions and the weighing of arguments more difficult and favors intense emotions and seemingly simple solutions. The dominant culture on social media is "focused on the accumulation and asymmetric distribution of online attention, influence, reputation, visibility, and voice," culminating in an "influencer capitalism" (Fuchs 2021a, 75). As we have already stressed, platform corporations are continuously optimizing their business models, algorithms, and data trading strategies. They encourage blockbuster trends, where flashy, cleverly launched entertainment videos grab all the attention and push the quieter voices and less pleasant topics into the background.

All these challenges contribute to making it increasingly difficult for video activists to expose grievances, create counterpublics, and have an impact on society through social media. To sustain these important functions of video activism, there is an urgent need for a clear and ethically grounded self-understanding of activists, increased media literacy, and diverse, complementary strategies and networks of activists that also include exile groups, diaspora communities, and allies at home and abroad. In the following outlook, we would like to bring such aspects together in the overarching idea of diversity in solidarity.

A Plea for Diversity in Solidarity

It does not take the recent wars and crises to recognize the values of social diversity and solidarity. But the more peace, democracy, justice, science, and the acceptance of proven facts are threatened and the more rifts open up within and between societies, the more important it becomes to defend both values in their combination. We would therefore like to conclude our investigations with a political plea for *diversity in solidarity*. As these two terms are sometimes used as empty phrases, they need to be clarified here. Our plea refers primarily to the diversity and solidarity of video activism itself, its actors, concerns, forms, and strategies. However, this is related to the pluralism of society as a whole, its groups, identities, interests and individuals, its public spheres, and media. In the following, we will first discuss how activism is related to the diversity and solidarity of societies, and then outline a more specific, pluristrategic, and solidary understanding of democratic video activism.

In video activism, as in society as a whole, diversity leads to complex situations and tensions that can only be overcome through specific forms of solidarity. Conceptually, political theory points out that solidarity should not be confused with other human relationships such as love, compassion, sympathy, or empathy. Hannah Arendt (1963, 79), for example, emphasizes the "generality" of solidarity, which is based on a "community of interest with the oppressed and exploited," but ultimately includes "all mankind." Following Arendt's approach, Assaf Sharon develops a conception of solidarity that aims to avoid both the "dangers of exclusivist tribalism and of moral kitsch" (Sharon 2018, 115). According to this view, solidarity is neither a "purely instrumental collaboration" nor a "fraternal association based on natural similarity or uniformity or a charitable association based on sentiment." Rather, it is an association based on principles, including mutual respect and the shared long-term self-interest in living together in a more just, equitable, and livable world. Moreover, Sharon (2018, 115) emphasizes the "commitment to take into account the interests and needs of others," to "eliminate injustice" and ensure "care and concern." This in turn raises the question of where the boundaries of solidarity lie and who is practicing solidarity with whom. In contrast to mere pity or boundless compassion, solidarity presupposes a fundamental willingness to reciprocate: those with whom solidarity is practiced are expected to share the principles of mutual respect and to be generally willing to show solidarity themselves. Of course, it is important to bear in mind that those who lack power and resources are particularly in need of solidarity.

But what can diversity and solidarity mean beyond such general definitions, especially in the field of video activism? In the context of this study, the plea for diversity in solidarity primarily refers to the relationships between the different forms and strategies of video activism itself. However, these in turn are based on characteristic relationships of activism to society, the public, and the media more generally. By advocating for marginalized positions and groups, democratic activism already presupposes the guiding idea of a diverse and solidary society. Since diversity, plurality, and difference are fundamental facts of social life, the idea of a homogeneous community, be it national, ethnic, religious, or otherwise, ultimately appears unreal and repressive, as it must either ignore all social and cultural differences or suppress them in favor of hegemonic group interests. Democratic activists, in contrast, start from the ideal of a society in which "people could be different without fear" (Adorno 2005, 103).

However, pluralist societies and public spheres inevitably also give rise to complex constellations of interests, difficult decisions, and conflicts over values and resources. Authoritarian states and video actors thus often legitimize their repressive policies as a response to such social tensions, which are perceived as threatening. For example, they refer to Carl Schmitt's legal theories from Nazi

Germany, which have regained influence in China, Russia, and global right-wing extremism (Auer 2015; Libin and Patapan 2020). In contrast, the long history of democracies shows that centrifugal forces and controversies in society can be handled in other ways that open up spaces for diversity and solidarity. Democracy is not only to be understood as an institutionalized political system but also as a permanent process, an ongoing movement of the many with different voices, driven by the promise of a "democracy to come" (Derrida 1994, 81). Civil society activism, as epitomized by the Spanish grassroots alliance ¡Democracia Real Ya! ("Real Democracy Now!"), is a decisive part of that movement. Similarly, pluralism is not something static and ahistorical, but at the same time an integral part, prerequisite, and goal of democratic processes. Activists in totalitarian regimes are far from this goal, but even in democratic states it is necessary to constantly fight for it. Accordingly, it is not a contradiction for democratic activism to raise radical demands and at the same time recognize other actors and positions as legitimate. On the other hand, those who orient their own political actions exclusively toward the interests of their own group—however, justified these may be—and thus act at the expense of others, possibly even propagating violence against others and pursuing the goal of their own group dominance, cannot be understood as democratic activists.

Standing up for a diverse and solidary democracy requires agreeing on fundamental values and norms, making compromises, and empathizing with the perspectives of others, particularly those who think differently, thereby gaining insights, and not only practicing tolerance but also principled and respectful solidarity. It requires ensuring equal political and social participation, eliminating mechanisms of social exclusion, and opening up "spaces of legitimation" (Lessenich 2019, 24). This includes civil rights of self-determination, political participation, and social rights such as social security and labor rights. Those who are structurally disadvantaged due to social class, identity, or group deserve special opportunities for participation. Conversely, it is necessary to limit the concentration of power and resolutely oppose anti-democratic and anti-solidary forces. These include not only the declared enemies of an open society but also beneficiaries of it who claim to favor diversity, but in fact damage it through their actions: corporations that disregard or bend laws; media that sacrifice journalistic standards to their own interests; kleptocrats and plutocrats who buy political influence; oligarchs and nepotistic dynasties for whom the common good is only an annoying obstacle. Neoliberal capitalism has led to threats worldwide, including the economization of public and private relationships, increasing inequality, financial and economic crises, the overexploitation of planetary resources, and the destruction of the ecological foundations of life.

This results in a range of general political goals that could be shared by many otherwise different forms of democratic activism today, forming some common ground and a basis for solidary action. For example, the UN has set 17 Sustainable Development Goals and underpinned each of these with concrete demands. The scientific initiative Earth4All has bundled numerous measures for a sustainable, solidarity-based transformation of the economy and society in the areas of energy, food, poverty, inequality, and population (including health and education) (Dixson-Declève et al. 2022). Other proposals on political solidarity are more specific. For example, economist Thomas Piketty has proposed the model of a "participatory socialism" (Piketty 2014, 2020, 966–1034), a political program to combat global inequality through measures such as strengthening the power of workers in companies, more effective taxation of wealth, inheritance, income and carbon emissions, a basic capital endowment, a fairer education system, more democratic forms of financing political parties, and the restructuring of transnational organizations. These initiatives only serve as some examples of noteworthy approaches to national and transnational solidarity that are based on extensive research. Of course, such initiatives by no means exhaust the range of political solidarity and diversity that can underlie video activism.

Another field of diversity and solidarity concerns the public and the media. The struggle for political plurality can only be successful if it resists all attempts to restrict the public sphere and make it compliant, to exclude social groups from it, to control the media, to spread lies and hatred. Genuine diversity of opinion in a society presupposes that voices from outside existing power networks, especially the voices of the socially marginalized, are able to make themselves heard. Across societies, the same applies to perspectives from formerly colonized regions in which the historical exploitations by the centers of power live on in new ways. The diversity of opinion requires public forums and pluralistic media that give space to different positions and experiences. The democratic public sphere, based on the promise of equal participation, freedom of expression, and protection from discrimination, is intended to guarantee this. However, even in societies that strive for this ideal and have it enshrined in their constitution, the power to publicly represent one's own perspectives is unequally distributed and can be abused (see Chapters 1 and 6). It is therefore essential for pluralistic societies to draw clear boundaries against marginalization, hatred, and violence in the media, while at the same time maintaining freedom of the media and freedom of opinion and allowing controversial positions. The constitution of such a public sphere presupposes solidarity and represents an ongoing process of negotiation, difficult even in democratically constituted societies. This is why the video activists' central impetus is so significant: to stand up for unrecognized or suppressed political concerns and to make them public. Activists are part of marginalized groups or act in practical solidarity with their concerns—both with groups in their own social environment and with civil society in other countries, especially those under authoritarian rule.

By standing up for neglected groups and concerns, video activists simultaneously defend and strengthen the principle of a diverse and solidary public sphere on a performative level. Activism therefore participates not only in political debates *in* the public sphere but also in debates *about* the public sphere itself (see Chapter 6).

But how can the media of diverse societies, and video activism in particular, deal with the differences in power within the public sphere, with economic and media concentration and attacks on democracy? Where is the line between ethically based education and persuasion on the one hand and anti-democratic disinformation and manipulation on the other? How can activists adapt to the constant changes in the media system, to the increase in surveillance and disinformation? Such questions can ultimately only be answered in activist practice, but we would like to provide at least a brief overview of some guiding principles and approaches that could contribute to strengthening video activism as well as media diversity and democracy more generally.

First, video activism fighting for diversity and solidarity is committed to fundamental principles of ethical communication and media practice, without which it is impossible to achieve mutual trust, share perspectives, and negotiate compromises between different positions in society (Couldry 2012). These principles include trying to ensure the truthfulness, factual accuracy, and verifiability of verbal and audiovisual representations. They also include reflection on the effects of media, respect for all those involved (those portrayed, the media creators, and the addressees), and safeguarding the right to self-determination, safety, human dignity, and appropriate representation. Bernhard Pörksen, taking up an idea from John Hartley, has outlined the utopia of an "editorial society" (Pörksen 2022). According to this idea, basic principles of professional journalism—a focus on truth and understanding, critical skepticism, the consideration of diverse perspectives, relevance, ethical reflection, and communicative transparency—should be spread as broadly as possible in all of society. The question arises as to how realistic this comprehensive ideal is: How many people are actually able to invest the effort, time, and resources to acquire such abilities and to what extent do the education systems make this possible? However, the principles of an editorial society can serve as a guiding ideal for democratic video activism.

As a consequence of such principles, it follows that society as a whole requires an increase in media literacy, cross-generational and cross-class media education, which is understood as part of political education.[62] This seems to be a truism, but so far has not been adequately implemented even in rich democracies. Competent use of audiovisual, digital, and social media requires more than just basic technical knowledge and the routine use of common interfaces. Above all, it is important that media users be aware of the essential structures, functions, and effects of the various media and informed about the logic and business models they follow, how they convey information, determine discourses, arouse emotions, trigger actions, and generate effects. Even the so-called digital natives constantly need to renegotiate questions of the private and public on the internet, of image manipulation, disinformation, hate, and waves of outrage (boyd 2014; Einspänner-Pflock 2016). This kind of media education is about being aware of the political and ethical issues of media and their use, and it is essential not only in schools, vocational training, higher education, and adult education. Political media literacy also needs to be improved in other subsystems of society such as the legal system or law enforcement agencies. Even professional journalism is all too often carried away by the attention-grabbing dynamics of social media and is sometimes based on misinformation. Video activism can contribute to spreading relevant knowledge about social media.

Media literacy is also confronted with the constant changes in digital and social media, for example, with regard to AI systems and the spread of deep fakes in recent years. Civil society initiatives have therefore developed their own tools for recognizing such imagery and offer forums for the responsible use of AI; the video activist NGO WITNESS is a pioneer in this field (anlen and Vazquez Llorente 2023; Gregory 2023; WITNESS 2023). The demands made of states and corporations include the mandatory labeling of AI outputs ("watermarks"), the mandatory integration of metadata, and invisible fingerprints in order to trace the origin of AI-generated content and make the violation of personal rights and copyrights by deep fakes justiciable. (In contrast, AI works of art or satire that identify their sources and manipulations are to be protected from prosecution.)

Beyond digital media literacy, the defense of democracy and diversity on social media requires concrete activities and practices of solidarity by civil society. There are numerous investigative journalists, critical media collectives, foundations, not-for-profit organizations, or think tanks such as Amnesty International's Citizen Evidence Lab, the Responsible Tech Hub, the Tactical Technology Collective, WITNESS, the International Fact-Checking Network, or, correspondingly, Correctiv in Germany, but also a multitude of vigilant individual users who are fighting against fakes, disinformation, and hate speech on social media using a variety of tactics that take account of the changing media landscape.[63] Some organizations such as Learning for Action collect relevant resources for activism,[64] while others, for example, the New Tactics in Human Rights group provide strategy training.[65] Independent initiatives against online hate like the solidarity initiative #iamhere, organized in Facebook groups, directly implement creative strategies on social media or work to create networks among relevant initiatives.[66] More specialized projects are dedicated to protecting specific vulnerable groups online.[67]

Such interventions from civil society are essential, but the fight against disinformation and hate can only be won if democratic states and supranational formations (in dialogue with experts and civil society) create clear legal frameworks for social media platforms. For example, the EU and a growing number of individual countries have regulated gatekeeper platforms and other online providers since 2022 (e.g., via the EU Digital Services Act and the Digital Markets Act or the Online Safety Bill in the United Kingdom), and many governments have set up public reporting centers against online hate or support NGOs in their relevant initiatives.[68] The aim of state regulation and control of platforms should be to recognize and punish legal violations and threats on the internet without restricting civil society engagement and the diversity of the public sphere. State action is thus faced with the dilemma of either intervening too little or too much (Bennett 2021). It must be judged by whether it protects courageous voices in civil society from hate storms and trolling, supports them, and ensures that they are not silenced for fear of attack. Again, the situation is very different in authoritarian states, where the major platforms often behave opportunistically and actively contribute to the suppression of freedom of expression.

The platforms themselves operate within the legal framework by setting their own usage guidelines and anchoring them in their general terms and conditions. They attempt to fulfill both the prescribed and self-imposed regulatory tasks through automated filtering, manual content moderation, or their own educational projects and counterspeech initiatives. However, the practices of large social media organizations need constant critical scrutiny. It is striking that the major providers have often only met their obligations after enormous damage had already been incurred (in the case of Facebook: election campaign manipulation, genocide against the Rohingya), scandals (e.g., spying and manipulation by companies such as Cambridge Analytica), and sustained public pressure. The design of adequate algorithms and moderation by linguistically and culturally competent emergency teams is costly, and the self-regulation of platforms is also heavily dependent on market fluctuations.[69] Video activism is constantly confronted with such problems and can draw attention to them.

Beyond legislative initiatives and their mostly unsatisfactory implementation by the platforms, utopias for the Internet of the future are also important and inspire activism. The vision of a democratic internet oriented toward the common good is being discussed under the heading of digital commons: for instance, the Public Service Internet Manifesto outlines the vision of a materially sustainable, non-commercial, public-law structure of platforms on which open-source software and open-access content are provided and spaces are cultivated for deliberately slowed-down, and therefore more considered and sustainable, political communication and co-determination (Fuchs and Unterberger 2021). Such democratic platforms would give activists greater visibility and power to act.

All these general conditions for diverse and solidary public spheres have consequences for video activism. But what does the idea of diversity in solidarity mean more specifically for the concrete work of video activists themselves? Implicit answers to this question have already run through the previous chapters of this book. Their examples show how video activists join forces with each other and with other social actors in order to exert political influence. This can already be seen in the historical precursors of video activism discussed in Chapter 2, for example, in films in the context of social movements; in participatory forms of production and ethical reflections on the relationship between filmmakers and filmed subjects; in the solidarity with workers proclaimed by films of the student movement; or in the Third Cinema as part of a common anti-colonial liberation struggle. Such practices of solidarity are supplemented and enhanced by new ones in current video activism. For example, when the *Most Shocking Second a Day Video* (Chapter 3) promotes solidarity with refugees and support for an NGO, it relies on both interviews with refugee children and collaboration with professional film production companies and agencies. The influencer Rezo (Chapter 4) combines the provocation of political opponents with the presentation of scientific facts to build an alliance of different social groups in the fight for climate and social justice. The diversity and solidarity of video activists are also evident in Chapter 5, which explores how small collectives, influencer networks, large NGOs, and hashtag movements tackle overarching issues such as racism, capitalism, and the climate crisis with a variety of different strategies. And in Chapter 6, we saw how the hashtag strategies of the Black Lives Matter movement have created international waves of solidarity and a diverse alliance of affected communities, activists, and policymakers.

All these examples underline that diversity in solidarity means at least three things for video activists. In terms of *content*, it means working together on pressing social issues and striving to create and strengthen diverse but solidary democratic public spheres. In terms of *media practice*, it means using diverse video forms and strategies, interlinking them in hybrid media systems, and anchoring them in broader discourses. And *politically*, it means cooperating in solidarity with diverse social actors and movements online and offline. Approaches such as Bennett's "Idea Flow Model" of transformation communication also indicate that individual activists can rarely achieve much alone (Bennett 2020, 14, 50–61). Instead, their social impact depends on their collective actions and alliances, and thus on seeking common ground, on the strategic linking of various communities and networks that pursue shared overarching goals with different strategies, and on their unification into larger movements that exert political pressure. This is not easy because the diversity of video activism encompasses such different political, ethical, and aesthetic positions and practices, ranging from radical to more reformist stances. However, if strategic connections between these strands of activism can be established, their diversity proves to be a clear advantage.

First, the different *strategies and practices of activist video production, design, distribution, and networking* can complement each other (see Chapter 4). For example, in some situations, it may be more effective to use video strategies that maximize short-term attention and online reach, while in other cases strategies that have a longer-term impact on smaller, specific audiences may be more appropriate. For this reason, both activist influencers and NGOs that adapt to the logic of large platforms as well as small, radical video collectives that consciously reject this logic are important. However, it is crucial that groups with different strategies network with each other. Their approaches to cooperation are also diverse, and even within the field of smaller, more radical collectives, they range from the classic grassroots principle, as with Labournet.tv, to newer subscription models on left-wing streaming platforms such as Means.tv.

The diversity of activist strategies also produces a *variety of video forms* that influence and emotionally move different audiences in specific ways. This concerns both the main functional types of videos, such as witness and mobilization videos (see Chapter 1), and the various more specific aesthetic forms of audiovisual showing, narrating, arguing, symbolizing, and experimenting (see Chapter 3). Reflection on the political and ethical implications of such aesthetic forms and the development of practical media competence has a long tradition in the history of video activism (see Chapter 2). This includes knowing how videos evoke and spread political emotions, or how to evaluate video evidence, question narrative perspectives, and analyze audiovisual arguments and symbols. In these contexts of designing and assessing videos, diversity in solidarity means, among other things, that both the audience and the people portrayed are taken into account. This is of particular relevance in the case of vulnerable communities, their specific experiences, and their empowerment to do own media work.

The notion of diversity in solidarity applies most clearly to *video activist groups with different identities, practices, and forms of organization* (see Chapter 5). When local witnesses, affected communities, activist organizers, political collectives, committed filmmakers, NGO strategists, or semi-professional influencers work together across different platforms, they are usually better able to achieve common political goals. However, most activists rarely cooperate in a targeted and planned manner. All too often, they eye each other with suspicion or prejudice and disagree on specific political goals and means. For example, when is it appropriate to be politically or ethically uncompromising, and when is it inevitable to seek compromise? When should video activism be open, balanced, and rational, when should it take sides, arouse emotions, and act with decisive strength of opinion? Confronted with questions like these, activists must rely on their own political judgment and self-critically reflect on their actions.

However, in our view, the mutual accusations of being too compromising and conformist or, conversely, too dogmatic and ineffective are often unnecessary and block productive and necessary cooperation. We therefore also see this book as an invitation to democratic activists to share their experiences and look for new forms of cooperation. In view of the increasing threats to democracy that we are facing today, we are in favor of uniting the various progressive movements and civil society forces. Together, these forces can use their specific knowledge of different media strategies to fight back against manipulation, disinformation, and the suppression of relevant issues. After all, as explained above, many democratic activists share essential goals and opponents in their struggles against capitalist extractivism, chauvinism, racism, sexism, economic inequality, and other anti-democratic structures. Furthermore, the principles outlined above on diversity and solidarity in society, the public sphere, and the media could provide a common ground for different strands of video activism to work together in solidarity.

This solidarity among video activists concerns a wide range of specific practices, including sousveillance, the production of "counter-information," the organization of local events, the verification and archiving of visible evidence, the empowerment of vulnerable communities, and the amplification of social movement demands. Video activists can join forces to carry out crowd productions or produce video series and campaigns together. They can help each other seed videos and build networked narratives through linking their channels and videos and using each other's frames and hashtags. They can support each other in monitoring user engagement, managing comments, responding to reactions, involving multipliers, building communities of followers over time, or protesting against the deletion of videos by platforms. Together they can create curated websites, collective workshops or archives, and collaborate in long-term networks. Such solidarity-based networking strategies could significantly increase the visibility and impact of democratic video activism and thus create a stronger counterweight against anti-democratic trolls and right-wing extremists.

Following the traditions of critical theory from Gayatri Chakravorty Spivak (1988) to Judith Butler (2004, 2015), the call for diversity *in solidarity* also includes reflecting on and counteracting the unequal distribution of power, resources, and agency among activists themselves. Which voices are able to speak publicly and which are actually heard? Whose lives are considered important or worthy of mourning? Which issues or regions are marginalized? And how can activists in the Global South and North, in democratic and non-democratic countries, relate to each other, learn from each other, and support each other? Activists from the wealthy liberal-democratic countries of the Global Northwest are particularly called upon to show solidarity with communities under threat in authoritarian states and to support activists in exile who have been forced to flee such states due to repression and persecution.

However, democratic states are also increasingly under attack from within, and many people there have wrongly assumed for too long that they live in a natural state of security and stability. The fact that this state of affairs can never be taken for granted is not only demonstrated by the increasing attacks on democratic achievements and the rise of anti-democratic nationalism, fundamentalism, and conspiracy ideologies. The global grievances and threats are just as evident as the tireless and determined resistance against them: protests against human rights violations, unleashed capitalism, economic injustice, authoritarian governments, wars, racist violence, deadly border regimes, the destruction of natural resources; as well as campaigns for climate justice, sexual and gender diversity, labor rights or humanitarian aid. In this context of resistance, video activists, in all their diversity, use social media, despite all pitfalls, to fight for diverse and solidary societies again and again. And so we conclude with a plea to build networks of solidarity and plural alliances for social change: democratic activists of the world, unite!

Notes

1. It must be said, however, that such data are usually not available to the public in a verifiable form; it does not predominantly come from independent research, but from the annual reports of platform companies, from estimates by journalists and NGOs, or from advertising companies or industry journals that accumulate and process it (Constine 2015; Meeker 2019; Sandvine 2023). Some independent data can be found in Chapter 3.
2. Vaidhyanathan stresses how social media spread disinformation, incite hatred, and distort democratic processes. In his view, we need a global movement to "put pressure on Facebook and other companies through markets and competition, through legislatures, and through multilateral standard-setting organisations" (Vaidhyanathan 2018, 219). However, he seems to believe that it is utterly hopeless that such a movement could emerge and be successful.
3. On the concept of activism more generally, see Neumayer (2021).
4. See, for instance, the important work done by the Syrian Archive.
5. A condensed overview of the main concepts and positions in Social Movement Studies can be found in Sorg (2022). A helpful handbook about this field of research is Della Porta and Diani (2014).
6. A classic, albeit controversial, theory on the reasons for this alignment is offered by Herman and Chomsky ([1988] 2002).
7. This is also the case in Germany, a country with an average use of online media; see Kantar TNS/Die Medienanstalten (2018) and Matsa et al. (2018).
8. For the following functions, see also Eder and Klonk (2017).
9. Askanius (2013, 5–8) distinguishes between mobilization, witness, documentation, and archived radical and political mash-up videos. Mateos and Gaona (2015) arrive at a related but somewhat different functional taxonomy: document (including witness videos), rally call (including mobilization videos), re-discursive reaction (critical processing of dominant discourses), identity construction, and didactic (i.e., explanatory and educational) videos.
10. The functions of the video include observing/documenting, reporting/arguing, commenting/criticizing, mobilizing/networking, and provoking/disseminating/entertaining. The video form includes genre and (non-)fictionality markers, narrative and rhetorical structure, audiovisual design, affective structure, as well as inter- and transtextuality. Video

production and distribution differ in terms of level of professionalization, budget, individual or collective production, target audience, typical platform, position in campaigns, and opportunities for interaction and participation.

11. Warning: The site contains descriptions and video material of graphic violence.
12. See also Castells (2013), van Dijck et al. (2018), and van Dijck (2013).
13. The more optimistic position can be found in Castells (2012) and Shirky (2011); for pessimistic critiques, see Sunstein (2017), Gladwell (2010), and Morozov (2011).
14. Wikipedia currently offers a helpful overview that is more detailed than most academic publications, see Wikipedia (n.d.), Social media, https://en.wikipedia.org/wiki/Social_media. Accessed April 1, 2022.
15. See also the organization's response to their critics: The Shift Project (2020).
16. The full documentary can be accessed on the site of the Bundeszentrale für politische Bildung: https://www.bpb.de/mediathek/video/273199/the-cleaners/. Accessed July 17, 2024.
17. Warning: Please note that the video contains scenes of graphic violence.
18. Thanks to David Liftinger for this reference.
19. In the 1920s, WIR was responsible for setting up the Russian production firm Mezhrabpom-Film and founded Prometheus-Film in Germany, see Agde and Schwarz (2012).
20. The documentaries *The Black Power Mixtape 1967–1975* (Göran Olsson, Sweden 2011) and *Conversations: The Black Radical Tradition* (Edwian Eze Stokes, USA 2021) offer insights into the history of the Black liberation movement and its film and media practice.
21. The Axel Springer publishing house, and particularly its tabloid *Bild*, dominated the West German newspaper market and was a prime target of leftists at the time, since its conservative politics and often inflammatory writing were seen as spreading lies and propaganda, particularly defaming the left (translator's note).
22. See Video4Change (toolkit.video4change.org, accessed April 25, 2022), WITNESS (blog.witness.org/category/video-for-change/how-to-toolkits, accessed April 25, 2022), and the "Breadtube" playlists on YouTube (https://www.youtube.com/hashtag/breadtube, accessed April 25, 2022).
23. Self-description in the YouTube channel info on www.youtube.com/@democracyatwrk. Accessed May 13, 2023.
24. See the conversation between Harun Farocki and Hartmut Bitomsky (Feurich 1970).
25. On this, see the online resource www.filmingrevolution.org (accessed May 1, 2022), developed by the media scholar Alisa Lebow, which puts film and video work on the so-called Arab Spring in a network-like context.
26. To arrive at this formula, we have combined models from the following sources: Learning for Action (2013), Doc Society (2019), and Kurz and Kubek (2021). Compare also the "continuum of participation" in Dennis (2019).
27. This kind of effect has been examined more thoroughly in theories of documentary film; for an overview, see Chattoo and Jenkins (2019).

28. A similar, but less developed distinction was proposed in Eder (2023).
29. It must be added, however, that only three seconds of viewing was enough to be counted as a "view." Zuckerberg's announcement itself no longer seems to be available on the Meta website, but many trade journals such as *TechCrunch* reported on it, see Constine (2015). Further data with links to sources can be found in Gilbert (2023).
30. These figures are only estimates based on preliminary research and require more detailed examination. Other authors, however, seem to recognize similar trends, for example, Liedtke and Marwecki (2019).
31. When Richard Waters and Paul Jones examined YouTube videos on the 100 most popular non-profit channels in 2011, they found that videos were viewed an average of 872,556 times (ranging from 40 to more than five million views). The videos lasted about five minutes on average (from 30 seconds to 94 minutes) and received many, predominantly positive ratings.
32. For YouTube, see Park et al. (2016). According to the Socialbakers 2019 Q4 Trends Report, the average view duration for brand videos on Facebook was 4.57 seconds, see SMK (2020). After Socialbakers was merged into the new company Emplifi, their original quarterly report with the study seems to be no longer freely accessible.
33. Empirical research is found in countless separate studies, but some textbooks summarize their general findings, for example, Cooney (2011) and Stoknes (2015).
34. On the following, see Eder (2020). Several researchers and centers, such as Nicole Doerr at the Copenhagen Research Centre for Political Mobilisation and Social Movement Studies, currently study the visual communication of extremist groups in Europe and elsewhere.
35. Some of this has also been documented by Evon (2015).
36. Today, those comments have been removed from the YouTube page.
37. Jones, Marc Owen (@marcowenjones) (2022), "There are now over 274 000 000 (274 million) tweets on the Persian version of the Mahsa Amini hashtag. For context, since mid-2013, the #BlackLivesMatter hashtag has accumulated 63 000 000 (63 million) tweets. #IranRevolution," X/Twitter. October 12, https://x.com/marcowenjones?lang=de. Accessed May 13, 2023.
38. Personal interview by Jens Eder with the director David Knight in the context of the symposium "Social Impact of Audiovisual Media," online video conference, August 13, 2021.
39. Such proposals are scattered across numerous specialist blogs on the net. We would also like to thank Julia Althoff, Floris Asche, Moritz Hohenfelder, Dana Regev, and many other social media experts at the Social Storytelling Labs 2018 and 2020 at the Film University Babelsberg for their information and discussions.
40. See, for instance, Mobile Marketing Association (2019), Animoto (n.d.), and Duvan (2023).
41. On X/Twitter, however, this networked narrative may not be as tight and substantial as one might think, as a study by Kim Albrecht and his team indicates, https://metoo.kimalbrecht.com/. Accessed May 1, 2022.
42. Thanks to Giacomo Tagliani who directed our attention to this project.

43. YouTube channels: rezo (2015a–present, 1.8 million followers in 2023, no new video uploads since 2020), Rezo ja lol ey (2018–present, 1.7 million followers in 2023), Renzo (2021–present, one million followers in 2023), Schlumpf (2020–present, 230,000 followers in 2023), Instagram channel: Rezo (2015–present, 1.2 million followers in 2023), and Twitch channel rezo (530,000 followers in 2023).
44. All quotes from interviews in this chapter have been translated from German by the authors.
45. Of course, there are also right-wing equivalents with even more followers such as Steven Crowder (5.9 million) or Ben Shapiro (six million).
46. In Germany, all political parties in the national parliament receive public funding for political education offered through formally independent foundations. The RLS has commissioned several studies on social media activism, see Liedtke and Marwecki (2019), Bösch and Köver (2021), Maier (2021), and Jendrzejewski and Strufe (2022).
47. Statement at the roundtable discussion "Politische Performances: Digitaler Videoaktivismus auf TikTok," University of Vienna, May 12, 2022, in which our research project participated.
48. Archival footage of the interview with Bob Hunter is used in the documentary *A Fierce Green Fire: The Battle for a Living Planet* (Mark Kitchell, USA 2012). For more information on the life and work of Bob Hunter, see Hunter (2023).
49. See American Masters PBS (2014).
50. For another early example of action on the high sea, see Greenpeace (1979) SYND 16 7 79 *Ship Carrying Nuclear Waste Harried by Greenpeace Boats*. See also the short video analysis by da Ponte (2018).
51. Among these agencies were Ogilvy UK, Don't Panic London, and Freundliche Grüsse, Zurich. For a selection, visit https://bit.ly/3H3rpMk. Accessed February 4, 2022.
52. However, as Julie Doyle has shown in a diachronic study of Greenpeace campaign videos featuring footage from the Arctic, they can no longer be read as sublime documents of nature that assert rather than prove the danger of climate change. Climate change has reached such a scale that its consequences are now clearly visible, even and especially in the Arctic, see Doyle (2017, 2011) as well as Abbamonte (2021).
53. "Environmental campaigns with heart and mind" is what one employee in the Greenpeace Germany communications department once called it, see Koch (2009).
54. On the distinction between "the public" and "a public," see Warner (2002).
55. In an online talk on October 11, 2022, organized by Sylvia Sasse and colleagues in Zurich, Mykhola Makhortykh presented a different but compatible typology of activism in the war on Ukraine. Taking a functional focus, it distinguished between activist archives, memory battlegrounds, digital border-makers, echo chambers, hate speech amplifiers, and information warriors.
56. A TikTok by user @vitaliyvendeta uses a musical mash-up of a speech by Oleksandr Porovozniuk (president of a small Ukrainian football club), which garnered over 250,000 views. The video is no longer available, but the music used in TikTok can still be found on

YouTube, see, for example, https://www.youtube.com/watch?v=CrWI9EpVKms. Accessed July 17, 2024.

57. A notable collection of materials translated to English can be found through the project WarTranslated: https://linktr.ee/wartranslated. Accessed July 17, 2024.
58. See, for example, X/Twitter user JohnB_Schneider: https://twitter.com/JohnB_Schneider. Accessed July 17, 2024.
59. Additionally, a notable German short documentary was produced in 2022 under the title *Following Valeria* (Nicola Fegg, Germany 2022): https://www.magnetfilm.de/short-film/films/details/following-valeria.html. Accessed July 17, 2024.
60. Captured, for example, by TikTok user @darkangelizuminka2804. This account no longer exists.
61. See, for example, this tutorial on wistia.com: https://tinyurl.com/mtpytrd8. Accessed July 17, 2024. At the same time, human rights advocacy groups such as WITNESS point out that these misleading manipulations should be fundamentally distinguished from AI-supported content produced for satirical or artistic purposes (anlen and Vazquez Llorente 2023). Among these are also artivist video fakes.
62. A good example of such media education is provided by the podcast "Social Media and Politics," https://socialmediaandpolitics.org/. Accessed May 2, 2023.
63. See, for example, the Citizen Evidence Lab of Amnesty International (https://citizenevidence.org/, accessed July 17, 2024), the Responsible Tech Hub (https://www.responsibletechhub.com/about, accessed July 17, 2024), Tactical Tech (https://tacticaltech.org/, accessed July 17, 2024), WITNESS (https://www.witness.org, accessed July 17, 2023), the International Fact-Checking Network (https://www.poynter.org/ifcn/, accessed July 17, 2023), and Correctiv (https://correctiv.org/, accessed July 17, 2023).
64. See the Platform Governance Archive (https://www.platformgovernancearchive.org/, accessed July 18, 2024), the Persuasion Lab (https://ad.watch/index.html, accessed July 18, 2024), Learning for Action (http://learningforaction.com/resource-library, accessed July 18, 2024), or Americans for the Arts with their overview of "Arts and Social Impact" (https://ww2.americansforthearts.org/explorer, accessed July 18, 2024).
65. See the New Tactics in Human Rights group initiated by the Centre for Victims of Torture (CVT) with its tactical mapping approach (https://tmt.newtactics.org/, accessed July 18, 2024). Other networks that support media education and activism include the Ulex Project (https://ulexproject.org, accessed July 18, 2024), the European Community Organizing Network (https://organizeeurope.org, accessed July 18, 2024), or European Alternatives (https://euroalter.com, accessed July 18, 2024).
66. The solidarity initiative #iamhere, organized in Facebook groups, provides a defense against hate storms in comment threads. An international overview of English-language initiatives against online hate can be found on the International Network for Hate Studies (INHS) (https://internationalhatestudies.com/cyber-hate-initiatives-3/, accessed July 18, 2024).
67. On the protection of refugees, see https://tinyurl.com/3s5ze4yj. Accessed July 18, 2024.

68. For the EU regulations, see https://digital-strategy.ec.europa.eu/en/policies/digital-services-act-package (accessed July 18, 2024). In the United States, for example, the Southern Poverty Law Center (https://www.splcenter.org/, accessed July 18, 2024), in the United Kingdom Stop Hate (https://www.stophateuk.org, accessed July 18, 2024), and in Germany Hass im Netz / Melden (https://www.hass-im-netz.info/melden, accessed July 18, 2024).
69. For example, numerous moderator positions were cut during mass redundancies at Facebook in 2023, instead of revising this area conceptually and expanding it in line with demand (Nix 2023). The platforms often react inadequately also in other ways. For example, in some cases, the obligation to use a clear name proves to be a problem for activists, members of the opposition, and vulnerable groups, for example, trans* people, who can be persecuted or excluded as a result. For all those reasons, platform-critical activism is indispensable, for example, in the form of complaints against the non-deletion of anti-Semitic and anti-Muslim posts or vice versa: through protests against the unjustified deletion of activist videos and accounts.

Media References

Abounaddara (2011–present), Vimeo channel, https://vimeo.com/user6924378. Accessed August 1, 2024.

ACTUPNY (2012–present), YouTube channel, https://www.youtube.com/@ACTUPNY. Accessed July 30, 2024.

Adair, Peter, Nancy Adair, Lucy Massie Phenix, Veronica Selver, Andrew Brown, and Rob Epstein (1977), *Word Is Out: Stories of Some of Our Lives*, directed by Mariposa Film Group, Nancy Adair, Andrew Brown, Lucy Massie Phenix, Veronica Selver, produced by Nancy Adair, Andrew Brown, Lucy Massie Phenix, Veronica Selver, USA.

Airwars (2015–present), YouTube channel, http://www.youtube.com/@Airwarsorg. Accessed July 31, 2024.

Al-Aloul, Ayman, and Yusef Maysam (2014), الركام دلو - العالول أيمن (Rubble Bucket Challenge), YouTube, August 23, https://www.youtube.com/watch?v=duSBig1-VUA. Accessed July 23, 2024.

Al-Kateab, Waad, and Edward Watts (2020), *For Sama*, Syria, UK and USA: PBS Frontline, Channel 4 News, ITN Productions.

Alk, Howard (1971), *The Murder of Fred Hampton*, USA: Chicago Film Group, MGA Inc.

Allen, Taisha, and R. Sylon (2014), *Unseen Video of Eric Garner Death—Over 7 Minutes Handcuffed Not Breathing NYPD Chokehold AFTERMATH*, YouTube, July 19, http://tinyurl.com/2w2czwd4. Accessed January 5, 2024. Trigger warning: This video contains disturbing scenes.

Álvarez, Santiago (1965), *Now!*, Cuba: Instituto Cubano del Arte e Industria Cinematográficos (ICAIC).

American Masters PBS (2014), *First Greenpeace Whale Rescue Mission | A Fierce Green Fire | American Masters*, YouTube, April 2, https://tinyurl.com/2emdaa9b. Accessed August 26, 2023.

Amnesty International (n.d.), Citizen Evidence Lab, Website, https://citizenevidence.org/. Accessed July 17, 2024.

Amnesty International (2006–present), YouTube channel, https://www.youtube.com/user/amnestyinternational. Accessed July 30, 2024.

Amnesty International, and Max Hattler (2013), *Amnesty International: Stop the Show*, YouTube, April 6, 2013, https://www.youtube.com/watch?v=Wre5VWHxSug. Accessed July 13, 2024.

Amnesty International UK (2008), *The Stuff of Life / Exposing Waterboarding / International Law*, YouTube, UK, https://www.youtube.com/watch?v=yLL7O9hIloA. Accessed July 23, 2024. Trigger warning: This video contains disturbing scenes.

Anders, Rayk (2013–present), YouTube channel, http://www.youtube.com/@RaykAnders. Accessed August 1, 2024.

Antonio, Emile de (1968), *In the Year of the Pig*, USA: Monday Film Production, Turin Film Productions.

Antonio, Emile de (1971), *Millhouse: A White Comedy*, USA: Whittier Film Corp./Turin Film Corp.

@aperegarom (Peregarom, Dana S.) (2022), *Russian Pensioner Who Survived Siege of Leningrad Arrested for Protest Against Ukraine War*, Russia, X/Twitter, March 2, https://twitter.com/aperegarom?lang=de. Accessed December 29, 2023.

Antonio, Emile de, Mary Lampson, and Wexler Haskell (1976), *Underground*, USA: Action 27.

Arrels fundació (2015), *The Most Boring Viral Video*, YouTube, May 3. Deleted, available at https://adsspot.me/media/tv-commercials/arrels-fundacio-the-most-boring-viral-video-3340e64c4084. Accessed July 20, 2016.

bak.ma (n.d.), Website, https://bak.ma/. Accessed July 23, 2024.

@bait.faktencheck (n.d.), TikTok channel, https://www.tiktok.com/@bait.faktencheck. Accessed July 30, 2024.

Bellingcat (2014–present), YouTube channel, https://www.youtube.com/@bellingcatofficial. Accessed July 31, 2024.

Black Lives Matter (n.d.), Website, https://blacklivesmatter.com/. Accessed July 31, 2024.

Bliss, Rob (2014), *10 Hours of Walking in NYC as a Woman*, YouTube, October 28, https://www.youtube.com/watch?v=b1XGPvbWn0A. Accessed July 31, 2024.

Block, Hans, and Moritz Riesewieck (2018), *The Cleaners*, Germany: Gebrueder Beetz Filmproduktion. [See Website, https://www.bpb.de/mediathek/video/273199/the-cleaners/. Accessed July 17, 2024.]

Boe, Henrik and Nicolai Bjorke (2022), Worlds Apart, nrk, April 5, https://tinyurl.com/d4nmcabe. Accessed November 3, 2023.

Brave New Films (n.d.), Website, https://www.bravenewfilms.org/. Accessed July 23, 2024.

Brown, Matthew, Evan Cass-Kavanagh, Mary Ryder, and Jane Slater (2018), *Anyone's Child: Mexico: A Living Documentary about Families Affected by Mexico's Drug War*, Mexico, UK: Anyone's Child. [See Website: http://mexico.anyoneschild.org/. Accessed April 18, 2023.]

B'Tselem (n.d.), Website, https://www.btselem.org/. Accessed July 23, 2024.

Calais Migrant Solidarity (2016), *Calais Jungle Police Assaults (5th and 6th of January)*, YouTube, January 7, https://tinyurl.com/3aac6x2v. Accessed May 16, 2023.

Campact (n.d.), Website, https://www.campact.de/. Accessed August 1, 2024.

Cassetteboy (2006–present), YouTube channel, https://www.youtube.com/user/cassetteboy. Accessed July 30, 2024.

Chai, Jing (2015), 穹顶之下 (*Under the Dome*), China. [See: *Under the Dome* (English subtitle, complete) by Chai Jing: *Air pollution in China*, YouTube, March 9, 2015, https://tinyurl.com/2kd9dthw. Accessed April 6, 2023.]

Cinemata. Social Issue Films about the Asia-Pacific (n.d.), Website, https://cinemata.org/Cinemata.org. Accessed July 23, 2024.

Critical Art Ensemble (n.d.), Website, http://critical-art.net/. Accessed August 1, 2024.

Daopoulos, Rony (1971), *L'Aggettivo donna* ("The Adjective Woman"), Italy: Collettivo Femminista di Cinema.

Dellert, Louisa (2016–20), Instagram account, #louisadellert. Accessed August 1, 2024.

Democracy at Work (2012–present), YouTube channel, www.youtube.com/@democracyatwrk. Accessed May 13, 2023.

Democracy Now! Independent Global News (n.d.), Website, https://www.democracynow.org/. Accessed July, 30, 2024.

Doc Society (n.d.), Website, https://docsociety.org/. Accessed July 31, 2024.

_docubase: The MIT Open Documentary Lab (2015), *The Quipu Project*, directed by Maria Court and Rosemarie Lerner, Chaka Studio, Website, https://docubase.mit.edu/project/quipu-project/. Accessed December 28, 2023.

The Documentary Channel (TDC) (2015), *Climate Change Explained Simply*, YouTube, December 2, https://tinyurl.com/53p7est4. Accessed April 13, 2023.

Ellis, Lindsay (2013–present), YouTube channel, http://www.youtube.com/@LindsayEllisVids. Accessed August 1, 2024.

Emmerich, Roland (2004), *The Day after Tomorrow*, USA: Twentieth Century Fox.

Ende Gelände (2019), *Ende Gelände 19–24.6. 2019 Rheinland*, YouTube, March 30, https://tinyurl.com/3rruyxwh. Accessed June 3, 2023.

Engage Media (n.d.), Website, https://engagemedia.org/. Accessed July 30, 2024.

European Alternatives (n.d.), Website, https://euroalter.com. Accessed July 18, 2024.

European Community Organizing Network (ECON) (n.d.), Website, https://organizeeurope.org. Accessed July 18, 2024.

Exodus: Our Journey to Europe (2016–present), TV documentary series, UK: KEO Films.

Extinction Rebellion Deutschland (2019–present), YouTube channel, https://www.youtube.com/@ExtinctionRebellionDeutschland. Accessed July 31, 2024.

Extinction Rebellion (XR) UK (2017–present), YouTube channel, https://www.youtube.com/@ExtinctionRebellionUK. Accessed July 31, 2024.

Fegg, Nicola (2022), *Following Valeria*, Germany: Chromosom Film. [See: https://www.magnetfilm.de/short-film/films/details/following-valeria.html. Accessed July 17, 2024.]

The Fifth Estate (2016), *Whalers vs. Greenpeace: Standoff on the High Seas—The Fifth Estate*, YouTube, July 5, https://tinyurl.com/4etnvsxa. Accessed April 19, 2023.

The Film Group (1966), *Cicero March*, USA: The Film Group.

FilmsForAction (n.d.), Website, https://www.filmsforaction.org/. Accessed July 23, 2024.

Fincher, David (2010), *The Social Network*, USA: Columbia Pictures, Relativity Media, Scott Rudin Productions, Michael De Luca Productions, Trigger Street Productions.

Forensic Architecture (n.d.), Website, https://forensic-architecture.org/. Accessed July 23, 2024.

Fox, Louis (2007), *The Story of Stuff*, USA: Free Range Studios, YouTube, April 22, 2009, https://www.youtube.com/watch?v=9GorqroigqM. Accessed July 23, 2024.

Grant, Laurens (2016), *Stay Woke: The Black Lives Matter Movement*, USA: FarWord.

Greenpeace (1979), *SYND 16 7 79 Ship Carrying Nuclear Waste Harried by Greenpeace Boats*, YouTube (AP Archive), https://www.youtube.com/watch?v=2bd8cOlIXjo. Accessed December 30, 2023.

Greenpeace Deutschland (2007), *Bei Vattenfall: Neulich in Krümmel …*, YouTube, August 27, https://tinyurl.com/3avmevr5. Accessed August 16, 2023.

Greenpeace International (2006–present), YouTube channel, http://www.youtube.com/@greenpeace. Accessed August 1, 2024.

Greenpeace International (2010), *Facebook: Unfriend Coal*, YouTube, September 13, https://tinyurl.com/58y54e5y. Accessed April 6, 2023.

Greenpeace International (2010), *Give the Orangutan a Break: Nestle KitKat Spoof Video*, Greenpeace media, March 17, 2010, https://tinyurl.com/mdjxtx22. Accessed August 10, 2023.

Greenpeace International (2012), *A Homeless Polar Bear in London—Ft. Jude Law and Radiohead*, YouTube, July 3, https://tinyurl.com/yeyujea2. Accessed April 6, 2023.

Greenpeace International (2015), *A Song of Oil, Ice and Fire*, YouTube, May 27, https://tinyurl.com/3evm3ap9. Accessed April 6, 2023.

Greenpeace International (2018), *There's a Rang Tan in My Bedroom*, August 14, https://media.greenpeace.org/Detail/27MZIFJWY4WSN. Accessed August 16, 2023.

Greenpeace Media (n.d.), Website, https://media.greenpeace.org/. Accessed July, 30, 2024.

Guzmán, Patricio (1975–79), *La Batalla de Chile* ("The Battle of Chile"), Chile: Equipe Tercer Ano.

Hamed Rad (2009), *Neda Agha Soltan Killing Scene*, YouTube, June 20, https://tinyurl.com/mr2tyx3n. Accessed April 7, 2023. Trigger warning: This video contains scenes of graphic violence.

Happen Films (n.d.), Website, https://happenfilms.com/. Accessed July 23, 2024.

Heinig, Marco, and Steffen Maurer (2018), *Hamburger Gitter*, Germany: Leftvision.

Heinig, Marco, Steffen Maurer, Luise Burchard, and Luca Vogel (2022), *Rise Up*, Germany: Freischwimmer Film and Leftvision.

The Humane Society of the United Stetes, and Spencer Susser (2021), *Save Ralph—A Short Film with Taika Waititi*, YouTube, April 6, USA, Australia and UK: Arch Model Studio, Blue-Tongue Films, Humane Society International and Vespa Pictures, https://www.youtube.com/watch?v=G393z8s8nFY. Accessed July 23, 2024.

Hurwitz, Leo (1932), *Detroit Workers News Special 1932: Ford Massacre*, YouTube, USA: Workers Film and Photo League. https://www.youtube.com/watch?v=HFEskpjPbfE. Accessed July 23, 2024.

Indigenous Rising Media (2014–present), YouTube channel, https://www.youtube.com/c/IndigenousRising/. Accessed July 30, 2024.

Invisible Children, and Jason Russell (2012), *KONY 2012*, YouTube, March 5, https://tinyurl.com/46jxazkf. Accessed April 13, 2023.

Ivens, Joris (1937), *The Spanish Earth*, USA: Contemporary Historians Inc.

Jones, Owen (2015–present), YouTube channel, https://www.youtube.com/@owenjonestalks. Accessed July 31, 2024.

Kitchell, Mark (2012), *A Fierce Green Fire: The Battle for a Living Planet*, USA: Zoetrope Aubry Productions.

Kitidi, Katerina, and Aris Chatzistefanou (2011), *Debtocracy*, Greece: Creative Commons, YouTube, https://www.youtube.com/watch?v=qKpxPo-lInk. Accessed July 30, 2024.

Lebow, Alisa (2018), Website, www.filmingrevolution.org. Accessed May 1, 2022.

Leftvision (2017), *Welcome to Hell—Polizei zerschlägt G20-Demo in Hamburg 2017* ("Police Smashes G20 Demonstration in Hamburg, Germany 2017"), YouTube, n.d., https://bit.ly/3S31OcN. Accessed January 5, 2024.

Leftvision (2020), *Gefangen auf Lesbos (Reportage)*, YouTube, March 14, https://tinyurl.com/yc688mhw. Accessed April 13, 2023.

Leftvision (2020), *Prozessauftakt gegen den Attentäter von Halle—Zeugin und Nebenklägerin blickt kritisch zurück* ("Start of Trial Against the Halle Assassin: Witness and Joint Plaintiff Takes a Critical Look Back"), YouTube, July 21, https://tinyurl.com/4fjm7c8h. Accessed April 12, 2023.

Letzte Generation (2021–present), YouTube channel, https://www.youtube.com/channel/UCBeUnC1ky0b_Hwpjf9bA_qw. Accessed July 31, 2024.

Linke Sau (2018–present), YouTube channel, http://www.youtube.com/@linkesau7595. Accessed August 1, 2024.

LoveTapesCollective (2019), *L020A Sylvia Rivera, "Y'All Better Quiet Down", Original Authorized Video, 1973 Gay Pride Rally NYC*, YouTube, May 23, https://tinyurl.com/xvm22u6w. Accessed April 5, 2023.

Mesh Collective (2010–present), YouTube channel, https://www.youtube.com/c/meshcollective. Accessed July 31, 2024.

Minow, Hans-Rüdiger, and Thomas Giefer (1967), *Berlin, 2. Juni '67*, Germany: AStA der Freien Universität Berlin.

Navalny, Alexei (2021), *Putin's Palace: The Story of the World's Biggest Bribe*, YouTube, February 4, https://tinyurl.com/2vnvevke. Accessed April 5, 2023.

New Tactics (n.d.), Website, https://tmt.newtactics.org/. Accessed July 18, 2024.

Nexta TV (2015–present), YouTube channel, https://www.youtube.com/nexta_tv. Accessed July 31, 2024.

¡Ni Una Menos! (n.d.), Website, https://niunamenos.org.ar/. Accessed July 31, 2024.

Office of the President of Ukraine (2013–present), YouTube channel, https://www.youtube.com/@PresidentGovUa. Accessed April 26, 2023.

Olsson, Göran (2011), *The Black Power Mixtape 1967–1975*, Sweden: Louverture Films.

Orlowski, Jeff (2020), *The Social Dilemma*, USA: Agent Pictures.

Orta, Ramsey (2014), *Eric Garner Fatal Arrest Video*, New York Daily News Exclusive. [No longer retrievable online.]

Papo Reto (2013–present), YouTube channel, http://www.youtube.com/@paporeto2279. Accessed July 31, 2024.

Pataxó, Alice (2015–present), alice_pataxo. Instagram account. Accessed August 1, 2024.

Pataxó, Tukumã (2013–present), tukuma_pataxo. Instagram account. Accessed August 1, 2024.

Peng! Kollektiv (n.d.), Website, http://pen.gg/de/. Accessed July 30, 2022.

Peng! Kollektiv (2018), *Seebrücke des Bundes* ("Federal Sea Bridge"), Berlin: Peng! [See: *Seebrücke des Bundes Reup* (2019), YouTube, February 26, http://tinyurl.com/mr3d33eh. Accessed January 5, 2024.]

Perincioli, Cristina (1971), *Für Frauen: 1. Kapitel* ("For Women: Chapter 1"), Germany: Deutsche Film- und Fernsehakademie Berlin.

Perlman, Michael (2013), *Occupy Wall Street: We Are the 99%*, USA.

PETA Deutschland (2006–present), YouTube channel, https://www.youtube.com/user/peta-deutschland. Accessed July 31, 2024.

PhilosophyTube (2013–present), YouTube channel, http://www.youtube.com/@PhilosophyTube. Accessed August 1, 2024.

Piker, Hasan (n.d.), HasanAbi, Twitch channel, www.twitch.tv/hasanabi. Accessed August 1, 2024.

Politizane (2012), *Wealth Inequality in America*, YouTube, November 20, https://tinyurl.com/2p8a86dr. Accessed April 5, 2023.

Praunheim, Rosa von (1971), *Nicht der Homosexuelle ist pervers, sondern die Situation, in der er lebt* ("It Is Not the Homosexual Who Is Perverse, but the Society in Which He Lives"), Germany: Bavaria.

Pro Asyl (2011–present), YouTube channel, https://www.youtube.com/@proasylEU. Accessed July 31, 2024.

Radical Film Network (n.d.), Website, https://radicalfilmnetwork.com/. Accessed July 23, 2024.

ReelNews (2006–present), YouTube channel, https://www.youtube.com/@ReelNews. Accessed July 23, 2024.

refugee.tv (2015–present), YouTube channel, https://www.youtube.com/@refugeetv. Accessed July 31, 2024.

Reidemeister, Helga (1979), *Von wegen "Schicksal"* ("Is This Fate?"), Germany: Deutsche Film- und Fernsehakademie Berlin.

Renzo (2021a), *Zerstörung Teil 1: Inkompetenz*, YouTube, August 21, https://tinyurl.com/4f34am5c. Accessed June 4, 2023.

Renzo (2021b), *Zerstörung Teil 2: Klima-Katastrophe*, YouTube, September 4, https://tinyurl.com/ycpzfjhw. Accessed June 4, 2023.

Renzo (2021c), *Zerstörung FINALE: Korruption*, YouTube, September 18, https://tinyurl.com/b92wpxyp. Accessed June 4, 2023.

Rezo (@rezomusik) (2019), *Jo Leute, hab in den letzten Tagen sau viele Fragen bekommen und dachte, dass ich die aus meiner Sicht am häufigsten gestellten Themen hier mal kurz ansprechen und beantworten kann (Ein Thread)* ("Guys, [...] (a thread)"), X/Twitter May 29, https://tinyurl.com/y8ajyr7x. Accessed June 4, 2023.

Rezo ja lol ey (2019a), *Die Zerstörung der CDU* ("The Destruction of the CDU"), YouTube, May 18, https://tinyurl.com/y76tmz2u. Accessed April 13, 2023.

Rezo ja lol eye (2019b), *Ein Statement von 90+ YouTubern* ("Statement of 90+ YouTubers"), YouTube, May 24, https://tinyurl.com/2s3zphmp. Accessed June 4, 2023.

Rezo ja lol eye (2020), *Die Zerstörung der Presse* ("The Destruction of the Press"), YouTube, May 31, https://tinyurl.com/4pxvxupc. Accessed June 4, 2023.

RobBubble (2006–present), YouTube channel, http://www.youtube.com/@RobBubble. Accessed August 1, 2024.

Roca de Viñals, Jose Maria, Guillermo Santaisabel, Javier Urbaneja, Cristina Rodríguez, and Esteban Crespo (2015), *Hologramas por la Libertad* ("Holograms for Freedom"), No Somos Delito, YouTube channel, March 26, http://tinyurl.com/mpejcs6b. Accessed January 5, 2024.

Sander, Helke (1968), *Brecht die Macht der Manipulateure* ("Break the Manipulators' Power"), Germany: Deutsche Film- und Fernsehakademie Berlin (DFFB).

Sander, Helke (1978), *Die allseits reduzierte Persönlichkeit—Redupers* ("The All-Round Reduced Personality—Redupers"), Germany: Basis Filmverleih and Zweites Deutsches Fernsehen (ZDF).

San Francisco Newsreel (1967), *Black Panther a.k.a. Off the Pig (Newsreel #19)*, USA: Third World Newsreel.

Sasse, Elke (2016), *#My Escape/Meine Flucht*, Germany: Westdeutscher Rundfunk.

Save the Children (2006–present), YouTube channel, http://www.youtube.com/@savethechildrenuk. Accessed August 1, 2024.

Save the Children, and Martin Stirling (2014), *Most Shocking Second a Day Video*, YouTube, March 5, 2014, https://www.youtube.com/watch?v=RBQ-IoHfimQ. Accessed July 23, 2024.

Schneider, John B. (2018–present), X/Twitter account, JohnB_Schneider, https://twitter.com/JohnB_Schneider. Accessed July 17, 2024.

Shashenok, Valeria (n.d.), TikTok account, @valerisssh. Accessed August 1, 2024.

SITU Research (2011–present), Vimeo channel, https://vimeo.com/situnyc. Accessed July 31, 2024.

Solanas, Fernando E., and Octavio Getino (1968), *La Hora de las Hornos* ("The Hour of the Furnaces"), Argentina: Grupo Cine Liberacion and Solanas Productions.

Stokes, Edwin (2021), *Conversations: The Black Radical Tradition*, USA: self-produced.

Storck, Henri, and Ivens, Joris (1934), *Misère au Borinage* (Borinage), Belgium: self-produced.

Syrian Archive (n.d.), https://syrianarchive.org/. Accessed April 7, 2023.

Systemrelevant (2020-present), YouTube channel, http://www.youtube.com/@systemrelevant8233. Accessed August 1, 2024.

Tactical Tech (n.d.), Website, https://tacticaltech.org/. Accessed July 31, 2024.

Tagesschau (2019), *Zerstörung der CDU: YouTuber Rezo polarisiert mit viralem Video* ("Destruction of the CDU: YouTuber Rezo polarises with viral video"), YouTube, May 23, https://tinyurl.com/2exem7hj. Accessed April 5, 2023.

The Telegraph (2022), *Deep Fake Video of Volodymyr Zelenskiy Surrendering Surfaces on Social Media*, YouTube, March 17, https://tinyurl.com/2pf536xb. Accessed November 3, 2023.

Testing the Limits Collective (1988), *Testing the Limits: NYC*, USA: Testing the Limits Collective.

Three Arrows (2016–present), YouTube channel, http://www.youtube.com/@ThreeArrows. Accessed August 1, 2024.

TV Debout (2016), YouTube channel, http://www.youtube.com/@TVDeboutParis. Accessed July 31, 2024.

TV Fórum (2010–present), Youtube channel, http://www.youtube.com/@forumrevista. Accessed August 2, 2024.

Ulex Project (n.d.), Website, https://ulexproject.org. Accessed July 18, 2024.

Ushahidi (n.d.), Website, https://www.ushahidi.com/. Accessed July 31, 2024.

Vframe (n.d.), Website, https://vframe.io/. Accesssed July 31, 2024.

Video4Change (n.d.), Website, https://video4change.org/. Accessed July 23, 2024.

Videoccupy Türkiye (2013–14), YouTube channel, https://www.youtube.com/@videoccupy turkiye9204. Accesssed July 31, 2024.

Volksverpetzer (n.d.), Website, https://www.volksverpetzer.de/. Accessed August 1, 2024.

WikiLeaks (2010), *Collateral Murder, 5 Apr 2010*, 5 April, https://tinyurl.com/y2n56skv. Accessed April 6, 2023. Trigger warning: This video contains scenes with graphic violence.

WITNESS (n.d.), Website, https://www.witness.org/. Accessed July 23, 2024.

WITNESS Media Lab (n.d.), Website, https://lab.witness.org/. Accessed July 31, 2024.

Wölken, Tiemo (2019), *Reaktion auf Rezo/Tiemo Wölken*, YouTube, May 22, https://tinyurl.com/394br9jh. Accessed April 5, 2023.

Women's Film Group Munich (1975), *Wir haben lange geschwiegen* ("We Have Been Silent for a Long Time"), Germany: self-produced.

Workers Film & Photo League International (2018–present), YouTube channel, https://tinyurl.com/92hd94u2. Accessed April 6, 2023.

World Wildlife Fund Germany (2019), *Die Glyphosat-Vergiftung! Aber was ist Glyphosat? | WWF Deutschland* ("Intoxication by Glyphosate"), YouTube, December 5, 2017, https://www.youtube.com/watch?v=K1AOlp1Q950. Accessed July 23, 2024.

Wynn, Natalie (2011–present), ContraPoints, YouTube channel, https://www.youtube.com/user/contrapoints. Accessed July 23, 2024.

The Yes Men (n.d.), Website, https://theyesmen.org/#. Accessed July 30, 2024.

YouTube Advertisers (2017), *The High Diver | YouTube Advertisers*, YouTube, January 19, https://tinyurl.com/ystnv5s5. Accessed April 13, 2023.

Bibliography

Abbamonte, Lucia. "The 'Sustainable' Video-Narratives of Greenpeace—An Ecolinguistic Investigation." *Forum for Modern Language Studies* 57, no. 2 (2021): 145–85.

Adamson, Morgan. *Enduring Images: A Future History of New Left Cinema*. Minneapolis, MN and London: University of Minnesota Press, 2018.

Adorno, Theodor W. *Minima Moralia: Reflections on a Damaged Life*. New York and London: Verso, 2005.

Agde, Günter, and Alexander Schwarz, eds. *Die rote Traumfabrik: Meschrabpom-Film und Prometheus 1921–1936*. Berlin: Deutsche Kinemathek—Museum für Film und Fernsehen and Bertz + Fischer, 2012.

Agency France Press. "War-Themed Video Game Fuels Wave of Misinformation." *France24*, January 2, 2023, https://tinyurl.com/23bmepk2. Accessed November 3, 2023.

Aguayo, Angela J. *Documentary Resistance: Social Change and Participatory Media*. New York: Oxford University Press, 2019.

Akser, Murat, and Victoria McCollum, eds. *Alternative Media in Contemporary Turkey: Sustainability, Activism, and Resistance*. Lanham, MD: Rowman & Littlefield, 2018.

Alexander, Michelle. *The New Jim Crow: Mass Incarceration in the Age of Colourblindness*. London: Penguin, 2010.

Alexander, William. *Film on the Left: American Documentary Film from 1931 to 1942*. Princeton, NJ: Princeton University Press, 1981.

Alfter, Brigitte, Ralph Müller-Eiselt, and Matthias Spielkamp. "Introduction." In *Automating Society: Taking Stock of Automated Decision-Making in the EU*, edited by Matthias Spielkamp, 6–12. Berlin: AlgorithmWatch, 2019.

Allan, Stuart. *Citizen Witnessing: Revisioning Journalism in Times of Crisis, Key Concepts in Journalism*. Cambridge and Malden, MA: Polity, 2013.

Allgaier, Joachim. "Rezo and German Climate Change Policy: The Influence of Networked Expertise on YouTube and Beyond." *Media and Communication* 8, no. 2 (2020): 376–86.

Amnesty International. *Myanmar: The Social Atrocity: Meta and the Right to Remedy for the Rohingya*. Website of Amnesty International, 2022, https://www.amnesty.org/en/documents/ASA16/5933/2022/en/. Accessed November 3, 2023.

Andén-Papadopoulos, Kari. "Media Witnessing and the 'Crowd Sourced Video Revolution'." *Visual Communication* 12, no. 3 (2013): 341–57.

Andén-Papadopoulos, Kari. "Citizen Camera-Witnessing: Embodied Political Dissent in the Age of 'Mediated Mass Self-Communication'." *New Media & Society* 16, no. 5 (2014): 753–69.

Anders, Rayk. *Eure Dummheit kotzt mich an: Wie Bullshit unser Land vergiftet.* München: dtv, 2016.

Anders, Rayk. *Der Barbar in uns muss Liebe finden: Warum das Land verroht und wie wir uns wehren können.* München: dtv, 2021.

Andreasen, Alan R. "Marketing Social Marketing in the Social Change Marketplace." *Journal of Public Policy & Marketing* 21, no. 1 (2002): 3–13.

Animoto. "Easily Create Professional Videos" [online course], n.d. https://animoto.com/. Accessed April 12, 2023.

anlen, shirin, and Raquel Vazquez Llorente. "Using Generative AI for Human Rights Advocacy." WITNESS, June 28, 2023, https://tinyurl.com/27vmwh77. Accessed November 3, 2023.

Arendt, Hannah. *The Human Condition.* Chicago, IL: University of Chicago Press, 1958.

Arendt, Hannah. *On Revolution.* London: Penguin Books, 1963.

Arendt, Hannah. "Lying in Politics: Reflections on the Pentagon Papers." In *Crises of the Republic.* San Diego, CA, New York and London: Harcourt Brace & Company, 1972: 1–47.

Arkenbout, Chloë, Jack Wilson, and Daniel de Zeeuw, eds. *Critical Meme Reader: Global Mutations of the Viral Image.* Amsterdam: Institute of Network Cultures, 2021.

Arroyo Almaraz, Isidoro, Miguel Baños Gonzaléz, and Cliff Van-Wyck. "Analysis of the Campaign Videos Posted by the Third Sector on YouTube." *Revista Latina de Comunicación Social* 68 (2013): 328–54, https://doi.org/10.4185/RLCS-2013-980. Accessed September 11, 2023.

Askanius, Tina. *Radical Online Video: YouTube, Video Activism and Social Movement Media Practices.* Lund: Lund University, 2012.

Askanius, Tina. "Online Video Activism and Political Mash-Up Genres." *JOMEC Journal* 4 (2013), 1–17, https://tinyurl.com/2hwtm7ye. Accessed April 25, 2023.

Askanius, Tina. "Video as Text, Testimony, Technology—or Practices?" In *Citizen Media and Practice: Currents, Connections, Critiques*, edited by Hilde Stephansen and Emiliano Treré, 136–51. London: Routledge, 2019.

Aston, Judith, Sandra Gaudenzi, and Mandy Rose, eds. *i-Docs: The Evolving Practices of Interactive Documentary.* London and New York: Wallflower Press, 2017.

Atton, Chris, ed. *The Routledge Companion to Alternative and Community Media.* London: Routledge, 2015.

Auer, Stefan. "Carl Schmitt in the Kremlin: The Ukraine Crisis and the Return of Geopolitics." *International Affairs* 91, no. 5 (2015): 953–68.

Bach, Jonathan, and David Stark. "Link, Search, Interact: The Co-Evolution of NGOs and Interactive Technology." *Theory, Culture & Society* 21, no. 3 (2004): 101–07.

Baker, Al, J. David Goodman, and Benjamin Mueller. "Beyond the Chokehold: The Path to Eric Garner's Death." *The New York Times*, June 13, 2015, https://tinyurl.com/bdzx9z9b. Accessed October 2, 2023.

Baker, Mona, Bolette Blaagaard, Henry Jones, and Luis Pérez-González, eds. *The Routledge Encyclopedia of Citizen Media*. London: Routledge, 2021.

Barassi, Veronica. *Activism on the Web: Everyday Struggles against Digital Capitalism*. London: Routledge, 2015.

Barendregt, Bart, and Florian Schneider. "Digital Activism in Asia: Good, Bad, and Banal Politics Online." *Asiascape: Digital Asia* 7, no. 1&2 (2020): 5–19.

Barlow, John Perry. "A Declaration of the Independence of Cyberspace." *Electronic Frontier Foundation*, February 8, 1996, https://tinyurl.com/y8syj43j. Accessed April 21, 2023.

Barnouw, Erik. *Documentary: A History of the Non-Fiction Film*. 2nd rev. ed. New York and Oxford: Oxford University Press, [1974] 1993.

Bärtl, Mathias. "YouTube Channels, Uploads and Views: A Statistical Analysis of the Past 10 Years." *Convergence: The International Journal of Research Into New Media Technologies* 24, no. 1 (2018): 16–32.

Baú, Valentina. "What Killed Indymedia? Lessons from the IMC Experience of Australia." *Journal of Alternative & Community Media* 5, no. 2 (2020): 191–210.

Benjamin, Jack. "Misinformation Spreaders Surge on Twitter after Musk Takeover." *MediaLeader*, November 14, 2022, https://tinyurl.com/2vyhupp6. Accessed April 15, 2023.

Benkler, Yochai. *The Wealth of Networks: How Social Production Transforms Markets and Freedom*. New Haven, CT: Yale University Press, 2006.

Bennett, Bruce. "Becoming Refugees: Exodus and the Contemporary Meditations of the Refugee Crisis." *Transnational Cinemas* 9, no. 1 (2018): 13–30, https://doi.org/10.1080/20403526.2018.1471181. Accessed December 28, 2023.

Bennett, W. Lance. *Communicating the Future: Solutions for Environment, Economy and Democracy*. Cambridge and Malden, MA: Polity, 2020.

Bennett, W. Lance. "Killing the Golden Goose? A Framework for Regulating Disruptive Technologies." *Information, Communication & Society* 26, no. 1 (2021): 16–36.

Bennett, W. Lance, and Alexandra Segerberg. "The Logic of Connective Action: Digital Media and the Personalization of Contentious Politics." *Information, Communication & Society* 15, no. 5 (2012): 739–68.

Bennett, W. Lance, and Alexandra Segerberg. *The Logic of Connective Action: Digital Media and the Personalization of Contentious Politics*. Cambridge: Cambridge University Press, 2013.

Bennett, W. Lance, Alexandra Segerberg, and Yunkang Yang. "The Strength of Peripheral Networks: Negotiating Attention and Meaning in Complex Media Ecologies." *Journal of Communication* 68, no. 4 (2018): 659–84.

Bennett, W. Lance, and Barbara Pfetsch. "Rethinking Political Communication in a Time of Disrupted Public Spheres." *Journal of Communication* 68, no. 2 (2018): 243–53.

Berger, Jonah. *Contagious: Why Things Catch On*. New York: Simon & Schuster, 2013.

Beutelschmidt, Thomas. "Alternative Medienarbeit in Berlin—ein Überblick." In *Wer nicht produziert, lebt reduziert! Alternative Medienarbeit in Berlin West und Ost*, edited by Thomas Beutelschmidt and Kay Hoffmann, 21–30. Marburg: Schüren, 2018 (*Augenblick: Konstanzer Hefte zur Medienwissenschaft*, 72).

Beyerle, Mo, and Christine N. Brinckmann, eds. *Der amerikanische Dokumentarfilm der 60er Jahre: Direct Cinema und Radical Cinema*. Frankfurt a. M. and New York: Campus, 1991.

Biermann, Kai. "CSYou: CSU versucht eine Antwort auf Rezo." *Zeit Online*, September 1, 2019, https://tinyurl.com/ycxukfj4. Accessed April 5, 2023.

Boettger, Conny. "The Role of Photography in Greenpeace's Strategy. The Photograph as Witness." In *Greenpeace: Changing the World. The Photographic Record*, edited by Conny Boettger and Fouad Hamndan, 12–22. Steinfurt: Tecklenborg, 2001.

Boettger, Conny, and Fouad Hamndan. *Greenpeace: Changing the World. The Photographic Record*. Steinfurt: Tecklenborg, 2001.

Boichak, Olga. "Mapping the Russian Political Influence Ecosystem: The Night Wolves Biker Gang." *Social Media + Society* 9, no. 2 (2023), https://doi.org/10.1177/20563051231177920. Accessed April 13, 2023.

Borenstein, Eliot. *Meanwhile, in Russia ... Russian Internet Memes and Viral Video*. London: Bloomsbury Publishing, 2022.

Borum Chattoo, Caty. *Story Movements: How Documentaries Empower People and Inspire Social Change*. Oxford: Oxford University Press, 2020.

Borum Chattoo, Caty, and Will Jenkins. "From Reel Life to Real Social Change: The Role of Contemporary Social-Issue Documentary in U.S. Public Policy." *Media, Culture & Society* 41, no. 8 (2019): 1107–24.

Bösch, Marcus. "WARTOK—TikTok und der Krieg in der Ukraine." *Televizion* 35, no. 2 (2022): 4–7.

Bösch, Marcus. "Russian Disinformation." *Understanding TikTok*, July 3, 2023, https://tinyurl.com/2udjward. Accessed November 3, 2023.

Bösch, Marcus, and Chris Köver. *Schluss mit lustig? TikTok als Plattform für politische Kommunikation*. Berlin: Rosa-Luxemburg-Stiftung (*Studien*, 7), 2021, https://tinyurl.com/s4x7d78d(pdf). Accessed April 8, 2022.

boyd, danah. "Social Network Sites as Networked Publics: Affordances, Dynamics, and Implications." In *Networked Self: Identity, Community, and Culture on Social Network Sites*, edited by Zizi Papacharissi, 39–58. London and New York: Routledge, 2010.

boyd, danah. *It's Complicated: The Social Lives of Networked Teens*. New Haven, CT: Yale University Press, 2014.

Boyle, Deidre. "From Portapak to Camcorder: A Brief History of Guerilla Television." *Journal of Film and Video* 44, no. 1&2 (1992): 67–79.

Boyle, Deidre. *Subject to Change: Guerrilla Television Revisited*. New York: Oxford University Press, 1997.

Brecht, Bertolt. "The Radio as an Apparatus of Communication." [German 1932]. In *New Media: Theories and Practices of Digitextuality*, edited by Anna Everett and John T. Caldwell, 29–32. New York and London: Routledge, 2003.

Briese, Andreas, and Sabine Frank. "YouTube Rewind: Das sind die erfolgreichsten Videos des Jahres." *YouTube Official Blog*, December 5, 2019, https://tinyurl.com/5x6u567x. Accessed April 5, 2023.

Brown, Michael Harold, and John May. *The Greenpeace Story*. London: Dorling Kindersley, 1989.

Browne, Malachy. "YouTube Removes Videos Showing Atrocities in Syria." *The New York Times*, August 22, 2017, https://www.nytimes.com/2017/08/22/world/middleeast/syria-youtube-videos-isis.html. Accessed December 28, 2023.

Bruns, Axel, Gunn Enli, Eli Skogerbo, Anders Larsson, and Christian Christensen. *The Routledge Companion to Social Media and Politics*. London: Routledge, 2016.

Burgess, Jean, Anne Galloway, and Theresa Sauter. "Hashtag as Hybrid Forum: The Case of #agchatoz." In *Hashtag Publics: The Power and Politics of Discursive Networks*, edited by Nathan Rambukkana, 61–76. Digital Formations, New York: Peter Lang, 2015.

Butler, Judith. *Precarious Life: The Politics of Mourning and Violence*. New York and London: Verso, 2004.

Butler, Judith. *Notes Toward a Performative Theory of Assembly*. Cambridge, MA and London: Harvard University Press, 2015.

Casilli, Antonio A. "Never Mind the Algorithms: The Role of Click Farms and Exploited Digital Labor in Trump's Election." November 20, 2016, https://www.casilli.fr/2016/11/20/never-mind-the-algorithms-the-role-of-exploited-digital-labor-and-global-click-farms-in-trumps-election/. Accessed April 10, 2023.

Castells, Manuel. *Networks of Outrage and Hope: Social Movements in the Internet Age*. Cambridge and Malden, MA: Polity, 2012.

Castells, Manuel. *Communication Power*, 2nd ed. Oxford and New York: Oxford University Press, 2013.

Celikates, Robin. "Digital Publics, Digital Contestation: A New Structural Transformation of the Public Sphere?" In *Transformations of Democracy: Crisis, Protest and Legitimation*, edited by Robin Celikates, Regina Kreide, and Tilo Wesche, 159–76. London: Rowman & Littlefield, 2015.

De Certeau, Michel. *The Practice of Everyday Life*. Translated by S. Rendall. Berkeley, CA: University of California Press, 1988.

Cervi, Laura, and Tom Divon. "Playful Activism: Memetic Performances of Palestinian Resistance in TikTok #challenges." *Social Media and Society* 9, no. 1 (2023): 1–13.

Chadwick, Andrew. *The Hybrid Media System: Politics and Power*. Oxford and New York: Oxford University Press, 2013.

Chanan, Michael. *The Politics of Documentary*. London: British Film Institute, 2007.

Chartier, Denis. "Greenpeace." In *Dictionnaire de la pensée écologique*, edited by Dominique Bourg and Alain Papaux, 501–04. Paris: PUF, 2015.

Chayka, Kyle. "Watching the World's 'First TikTok War'." *The New Yorker*, March 3, 2022, https://tinyurl.com/248hfwjx. Accessed September 21, 2023.

Chouliaraki, Lilie. "Ordinary Witnessing in Post-Television News: Towards a New Moral Imagination." *Critical Discourse Studies* 7, no. 4 (2010): 305–19, http://eprints.lse.ac.uk/29740/. Accessed December 28, 2023.

Chouliaraki, Lilie. "Digital Witnessing in Conflict Zones: The Politics of Remediation." *Information, Communication & Society* 18, no. 11 (2015): 1362–77.

Citton, Yves. *The Ecology of Attention*. Cambridge and Malden, MA: Polity, 2017.

Clayton, James. "TikTok CEO Shou Zi Chew's Congress Showdown: Five Takeaways." *BBC News*, March 24, 2023, https://tinyurl.com/528pxkj8. Accessed May 11, 2023.

Coleman, Gabriella. *Hacker, Hoaxer, Whistleblower, Spy: The Many Faces of Anonymous*. New York and London: Verso, 2014.

Constine, Josh. "Facebook Hits 8 Billion Daily Video Views, Doubling from 4 Billion in April." *TechCrunch*, November 4, 2015, https://tinyurl.com/56y3shep. Accessed April 6, 2023.

Contreras, Brian, and Marisa Martinez. "Fed Up with TikTok, Black Creators Are Moving On." *Los Angeles Times*, September 16, 2021, https://tinyurl.com/5cah8ahj. Accessed April 24, 2023.

Cooney, Nick. *Change of Heart: What Psychology Can Teach Us About Spreading Social Change*. New York: Lantern Books, 2011.

Couldry, Nick. *Media, Society, World: Social Theory and Digital Media Practice*. Cambridge, MA: Polity Press, 2012.

Couldry, Nick, and Ulises A. Mejias. *The Costs of Connection. How Data Is Colonizing Human Life and Appropriating It for Capitalism*. Stanford, CA: Stanford University Press, 2019.

Crawford, Kate. "Can an Algorithm Be Agnostic? Ten Scenes from Life in Calculated Publics." *Science, Technology, & Human Values* 41, no. 1 (2016): 77–92.

Curtis, Polly, and Tom McCarthy. "*KONY 2012*: What's the Real Story?" *The Guardian*, March 8, 2012, https://tinyurl.com/2hu2emea. Accessed April 13, 2021.

Dahlgren, Peter. "The Internet, Public Spheres, and Political Communication: Dispersion and Deliberation." *Political Communication* 22, no. 2 (2005): 147–62, https://doi.org/10.1080/10584600590933160.

Daniels, Cheyanne M. "Here's What Changed Since George Floyd's Murder Three Years Ago." *The Hill*, May 25, 2023, https://tinyurl.com/3k5rpdc4. Accessed September 27, 2023.

Dawson, Paul. "Hashtag Narrative: Emergent Storytelling and Affective Publics in the Digital Age." *International Journal of Cultural Studies* 23, no. 6 (2020): 968–83.

Dawson, Paul, and Maria Mäkelä. "The Story Logic of Social Media: Co-construction and Emergent Narrative Authority." *Style* 54, no. 1 (2020): 21–35.

Dean, Jonathan. "From Solidarity to Self-promotion? Neoliberalism and Left Politics in the Age of the Social Media Influencer." *Capital & Class* (2023): 1–23, https://doi.org/10.1177/03098168231199907. Accessed December 2, 2023.

Dee, Juliet, ed. *From Tahrir Square to Ferguson: Social Networks as Facilitators of Social Movements*. New York: Peter Lang, 2018.

de Gregorio, Giovanni, and Catalina Goanta. "The Influencer Republic: Monetizing Political Speech on Social Media." *German Law Journal* 23, no. 2 (2022): 204–25.

Della Porta, Donatella. "Repertoires of Contention." In *The Wiley-Blackwell Encyclopedia of Social and Political Movements*, edited by David A. Snow, Donatella Della Porta, Dough McAdam, and Bert Klandermans. Hoboken, NJ: Wiley-Blackwell, 2013.

Della Porta, Donatella, and Alice Mattoni, eds. *Spreading Protest: Social Movements in Times of Crisis*. Colchester: ECPR Press, 2014.

Della Porta, Donatella, and Mario Diani, eds. *The Oxford Handbook of Social Movements*. Oxford: Oxford University Press, 2014.

Dellar, Hugh. "Day 411 of the War." *VK.com*, April 11, 2023, https://vk.com/wall438426825_9634. Accessed November 3, 2023.

Della Ratta, Donatella. *Shooting a Revolution: Visual Media and Warfare in Syria*. London: Pluto Press, 2018.

Dellert, Louisa. *Mein Herz schlägt grün: Weltverbessern für Anfänger—Herzblut statt moralischer Zeigefinger*. München: Komplett Media, 2018.

Dellert, Louisa. *WIR: Weil nicht egal sein darf, was morgen ist*. München: Komplett Media, 2021.

DeLuca, Kevin Michael. *Image Politics: The New Rhetoric of Environmental Activism*. New York and London: Routledge, [1999] 2005.

DeLuca, Kevin Michael. "Greenpeace International Media Analyst Reflects on Communicating Climate Change [Interview with Soenke Lorenzen, Greenpeace International]." *Environmental Communication* 3, no. 2 (2009): 263–9.

Denisova, Anastasia. *Internet Memes and Society: Social, Cultural, and Political Contexts*. London: Routledge, 2019.

Dennis, James. *Beyond Slacktivism: Political Participation on Social Media*. Basingstoke: Palgrave Macmillan, 2019.

Derrida, Jacques. *Spectres of Marx*. New York and London: Routledge, 1994.

Dietze, Gabriele. "Sich ein eigenes Bild machen: Selbstbestimmtheit in Filmen von Frauen in den 1960er- bis 1990er-Jahren." In *Selbstbestimmt: Perspektiven von Filmemacherinnen*, edited by Karin Herbst-Meßlinger and Rainer Rother, 17–45. Bonn: Bundeszentrale für politische Bildung, 2019.

van Dijck, José. *The Culture of Connectivity: A Critical History of Social Media*. Oxford: Oxford University Press, 2013.

van Dijck, José, and Thomas Poell. "Understanding Social Media Logic." *Media and Communication* 1, no. 1 (2013): 2–14.

van Dijck, José, Thomas Poell, and Martijn de Waal. *The Platform Society: Public Values in a Connective World.* Oxford and New York: Oxford University Press, 2018.

Dixson-Declève, Sandrine, Owen Gaffney, Jayati Ghosh, Jorgen Randers, Johan Rockström, and Per Espen Stoknes. *Earth for All: A Survival Guide for Humanity.* Gabriola, BC: New Society Publishers, 2022.

Doc Society. *The Impact Field Guide & Toolkit* (Website), 2019, www.impactguide.org. Accessed April 25, 2023.

Doll, Martin. *Fälschung und Fake: Zur diskurskritischen Dimension des Täuschens*, Berlin: Kadmos, 2012.

Don't Panic. *Save the Children: Most Shocking Second a Day* (Website), (n.d.), https://tinyurl.com/bdz9u5xn. Accessed April 5, 2023.

Dörr, Nicole, and Simon Teune. "The Imagery of Power Facing the Power of Imagery: Toward a Visual Analysis of Social Movements." In *The Establishment Responds: Power, Politics, and Protest since 1945*, edited by Kathrin Fahlenbrach, Martin Klimke, Joachim Scharloth, and Laura Wong, 43–55. New York: Palgrave Macmillan, 2012.

Dorsch, Timo. "Die Seebrücke nach Deutschland." *Frankfurter Rundschau*, January 4, 2019, https://www.fr.de/politik/seebruecke-nach-deutschland-10967122.html. Accessed September 21, 2023.

Dovey, Jon, and Mandy Rose. "This Great Mapping of Ourselves: New Documentary Forms Online." In *The Documentary Film Book*, edited by Brian Winston, 366–75. London: Palgrave Macmillan, 2013.

Doyle, Julie. "Picturing the Clima(c)tic: Greenpeace and the Representational Politics of Climate Change Communication." *Science as Culture* 16, no. 2 (2007): 129–50.

Doyle, Julie. *Mediating Climate Change.* Surrey: Ashgate, 2011.

Duvan, Carrie. "18 Strategien für erfolgreiche Social Media Videos bei Facebook, Twitter, Instagram und LinkedIn." *filmpuls*, March 21, 2023, https://tinyurl.com/46v54v8c. Accessed April 12, 2023.

Dyer-Witheford, Nick, and Svitlana Matviyenko. *Cyberwar and Revolution: Digital Subterfuge in Global Capitalism.* Minneapolis, MN: University of Minnesota Press, 2019.

Earl, Jennifer, Thomas V. Maher, and Jennifer Pan. "The Digital Repression of Social Movements, Protest, and Activism: A Synthetic Review." *Science Advances* 8, no. 10 (2022): 1–15, https://www.science.org/doi/10.1126/sciadv.abl8198. Accessed April 1, 2023.

Edel, Anastasia. "A Day Inside Putin's Surreal Television Empire." *Foreign Policy*, May 28, 2022, https://tinyurl.com/yvua7cdc. Accessed November 3, 2023.

Eder, Jens. "Collateral Emotions: Political Web Videos and Divergent Audience Responses." In *Cognitive Theory and Documentary Film*, edited by Catalin Brylla and Mette Kramer, 183–203. London: Palgrave Macmillan, 2018.

Eder, Jens. "Rechte Videos und Affekte in Sozialen Medien." In *Zwischen Feindsetzung und Selbstviktimisierung: Gefühlspolitik und Ästhetik populistischer Kommunikation*, edited by Lars Koch and Torsten König, 177–202. Frankfurt a. M.: Campus, 2020.

Eder, Jens. "Political Impact—On the Societal Vibrancy of Film." In *What Film Is Good For: On the Values of Spectatorship*, edited by Julian Hanich and Martin P. Rossouw, 102–14. Berkeley, CA: University of California Press, 2023.

Eder, Jens, and Charlotte Klonk. "Introduction." In *Image Operations: Visual Media and Political Conflict*, edited by Jens Eder and Charlotte Klonk, 1–22. Manchester: Manchester University Press, 2017.

Einspänner-Pflock, Jessica. *Privatheit im Netz: Konstruktions- und Gestaltungsstrategien von Online-Privatheit bei Jugendlichen*. Wiesbaden: Springer VS, 2016.

Elemia, Camille, and Gelo Gonzalez. "Stars, Influencers Get Paid to Boost Duterte Propaganda, Fake News." *Rappler*, February 27, 2021, https://tinyurl.com/ynms3kc3. Accessed April 8, 2023.

von Engelhardt, Johannes, and Jeroen Jansz. "Challenging Humanitarian Communication: An Empirical Exploration of *KONY 2012*." *International Communication Gazette* 76, no. 6 (2014): 464–84.

Entman, Robert M. "Framing: Toward Clarification of a Fractured Paradigm." *Journal of Communication* 43, no. 4 (1993): 51–58.

Eskjær, Mikkel Fugl, Stig Hjarvard, and Mette Mortensen, eds. *The Dynamics of Mediatized Conflicts*. New York: Peter Lang, 2015.

Evon, Dan. "With Gates Wide Open." *Snopes*, November 17, 2015, https://tinyurl.com/2vzcb-njp. Accessed February 21, 2020.

Fahlenbrach, Kathrin. "Video-Aktivismus: Formen und Strategien der audiovisuellen Mobilisierung im Netz." *Forschungsjournal Soziale Bewegungen* 33, no. 2 (2020): 457–73.

Farocki, Harun. "Die Agitation verwissenschaftlichen und die Wissenschaft politisieren." *Film* 3 (1969): 49–52.

Feng, Emily. "Zelenskiyy Has Consolidated Ukraine's TV Outlets and Dissolved Rival Political Parties." *npr*, July 8, 2022, https://tinyurl.com/3c9yps63. Accessed September 21, 2023.

Fenton, Natalie. *Digital, Political, Radical*. Cambridge: Polity, 2016.

Feurich, Jörg Peter. "Gespräch mit Harun Farocki und Hartmut Bitomsky." *Filmkritik* 8 (1970): 420–25.

Fielitz, Maik, and Laura Lotte Laloire, eds. *Trouble on the Far-Right: Contemporary Right-Wing Strategies and Practices in Europe*. Bielefeld: Transcript, 2016.

Fielitz, Maik, and Nick Thurston, eds. *Post-Digital Cultures of the Far Right: Online Actions and Offline Consequences in Europe and the US*. Bielefeld: Transcript, 2019.

Fisher, Ian. "Kelly Bans Choke Holds by Officers." *The New York Times*, November 24, 1993, https://tinyurl.com/yc6452s5. Accessed October 2, 2023.

Ford, Sam, Joshua Green, and Henry Jenkins. *Spreadable Media: Creating Value and Meaning in a Networked Culture*. New York: New York University Press, 2013.

Forestal, Jennifer. *Designing for Democracy: How to Build Community in Digital Environments*. Oxford: Oxford University Press, 2023.

Frank, Lauren B., and Paul Falzone, eds. *Entertainment-Education Behind the Scenes: Case Studies for Theory and Practice*. Cham: Palgrave Macmillan, 2021.

Fraser, Nancy. "Rethinking the Public Sphere: A Contribution to the Critique of Actually Existing Democracy." *Social Text* 25&26 (1990): 56–80.

Fraser, Nancy. "Neue Überlegungen zur Öffentlichkeit: Ein Beitrag zur Kritik der real existierenden Demokratie." In *Die halbierte Gerechtigkeit: Schlüsselbegriffe des postindustriellen Sozialismus*, translated by Karin Wördemann, 107–50. Frankfurt a. M.: Suhrkamp, 2001.

Fricker, Miranda. *Epistemic Injustice: Power and the Ethics of Knowing*. Oxford: Oxford University Press, 2007.

Fuchs, Christian. *OccupyMedia! The Occupy Movement and Social Media in Crisis Capitalism*. Winchester: John Hunt Publishing, 2014.

Fuchs, Christian. *Soziale Medien und Kritische Theorie. Eine Einführung*. 2nd ed. Stuttgart: UTB, 2021a.

Fuchs, Christian. "The Digital Commons and the Digital Public Sphere: How to Advance Digital Democracy Today." *Westminster Papers in Communication and Culture* 16, no. 1 (2021b): 9–26, https://doi.org/10.16997/wpcc.917. Accessed December 28, 2023.

Fuchs, Christian, and Klaus Unterberger, eds. *The Public Service Media and Public Service Internet Manifesto*. London: University of Westminster Press, 2021.

Fuller, Matthew, and Eyal Weizman. *Investigative Aesthetics: Conflicts and Commons in the Politics of Truth*. New York and London: Verso, 2021.

Funk, Allie, Adrian Shahbaz, and Kian Vesteinsson. "Freedom on the Net 2023: The Repressive Power of Artificial Intelligence." *Freedom House*, November 21, 2023, https://tinyurl.com/2ektra4y. Accessed November 29, 2023.

Galloway, Alexander R., and Eugene Thacker. *The Exploit: A Theory of Networks*. Minneapolis, MN and London: University of Minnesota Press, 2007.

Georgakopoulou, Alexandra. *Small Stories, Interaction and Identities*. Amsterdam: John Benjamins Publishing, 2007.

Gerbaudo, Paolo. *Tweets and the Streets: Social Media and Contemporary Activism*. London: Pluto Press, 2012.

Gerhardt, Christina, and Sara Saljoughi, eds. *1968 and Global Cinema*. Detroit, MI: Wayne State University Press, 2018.

Ghosh, Bishnupriya. *Global Icons: Apertures to the Popular*. Durham, NC: Duke University Press, 2011.

Gilbert, David. "Russian TikTok Influencers Are Being Paid to Spread Kremlin Propaganda." *Vice*, March 11, 2022, https://tinyurl.com/23m4zp2z. Accessed October 31, 2023.

Gilbert, Nestor. "64 Facebook Video Statistics You Can't Ignore: 2023 Data Analysis & Market Share." *FinancesOnline*, March 15, 2023, https://tinyurl.com/mpmnhn6p. Accessed April 6, 2023.

Gillespie, Tarleton. *Custodians of the Internet: Platforms, Content Moderation, and the Hidden Decisions That Shape Social Media*. New Haven, CT and London: Yale University Press, 2018.

Giraud, Eva. "Has Radical Participatory Online Media Really 'Failed'? Indymedia and Its Legacies." *Convergence: The International Journal of Research into New Media Technologies* 20, no. 4 (2014): 419–37.

Gladwell, Malcolm. "Small Change: Why the Revolution Will Not Be Tweeted." *The New Yorker*, October 4 (2010): 42–29.

Glazunova, Sofya. *Digital Activism in Russia: The Communication Tactics of Political Outsiders*. London: Palgrave Macmillan, 2022.

Götz, Norbert. "Reframing NGOs: The Identity of an International Relations Non-starter." *European Journal of International Relations* 14, no. 2 (2008): 231–58.

Gould, Deborah. *Moving Politics: Emotion and ACT UP's Fight against AIDS*. Chicago, IL and London: University of Chicago Press, 2009.

Grant, Paul Douglas. *Cinéma Militant: Political Filmmaking and May 1968*. London: Wallflower Press, 2016.

Gray, Jonathan. "Data Witnessing: Attending to Injustice with Data in Amnesty International's Decoders Project." *Information, Communication & Society* 22, no. 7 (2019): 971–91.

Greenpeace Deutschland. "Greenpeace-Jahresbericht 2020." July 15, 2021, https://www.greenpeace.de/publikationen/greenpeace-jahresbericht-2020-1. Accessed September 9, 2023.

Gregory, Sam. "Deepfakes, Misinformation and Disinformation and Authenticity Infrastructure Responses: Impacts on Frontline Witnessing, Distant Witnessing, and Civic Journalism." *Journalism* 23, no. 3 (2022): 708–29.

Gregory, Sam. "Testimony of Sam Gregory, Executive Director, WITNESS before the U.S. Senate Committee on Commerce, Science and Transportation, Subcommittee on Consumer Protection, Product Safety and Data Security. Date of Hearing: September 12, 2023. The Need for Transparency in Artificial Intelligence" (pdf), 2023, https://tinyurl.com/yckx7fd5. Accessed November 29, 2023.

Gritsenko, Daria, Mariëlle Wijermars, and Mikhail Kopotev, eds. *The Palgrave Handbook of Digital Russia Studies*. Cham: Palgrave Macmillan, 2021.

Habermas, Jürgen. *Vorstudien und Ergänzungen zur Theorie des kommunikativen Handelns*. Frankfurt a. M.: Suhrkamp, 1984.

Habermas, Jürgen. *The Structural Transformation of the Public Sphere: An Inquiry Into a Category of Bourgeois Society*. Translated by Thomas Burger. Cambridge, MA: MIT Press, [German 1962] 1991.

Habermas, Jürgen. "Further Reflections on the Public Sphere." In *Habermas and the Public Sphere*, edited by Craig Calhoun. Cambridge, MA and London: MIT Press, 1992.

Habermas, Jürgen. "Reflections and Hypotheses on a Further Structural Transformation of the Political Public Sphere." *Theory, Culture & Society* 39, no. 4 (2022): 145–71.

Habermas, Jürgen. *A New Structural Transformation of the Public Sphere and Deliberative Politics*. Cambridge and Malden, MA: Polity, 2023.

Habermas, Jürgen, Sigmar Gabriel, and Emmanuel Macron. "Europa neu denken." *Blätter* 17, no. 4 (2017): 41–54.

Hamblin, Sarah, and Ryan Watson. "Introduction: Radical Documentary Today." *Studies in Documentary Film* 13, no. 3 (2019): 187–95.

Hankey, Stephanie. "The Influence Industry: The Global Business of Using Your Data in Elections." *TacticalTech* (Website), April 20, 2018, https://tinyurl.com/526tx99w. Accessed April 10, 2023.

Happen Films. "About Happen Films." (n.d.), https://happenfilms.com/about. Accessed April 5, 2023.

Harcup, Tony, and Deirdre O'Neill. "What Is News? News Values Revisited (Again)." *Journalism Studies* 18, no. 12 (2017): 1470–88.

Harding, Thomas. *The Video Activist Handbook*, 2nd ed. London: Pluto Press, [1997] 2001.

Harrild, Lucie. "Lessons from the Palm Oil Showdown." *The Guardian*, October 27, 2010, http://tinyurl.com/2przsm3u. Accessed August 4, 2023.

Harris, Brandon C., Maxwell Foxman, and William C. Partin. "'Don't Make Me Ratio You Again': How Political Influencers Encourage Platformed Political Participation." *Social Media + Society* 9, no. 2 (2023), https://doi.org/10.1177/20563051231177944. Accessed December 29, 2023.

Hartley, John. "Silly Citizenship." *Critical Discourse Studies* 7, no. 4 (2010): 233–48.

Harwell, Drew. "The Gory Online Campaign Ukraine Hopes Will Sow Anti-Putin Dissent Probably Violates the Geneva Conventions." *The Washington Post*, March 3, 2022, https://www.washingtonpost.com/technology/2022/03/03/telegram-russian-war-dead-ukraine-pows/. Accessed April 26, 2023.

Herman, Edward S., and Noam Chomsky. *Manufacturing Consent: The Political Economy of the Mass Media*. New York: Random House, 1988.

Hern, Alex. "Revealed: How TikTok Censors Videos That Do Not Please Beijing." *The Guardian*, September 25, 2019, https://tinyurl.com/3vnptakv. Accessed April 10, 2023.

Herrmann, Boris. "WhatsApp im Wahlkampf: Brasilien, Land der bestellten Lügen." *Süddeutsche Zeitung*, October 23, 2018, https://tinyurl.com/f72m2kny. Accessed April 10, 2023.

Hesling, Willem. "Documentary Film and Rhetorical Analysis." In *Image—Reality—Spectator: Essays on Documentary Film and Television*, edited by Willem de Greef and Willem Hesling, 101–31. Leuven: Acco, 1989.

Highfield, Tim. *Social Media and Everyday Politics*. Cambridge and Malden, MA: Polity Press, 2016.

Highfield, Tim, and Tama Leaver. "Instagrammatics and Digital Methods: Studying Visual Social Media, from Selfies and GIFS to Memes and Emoji." *Communication Research and Practice* 2, no. 1 (2016): 47–62.

Himelboim, Itai, Marc A. Smith, Lee Rainie, Ben Shneiderman, and Camila Espina Young. "Classifying Twitter Topic-Networks Using Social Network Analysis." *Social Media + Society* 3, no. 1 (2017): 1–13, https://tinyurl.com/yn82yrse. Accessed June 3, 2023.

Hoffmann, Kay. "Die Technik verändert den Dokumentarfilm: Neue Formen durch synchrone 16 mm und Video-Kameras." In *Protest—Film—Bewegung: Neue Wege im Dokumentarischen*, edited by Kay Hoffmann, Erika Wottrich, Ursula von Keitz, and Thomas Weber, 38–51, München: Edition Text + Kritik, 2015.

Hoffmann, Kay. "Die Aufnahmetechnik prägt das Dokumentarische." In *Wer nicht produziert, lebt reduziert! Alternative Medienarbeit in Berlin West und Ost*, edited by Thomas

Beutelschmidt and Kay Hoffmann, 9–20. Marburg: Schüren, 2018 (=*Augenblick. Konstanzer Hefte zur Medienwissenschaft*, 72).

Hofmann, Martin Ludwig. *Mindbombs. Was Werbung und PR von Greenpeace & Co. lernen können*. München: Fink, 2008.

Hogenkamp, Bert. "The Radical Tradition in Documentary Film-Making, 1920s–50s." In *The Documentary Film Book*, edited by Brian Winston, 173–79. London: British Film Institute, 2013.

Holmlund, Chris, and Cynthia Fuchs, eds. *Between the Sheets, in the Streets: Queer, Lesbian, and Gay Documentary*. Minneapolis, MN: University of Minnesota Press, 1999.

Hund, Emily. *The Influencer Industry: The Quest for Authenticity on Social Media*. Princeton, NJ and Oxford: Princeton University Press, 2023.

Hunter, Bobbi, ed. *Mr. Mind Bomb: Eco-hero and Greenpeace Co-founder Bob Hunter—A Life in Stories*. Surrey, British Columbia: Rocky Mountain Books, 2023.

InfluenceMap. *Big Oil's Real Agenda on Climate Change: An InfluenceMap Report*, 2019, www.bit.ly/3exO7Nc. Accessed April 24, 2023.

The Influence Industry Project. *The Influence Industry Explorer* (Website), (n.d.), https://influenceindustry.org/en/explorer/. Accessed April 15, 2023.

Jackson, Sarah J., Moya Bailey, and Brooke Foucault Welles. *#HashtagActivism: Networks of Race and Gender Justice*. Cambridge, MA: MIT Press, 2020.

Jasper, James. *The Emotions of Protest*. Chicago, IL: The University of Chicago Press, 2018.

Jendrzejewski, Sophia, and Celine Strufe. *Don't Shoot the Messenger! Telegram als Instrument für linken Aktivismus*. Berlin: Rosa-Luxemburg-Stiftung (=*Studien*, 3), 2022, https://tinyurl.com/tdxz92ve. Accessed April 12, 2023.

Jenkins, Henry. "If It Doesn't Spread, It's Dead (Part One): Media Viruses and Memes." *Pop Junctions* (Website), February 11, 2009, www.bit.ly/2RV2MZc. Accessed April 12, 2023.

Jenkins, Henry, Sangita Shresthova, Liana Gamber-Thompson, Neta Kligler-Vilenchik, and Arely M. Zimmerman, eds. *By Any Media Necessary: The New Youth Activism, Connected Youth and Digital Futures*. New York: NYU Press, 2016a.

Jenkins, Henry, Sangita Shrestova, Liana Gamber-Thompson, and Neta Kligler-Vilenchik. "Superpowers to the People! How Young Activists are Tapping the Civic Imagination." In *Civic Media: Technology, Design, Practice*, edited by Eric Gordon and Paul Milhailidis, 295–320. Cambridge, MA: MIT Press, 2016b.

Johnson, Lauren. "Save the Children Spot Gets Another Run on YouTube Thanks to Ashton Kutcher." *Adweek*, November 12, 2014, https://tinyurl.com/5n6smc6j. Accessed April 12, 2023.

Johnston, Hank, and John A. Noakes, eds. *Frames of Protest: Social Movements and the Framing Perspective*. Lanham, MD: Rowman & Littlefield, 2005.

de Jong, Wilma, Martin Shaw, and Neil Stammer, eds. *Global Activism, Global Media*, London and Ann Arbor, MI: Pluto Press, 2005.

Juhasz, Alexandra. *AIDS TV: Identity, Community, and Alternative Video*. Durham, NC: Duke University Press, 1995.

Juhola, Sirkku, Tatiana Filatova, Stefan Hochrainer-Stigler, Reinhard Mechler, Jürgen Scheffran, and Pia-Johanna Schweizer. "Social Tipping Points and Adaptation Limits in the Context of Systemic Risk: Concepts, Models and Governance." *Frontiers in Climate* 4, September 21 (2022): 1009234, https://doi.org/10.3389/fclim.2022.1009234. Accessed December 30, 2023.

Kaap, Henry. "'I Can't Breathe!'—Polizeigewalt und anti-rassistischer Protest in den USA." *Kritische Berichte* 44, no. 1 (2016): 86–95.

Kácha, Ondřej, Jáchym Vintr, and Cameron Brick. "Four Europes: Climate Change Beliefs and Attitudes Predict Behavior and Policy Preferences Using a Latent Class Analysis on 23 countries." *Journal of Environmental Psychology* 81 (2022): 1–10, https://tinyurl.com/49sw3bp9. Accessed April 25, 2023.

Kahne, Joseph, and Benjamin Bowyer. "The Political Significance of Social Media Activity and Social Networks." *Political Communication* 35, no. 3 (2018): 470–93.

Kaiser, Jonas, and Adrian Rauchfleisch. "How the Right Takes Advantage of YouTube." *Encore: Magazine on Internet and Society* (2018): 34–45, https://www.hiig.de/encore/[pdf]. Accessed April 1, 2023.

Kaltseis, Magdalena. "Russisches YouTube." *Dekoder [Russland und Belarus entschlüsseln]*, April 6, 2023, https://tinyurl.com/mpt7vr7v. Accessed November 3, 2023.

Kant, Immanuel. "An Answer to the Question: What Is Enlightenment?" In *Practical Philosophy. The Cambridge Edition of the Works of Immanuel Kant*, edited by Mary J. Gregor, 11–22. Cambridge, UK and New York: Cambridge University Press, 1999.

Kantar TNS / Die Medienanstalten. *Gewichtungsstudie zur Relevanz der Medien für die Meinungsbildung in Deutschland: MedienGewichtungsStudie 2018 I Juli 2018*, 2018, https://tinyurl.com/32vn6a43. Accessed April 19, 2023.

Kara, Selmin. "Rebels Without Regret: Documentary Artivism in the Digital Age." *Studies in Documentary Film* 9, no.1 (2015): 42–54.

Kara, Selmin, and Camilla Møhring Reestorff. "Introduction: Unruly Documentary Artivism." *Studies in Documentary Film* 9, no. 1 (2015): 1–9.

Katz-Kimchi, Merav, and Idit Manosevitch. "Mobilizing Facebook Users Against Facebook's Energy Policy: The Case of Greenpeace Unfriend Coal Campaign." *Environmental Communication* 9, no. 2 (2015): 248–67.

Kavada, Anastasia. "Engagement, Bonding, and Identity across Multiple Platforms: Avaaz on Facebook, YouTube, and MySpace." *MedieKultur: Journal of Media and Communication Research* 52 (2012): 28–48, https://tidsskrift.dk/index.php/mediekultur/article/view/5486. Accessed August 8, 2023.

Kavada, Anastasia, Tina Askanius, Anne Kaun, Alice Mattoni, and Julie Udam. *Tying up Goliath: Activist Strategies for Confronting and Harnessing Digital Power*. Transnational Institute (TNI), February 14, 2023, https://www.tni.org/en/article/tying-up-goliath. Accessed December 29, 2023.

Kaye, D. Bondy Valdovinos, Jing Zeng, and Patrik Wikstrom. *TikTok: Creativity and Culture in Short Video*. Cambridge: Polity Press, 2022.

Kaye, D. Bondy Valdovinos, Xu Chen, and Jing Zeng. "The Co-evolution of Two Chinese Mobile Short Video Apps: Parallel Platformization of Douyin and TikTok." *Mobile Media & Communication* 9, no. 2 (2020): 229–53, https://doi.org/10.1177/2050157920952120. Accessed December 29, 2023.

Keenan, Thomas. "Counter-forensics and Photography." *Grey Room* 55 (2014): 58–77.

Kempkes, Sebastian. "Plastikmüll: Der Schrott und sein zweites Leben." *Die Zeit*, November 22 (2019).

Khan-Cullors, Patrisse, and asha bandele. *When They Call You a Terrorist: A Black Lives Matter Memoir*. Edinburgh: Canongate Books, 2018.

Kidd, Dorothy. "Indymedia." In *The Routledge Encyclopedia of Citizen Media*, edited by Mona Baker, Bolette B. Blaagaard, Henry Jones, and Luis Pérez-González, 215–20. London and New York: Routledge, 2021.

Kirchgaessner, Stephanie, Manisha Ganguly, David Pegg, Carole Cadwalladr, and Jason Burke. "Revealed: The Hacking and Disinformation Team Meddling in Elections." *The Guardian*, February 15, 2023, https://tinyurl.com/yc326xxp. Accessed April 13, 2023.

Kleinfeld, Philip. "Calling Bullshit on the Anti-refugee Video Taking the Internet by Storm." *Vice*, November 27, 2015, https://tinyurl.com/k2cwand3. Accessed April 12, 2023.

Koch, Svenja. "Greenpeace: Medienpräsent und spektakulär—ist das nachhaltig?" In *Handbuch Nachhaltigkeitskommunikation: Grundlagen und Praxis*, edited by Gerd Michelsen and Jasmin Godemann, 2nd ed., 902–07. München: Oekom, 2007.

Koch, Svenja. "Umweltkampagnen mit Herz und Verstand: Strategien der Greenpeace-Kommunikation." In *PR-Kampagnen: Über die Inszenierung von Öffentlichkeit*, edited by Ulrike Röttger, 109–15. Wiesbaden: VS-Verlag für Sozialwissenschaften, 2009.

Koc-Michalska, Karolina, Ulrike Klinger, Lance Bennett, and Andrea Römmele. "(Digital) Campaigning in Dissonant Public Spheres." *Political Communication* 40, no. 3 (2023): 255–62.

Koetsier, John. "Here are the 10 Most Downloaded Apps of 2020." *Forbes*, January 7, 2021, https://tinyurl.com/ymb2ex7j. Accessed April 15, 2023.

Köhler, Andreas. "Die Einflussnahme von NGOs auf den politischen Prozess: Lobbying als Kommunikationsinstrument." In *Handbuch NGO Kommunikation*, edited by Nadine Remus and Lars Rademacher, 147–62. Wiesbaden: Springer VS, 2018.

Köhler, Margret, ed. *Alternative Medienarbeit: Videogruppen in der Bundesrepublik*. Opladen: Leske & Budrich, 1980.

Kozinets, Robert. *Netnography*. London: Sage, 2020.

Kozinets, Robert V., Kristine de Valck, Andrea C. Wojnicki, and Sarah J. S. Wilner. "Networked Narratives: Understanding Word-of-Mouth Marketing in Online Communities." *Journal of Marketing* 74, no. 2 (2010): 71–89.

Krebber, Felix, Christian Biederstadt, and Ansgar Zerfaß. "Digitaler Lobbyismus? Die politische Kommunikation von Greenpeace Deutschland im Internet." In *Strategische Onlinekommunikation: Theoretische Konzepte und empirische Befunde*, edited by Olaf Hoffjann and Thomas Pleil, 291–310. Wiesbaden: Springer, 2015.

Kuo, Lily. "TikTok 'Makeup Tutorial' Goes Viral with Call to Action on China's Treatment of Uighurs." *The Guardian*, November 27, 2019, https://bit.ly/3NIImQ5. Accessed December 29, 2023.

Kurz, Bettina, and Doreen Kubek [on behalf of PHINEO]. *Social Impact Navigator. The Practical Guide for Organizations Targeting Better Results*, 2021, www.social-impact-navigator.org/. Accessed April 24, 2023.

Lancaster, Kurt. *Video Journalism for the Web: A Practical Introduction to Documentary Storytelling*. New York and London: Routledge, 2012.

Lang, Sabine. *NGOs, Civil Society, and the Public Sphere*. New York: Cambridge University Press, 2013.

Lang, Sabine. "Nongovernmental Organizations." In *The International Encyclopedia of Political Communication (Volume 2. Int-Pol)*, edited by Gianpietro Mazzoleni, 877–82. Hoboken, NJ: John Wiley & Sons, 2015.

Lasn, Kalle. *Culture Jam*. New York: Quill, 2000.

Lave, Jean, and Etienne Wenger. *Situated Learning: Legitimate Peripheral Participation*, Cambridge: Cambridge University Press, 1991.

Laville, Sandra. "Top Oil Firms Spending Millions Lobbying to Block Climate Change Policies, Says Report." *The Guardian*, March 22, 2019, www.bit.ly/2VKbIlj; https://www.theguardian.com/business/2019/mar/22/top-oil-firms-spending-millions-lobbying-to-block-climate-change-policies-says-repor. Accessed April 21, 2023.

Learning for Action. *Deepening Engagement for Lasting Impact: A Framework for Measuring Media Performance & Results*, 2013, www.bit.ly/2yutAbS. Accessed April 21, 2023.

Lebow, Alisa. *Filming Revolution* (Website), 2018, www.filmingrevolution.org. Accessed April 26, 2023.

Lefebvre, Henri, ed. "The Right to the City." In *Writings on Cities*, edited and translated by Eleonore Kofman and Elizabeth Lebas, 147–59. Oxford: Blackwell Publishers, [French 1968] 1996.

Lessenich, Stephan. *Grenzen der Demokratie: Teilhabe als Verteilungsproblem*. Stuttgart: Reclam, 2019.

Levin, Sam. "Did Russia Fake Black Activism on Facebook to Sow Division in the US?" *The Guardian*, September 30, 2017, https://tinyurl.com/43kjdj2j. Accessed October 2, 2023.

Lewis, Rebecca. "Alternative Influence: Broadcasting the Reactionary Right on YouTube." *Analysis & Policy Observatory (APO)*, September 18, 2018, https://apo.org.au/node/193281. Accessed October 20, 2024.

Libin, Xie, and Haig Patapan. "Schmitt Fever: The Use and Abuse of Carl Schmitt in Contemporary China." *International Journal of Constitutional Law* 18, no. 1 (2020): 130–46.

Liedtke, Marius, and Daniel Marwecki. *Von Influencer*innen lernen: YouTube & Co. als Spielfelder linker Politik und Bildungsarbeit*. Berlin: Rosa-Luxemburg-Stiftung (=Studien, 7), 2019, https://tinyurl.com/23hbumj9[pdf]. Accessed April 10, 2023.

Lindquist, Johan. "Illicit Economies of the Internet: Click Farming in Indonesia and Beyond." *Made in China Journal*, January 12, 2019, https://tinyurl.com/2p993fyj. Accessed April 10, 2023.

Lippert, Leopold. "Performance Labor, Im/Mobility, and Exhaustion in Nature Theater of Oklahoma's *Life and Times*." *Journal of Contemporary Drama in English* 5, no. 1 (2017): 140–55.

Literat, Ioana, and Neta Kligler-Vilenchik. "TikTok as a Key Platform for Youth Political Expression: Reflecting on the Opportunities and Stakes Involved." *Social Media + Society* 9, no. 1 (2023), https://tinyurl.com/25synu47. Accessed April 25, 2023.

Lovink, Geert. *Dark Fiber: Tracking Critical Internet Culture*. Cambridge, MA: MIT Press, 2002.

Maier, Tanja. *Visueller Aktivismus mit Instagram: Politische Kommunikation in sozialen Medien*. Berlin: Rosa-Luxemburg-Stiftung (=*Studien*, 10), 2021, https://tinyurl.com/42a7w9hk. Accessed April 12, 2023.

Makhortykh, Mykola, and Mariella Bastian. "Personalizing the War: Perspectives for the Adoption of News Recommendation Algorithms in the Media Coverage of the Conflict in Eastern Ukraine." *Media, War & Conflict* 15, no. 1 (2022): 25–45.

Malkowski, Jennifer. *Dying in Full Detail: Mortality and Digital Documentary*. Durham and London: Duke University Press, 2017.

Mateos, Concha, and Carmen Gaona. "Video Activism: A Descriptive Typology." *Global Media Journal*, Special Issue: "Use of Social media and Mediacoverage" (2015): 1–15, https://tinyurl.com/ynh9t9j6. Accessed April 18, 2023.

Matsa, Katerina Eva, Laura Silver, Elisa Shearer, and Mason Walker. "Western Europeans under 30 View News Media Less Positively, Rely More on Digital Platforms than Older Adults." *Pew Research Center*, October 30, 2018, https://tinyurl.com/me79t6bd. Accessed April 7, 2023.

McGarry, Aidan, Itir Erhart, Hande Eslen-Ziya, Olu Jenzen, and Umut Korkut. *The Aesthetics of Global Protest: Visual Culture and Communication, Protest and Social Movements*. Amsterdam: Amsterdam University Press, 2020.

McLagan, Meg, and Yates McKee, eds. *Sensible Politics: The Visual Culture of Nongovernmental Politics*. Princeton, NJ: Princeton University Press, 2012.

McLuhan, Marshall. *The Gutenberg Galaxy: The Making of Typographic Man*. Toronto: University of Toronto Press, 1962.

McQuater, Katie. "Anatomy of an Ad: Behind the Scenes of Save the Children's *Second a Day* Syria Ad." *The Drum*, April 7, 2014, https://tinyurl.com/4kdd2cwc. Accessed April 12, 2023.

Meeker, Mary (on behalf of BOND). *Internet Trends 2019* (Website), 2019, https://www.bond-cap.com/report/it19/. Accessed December 14, 2023.

Mehrabov, Ilkin. *Video Activism in Turkey: Empowerment of Oppressed or Another Kind of Surveillance? The Curious Case of Karahaber*. Saarbrücken: VDM, 2010.

Mehrabov, Ilkin. "When States Strike Back: Failures of Mediatized Activism in Azerbaijan and Turkey." *tripleC* 14, no. 2 (2016): 496–515.

Melchior, Moritz, and Manuel Rivera. *Klimagerechtigkeit erzählen: Narrative, Wertbezüge und Frames bei Extinction Rebellion, Ende Gelände und Fridays for Future*. Potsdam: Institute for Advanced Sustainability Studies (IASS), 2021, https://tinyurl.com/bdcm3ekx. Accessed May 22, 2023.

Metag, Julia, Tobias Füchslin, and Mike S. Schäfer. "Global Warming's Five Germanys: A Typology of Germans' Views on Climate Change and Patterns of Media Use and Information." *Public Understanding of Science* 26, no. 4 (2017): 434–51.

Meyer, David S. "Protest and Political Opportunities." *Annual Review of Sociology* 30 (2004): 125–45.

Milmo, Dan. "TikTok Users in Russia Can See Only Old Russian-made Content." *The Guardian*, March 10, 2022, https://tinyurl.com/5n839rd9. Accessed November 3, 2023.

Milmo, Dan, and Pjotr Sauer. "Deepfakes v Pre-bunking: Is Russia Losing the Infowar?" *The Guardian*, March 19, 2022, https://tinyurl.com/4c2vktaf. Accessed November 3, 2023.

Milne, Elizabeth-Jane, Claudia Mitchell, and Naydene de Lange, eds. *Handbook of Participatory Video*. Lanham and Plymouth: Rowman & Littlefield, 2012.

Mitchell, Mary. "Where Voice and Listening Meet: Participation in and Through Interactive Documentary in Peru." *Glocal Times* 22&23 (September 2015): 1–13, https://ojs.mau.se/index.php/glocaltimes/article/view/248. Accessed December 29, 2023

Mobile Marketing Association (MMA). "From a Blink to a Heartbeat." 2019, https://www.mmaglobal.com/documents/blink-heartbeat. Accessed April 12, 2023.

Moody-Ramirez, Mia, and Hazel Cole. "Victim Blaming in Twitter Users' Framing of Eric Garner and Michael Brown." *Journal of Black Studies* 49, no. 4 (2018): 383–407.

Morgan, Michael, James Shanahan, and Nancy Signorielli. "Cultivation Theory in the Twenty-First Century." In *The Handbook of Media and Mass Communication Theory*, edited by Robert S. Fortner and P. Mark Fackler, 480–97. Chichester: John Wiley, 2014.

Morozov, Evgeny. *The Net Delusion: The Dark Side of Internet Freedom*. New York and Philadelphia, PA: Public Affairs, 2011.

Mortensen, Mette. "Connective Witnessing: Reconfiguring the Relationship Between the Individual and the Collective." *Information, Communication & Society* 18, no. 11 (2015): 1393–406.

Moser, Susanne C. "Communicating Climate Change: History, Challenges, Process and Future Directions." *Wiley Interdisciplinary Reviews: Climate Change* 1, no. 1 (2010): 31–53.

Mouffe, Chantal. *Über das Politische: Wider die kosmopolitische Illusion*. Frankfurt a. M.: Suhrkamp, 2007.

Nagel, Laura. *Tales of Doom, Tales of Opportunity: How Climate Communication Can Help to Overcome Psychological Barriers to Sustainable Action*. Potsdam: Institute for Advanced Sustainability Studies (IASS), 2021, https://tinyurl.com/bdkfb934. Accessed May 22, 2023.

Napoli, Philip M. *Social Media and the Public Interest: Media Regulation in the Disinformation Age*. New York: Columbia University Press, 2019.

Nash, Kate. *Interactive Documentary: Theory and Debate*. London and New York: Routledge, 2022.

Nash, Kate, and John Corner. "Strategic Impact Documentary: Contexts of Production and Social Intervention." *European Journal of Communication* 31, no. 3 (2016): 227–42.

Negt, Oskar, and Alexander Kluge. *Public Sphere and Experience: Towards an Analysis of the Bourgeois and Proletarian Public Sphere*. Minneapolis, MN and London: University of Minnesota Press, 1993.

Neumayer, Christina. "Activism." In *The Routledge Encyclopedia of Citizen Media*, edited by Mona Baker, Bolette B. Blaagaard, Henry Jones, and Luis Pérez-González, 1–6. London and New York: Routledge, 2021.

Neumayer, Christina, and Jakob Svensson. "Activism and Radical Politics in the Digital Age: Towards a Typology." *Convergence* 22, no. 2 (2016): 131–14, https://doi.org/10.1177/1354856514553395. Accessed December 29, 2023.

Nichols, Bill. *Newsreel: Documentary Filmmaking on the American Left, 1969–1974*. New York: Ayer Co. Pub, 1980.

Nichols, Bill. "The Voice of Documentary." *Film Quarterly* 36, no. 3 (1983): 17–30.

Nichols, Bill. *Representing Reality: Issues and Concepts in Documentary*. Bloomington, IN: Indiana University Press, 1991.

Nichols, Bill. *Engaging Cinema: An Introduction to Film Studies*. New York: W. W. Norton & Company, 2010.

Nigg, Heinz, ed. *Rebel Video: Die Videobewegung der 1970er- und 1980er-Jahre*. London, Bern, Lausanne, Basel and Zürich: Scheidegger & Spiess, 2017.

Nix, Naomi. "Meta to Begin Fresh Layoffs, Cutting Heavily Among Business Staff." *The Washington Post*, May 23, 2023, https://tinyurl.com/mwusbj5v. Accessed November 29, 2023.

Noelle-Neumann, Elisabeth. *The Spiral of Silence: Public Opinion, Our Social Skin*. Chicago, IL and London: University of Chicago Press, [German 1984] 1993.

Noelle-Neumann, Elisabeth. *Die Schweigespirale: Öffentliche Meinung—unsere soziale Haut*. München: Langen Müller, [German 1980] 2001.

Notley, Tanya, Sam Gregory, and Andrew Lowenthal. "Video for Change: Creating and Measuring Ethical Impact." *Journal of Human Rights Practice* 9, no. 2 (2017): 223–46.

Nunes, Rodrigo. *The Organisation of the Organisationless: Collective Action After Networks*. London: Mute, 2014.

Nussbaum, Martha. *Political Emotions: Why Love Matters for Justice*. Cambridge, MA and London: Harvard University Press, 2013.

Nymoen, Ole, and Wolfgang M. Schmitt. *Influencer: Die Ideologie der Werbekörper*. Berlin: Suhrkamp, 2021.

Ollis, Tracey. "The 'Accidental Activist': Learning, Embodiment and Action." *Australian Journal of Adult Learning* 48, no. 2 (2008): 316–35.

Ong, Jonathan Corpus, and Jason Vincent A. Cabañes. *Architects of Network Disinformation: Behind the Scenes of Troll Accounts and Fake News Production in the Philippines*. UMass Amherst: Communication Department Faculty Publication Series, 2018, https://doi.org/10.7275/2cq4-5396. Accessed April 24, 2023.

O'Reilly, Tim. "What is Web 2.0: Design Patterns and Business Models for the Next Generation of Software." *O'Reilly* (Website), September 30, 2005, https://tinyurl.com/3s93rk6m. Accessed May 22, 2023.

Oreskes, Naomi, and Erik M. Conway. *Merchants of Doubt: How a Handful of Scientists Obscured the Truth on Issues from Tobacco Smoke to Global Warming*. London: Bloomsbury Publishing, 2011.

Otto, Isabell. *TikTok. Ästhetik, Ökonomie und Mikropolitik überraschender Transformationen*. Berlin: Wagenbach, 2023.

Page, Ruth E. *Stories and Social Media: Identities and Interaction*. London: Routledge, 2013.

Papacharissi, Zizi. *Affective Publics: Sentiment, Technology, and Politics*. Oxford: Oxford University Press, 2014.

Papacharissi, Zizi. "Affective Publics and Structures of Storytelling: Sentiment, Events and Mediality." *Information, Communication & Society*, 19, no. 3 (2015): 307–24.

Pariser, Eli. *The Filter Bubble: What the Internet Is Hiding from You*. London: Viking, 2011.

Park, Minsu, Naaman, Mor, and Jonah Berger. "A Data-Driven Study of View Duration on YouTube." *Proceedings of the 10th International Conference on Web and Social Media* 10, no. 1 (2016): 1–4, https://tinyurl.com/559jrsna. Accessed April 12, 2023.

Pasquale, Frank. "The Automated Public Sphere." In *The Politics and Policies of Big Data: Big Data, Big Brother?*, edited by Ann Rudinow Sætnan, Ingrid Schneider, and Nicola Green, 110–28. London and New York: Routledge, 2018.

Perez, Christian, and Anjana Nair. "Information Warfare in Russia's War in Ukraine." *Foreign Policy*, March 1, 2022, https://tinyurl.com/3938zteb. Accessed November 3, 2023.

Piketty, Thomas. *Capital in the Twenty-First Century*. Cambridge, MA and London: Harvard University Press, 2014.

Piketty, Thomas. *Capital and Ideology*. Cambridge, MA and London: Harvard University Press, 2020.

da Ponte, Alexander Campos. "Ship Carrying Nuclear Waste Harried by Greenpeace Boats." Video Activism (Website), March 14, 2018, https://videoactivism.net/en/greenpeace-nuclear-waste/. Accessed September 11, 2023.

Pörksen, Bernhard. *Die große Gereiztheit: Wege aus der kollektiven Erregung*. Munich: Carl Hanser, 2018.

Pörksen, Bernhard. *Digital Fever: Taming the Big Businesses of Misinformation*. London: Palgrave Macmillan, 2022.

Presence, Steve. "Reel News in the Digital Age: Framing Britain's Radical Video-Activists." In *The Routledge Companion to Cinema and Politics*, edited by Yannis Tzioumakis and Claire Mulloy, 103–11. Abingdon: Routledge, 2016.

Presence, Steve, Mike Wayne, and Jack Newsinger. *Contemporary Radical Film Culture: Networks, Organisations and Activists*. London: Routledge, 2021.

Rabinowitz, Paula. *They Must Be Represented: The Politics of Documentary*. London and New York: Verso, 1994.

Rainie, Lee. "Mapping Twitter Topic Networks: From Polarized Crowds to Community Clusters." *Pew Research Center*, February 20, 2014, https://www.pewresearch.org/internet/2014/02/20/mapping-twitter-topic-networks-from-polarized-crowds-to-community-clusters/. Accessed June 3, 2023.

Raley, Rita. *Tactical Media*. Minneapolis, MN: University of Minnesota Press, 2009.

Rambukkana, Nathan, ed. *Hashtag Publics: The Power and Politics of Discursive Networks*. New York: Peter Lang, 2015.

Raworth, Kate. *Doughnut Economics: Seven Ways to Think Like a 21st-Century Economist*. New York: Random House, 2017.

Reilly, Paul. "Sousveillance." In *The Routledge Encyclopedia of Citizen Media*, edited by Mona Baker, Bolette B. Blaagaard, Henry Jones, and Luis Pérez-González, 390–04. London and New York: Routledge, 2021.

Reinsborough, Patrick, and Doyle Canning. *Re:Imagining Change: How to Use Story-Based Strategy to Win Campaigns, Build Movements, and Change the World*. Birmingham, NY: PM Press, [2010] 2017.

Reporters Without Borders. "2022 World Press Freedom Index." 2022, https://rsf.org/en/index. Accessed April 26, 2023.

Reporters Without Borders. "Press Freedom in Europe Overshadowed by the War in Ukraine." 2023, https://rsf.org/en/classement/2023/europe-central-asia. Accessed November 3, 2023.

Rettinger, Carl-Ludwig. *Lieber Video in der Hand als Film im Kopf*. Berlin: Chamisso, 1980.

Reuter, Markus, and Chris Köver. "Cheerfulness and Censorship." *Netzpolitik*, November 23, 2019, https://tinyurl.com/ya93bywm. Accessed April 8, 2023.

Ribeiro, Manuel Horta, Raphael Ottoni, Robert West, Virgilio A. F. Almeida, and Wagner Meira Jr. "Auditing Radicalization Pathways on YouTube." In *FAT* '20: Conference on Fairness, Accountability, and Transparency*, edited by Mireille Hildebrandt, Carlos Castillo, Elisa Celis, Salvatore Ruggieri, Linnet Taylor, and Gabriela Zanfir-Fortuna, 131–41. New York: ACM, 2020.

Richardson, Alissa V. *Bearing Witness While Black: African Americans, Smartphones, and the New Protest #Journalism*. New York: Oxford University Press, 2020.

Riedl, Martin J., Josephine Lukito, and Samuel C. Woolley. "Political Influencers on Social Media: An Introduction." *Social Media + Society* 9, no. 2 (2023), https://doi.org/10.1177/20563051231177798. Accessed December 29, 2023.

Ristovska, Sandra. "Strategic Witnessing in an Age of Video Activism." *Media, Culture & Society* 38, no. 7 (2016): 1034–47.

Ristovska, Sandra. *Seeing Human Rights: Video Activism as a Proxy Profession*. Cambridge, MA: MIT Press, 2021.

Robé, Chris. *Breaking the Spell: A History of Anarchist Filmmakers, Videotape Guerillas, and Digital Ninjas*. Oakland, CA: PM Press, 2017.

Robé, Chris. *Abolishing Surveillance: Digital Media Activism and State Repression*. Birmingham, NY: PM Press, 2023.

Robé, Chris, and Stephen Charbonneau, eds. *InsUrgent Media from the Front: A Media Activism Reader*. Bloomington, IN: Indiana University Press, 2020.

Robertson, Alexa. *Media and Politics in a Globalizing World*. Cambridge: Polity, 2015.

Rocha, Glauber. "The Aesthetics of Hunger." In *Twenty-Five Years of the New Latin American Cinema*, edited by Michael Chanan, 13–14. London: BFI, [Portuguese 1965] 1983.

Roosvall, Anna, and Matthew Tegelberg. "Introduction to Climate Justice Communication." In *Research Handbook on Communicating Climate Change*, edited by David C. Holmes and Lucy M. Richardson, 291–92. Cheltenham: Edward Elgar Publishing, 2020.

Rotich, Juliane. "Ushahidi: Empowering Citizens Through Crowdsourcing and Digital Data Collection." *Field Actions Science Reports*, Special Issue: "Smart Cities at the Crossroads" 16 (2017): 36–38.

Roudé, Catherine. *Le cinéma militant à l'heure des collectifs: Slon et Iskra dans la France de l'après-1968*. Rennes: Presses Universitaire de Rennes, 2017.

Rucht, Dieter. "The Quadruple 'A': Media Strategies of Protest Movements Since the 1960s." In *Cyberprotest: New Media, Citizens and Social Movements*, edited by Wim van de Donk, Brian Loader, Paul G. Nixon, and Dieter Rucht, 25–48. London and New York: Routledge, 2004.

Ryan-Mosley, Tate. "This Huge Chinese Company Is Selling Video Surveillance Systems to Iran." *MIT Technology Review*, December 15, 2021, https://tinyurl.com/mstuyehe. Accessed November 3, 2023.

Sachs, Jonah. *Winning the Story Wars: Why Those Who Tell (and Live) the Best Stories Will Rule the Future*. Boston, MA: Harvard Business Review Press, 2012.

Sadler, Neil. *Fragmented Narrative: Telling and Interpreting Stories in the Twitter Age*. London and New York: Routledge, 2022.

Sandvine. *The Global Internet Phenomena Report January 2023*, Reporters Without Borders, 2023, https://www.sandvine.com/global-internet-phenomena-report-2023. Accessed November 21, 2023.

Sasse, Sylvia. "Der 'forensische' Blick." *Geschichte der Gegenwart*, June 5, 2022, https://tinyurl.com/3vx89sxs. Accessed November 3, 2023.

Sato, Mia. "Ukrainian Influencers Bring the Frontline to TikTok." *The Verge*, March 16, 2022, https://tinyurl.com/3xtbrxss. Accessed November 3, 2023.

Sauter, Molly. *The Coming Swarm: DDOS Actions, Hacktivism, and Civil Disobedience on the Internet*. London: Bloomsbury Publishing, 2014.

Schäfer, Mike S. "Digital Public Sphere." In *The International Encyclopedia of Political Communication*, edited by Gianpietro Mazzoleni, 322–28. Hoboken, NJ: John Wiley & Sons, 2016, https://doi.org/10.1002/9781118541555.wbiepc087. Accessed December 29, 2023.

Schankweiler, Kerstin. *Bildproteste*. Berlin: Wagenbach, 2019.

Schankweiler, Kerstin, Verena Straub, and Tobias Wendl, eds. *Image Testimonies: Witnessing in Times of Social Media*. London and New York: Routledge, 2019.

Schicha, Christian. "Kommunikationsstrategien von Greenpeace: Eventmanagement zwischen dramatisierender Symbolik und konstruktivem Engagement." *Zeitschrift für Kommunikationsökologie* 1 (2001): 22–26.

Schmitt, Wolfgang M. "Werden Influencer jetzt politisch?" *Der Freitag*, August 28, 2021, https://tinyurl.com/ycxbbz6m. Accessed September 19, 2023.

Schneider, Jonas. "Die 10 stärksten NGOs in Social Media." *PR Report* 6 (2019): 38–45.

Schwenkenbecher, Anne. "How We Fail to Know: Group-Based Ignorance and Collective Epistemic Obligations." *Political Studies* 70, no. 4 (2021): 901–18, https://tinyurl.com/yk52nx8n. Accessed May 22, 2023.

Scott, Martin, Kate Wright, and Mel Bunce. *The State of Humanitarian Journalism*. Norwich: University of East Anglia, 2018, https://tinyurl.com/yckt5wt5. Accessed April 16, 2023.

Searls, Doc. "The Splinternet." *Doc Searls Weblog*, December 16, 2008, https://tinyurl.com/yzyy3zp6. Accessed April 10, 2023.

Sehl, Annika, and Jonas Schützeneder. "Political Knowledge to Go: An Analysis of Selected Political Influencers and Their Formats in the Context of the 2021 German Federal Election." *Social Media + Society* 9, no. 2 (2023), https://doi.org/10.1177/20563051231177916. Accessed December 29, 2023.

Sennet, Richard. *The Fall of Public Man*. New York: Alfred A. Knopf, 1977.

Sharon, Assaf. "Solidarity Without Sentimentality." *Raisons politiques* 77, no. 2 (2018): 97–116.

Shestopalova, Alona, Anna Litvinenko, Magdalena Kaltseis, and Tatiana Golova. "FAQ #9: Propaganda in Russland—Wie und warum funktioniert sie?" *Dekoder*, March 23, 2023, https://tinyurl.com/3djubz94. Accessed November 3, 2023.

Shifman, Limor. *Memes in Digital Culture*. Cambridge, MA: MIT Press, 2014.

The Shift Project. *Climate Crisis: The Unsustainable Use of Online Video: Our New Report on the Environmental Impact of ICT*, July 11, 2019, https://tinyurl.com/5n7u4ud8. Accessed June 30, 2023.

The Shift Project. *Did The Shift Project Really Overestimate the Carbon Footprint of Online Video? Our Analysis of the IEA and Carbonbrief Articles*, June 15, 2020, https://theshiftproject.org/en/article/shift-project-really-overestimate-carbon-footprint-video-analysis/. Accessed June 29, 2023.

Shirky, Clay. "The Political Power of Social Media: Technology, the Public Sphere, and Political Change." *Foreign Affairs* 90, no. 1 (2011): 28–41.

Shresthova, Sangita. "2. 'Watch 30 Minute Video on Internet, Become Social Activist'? *KONY 2012*, Invisible Children, and the Paradoxes of Participatory Politics." In *By Any Media Necessary: The New Youth Activism*, edited by Henry Jenkins, Sangita Shresthova, Liana Gamber-Thompson, Neta Kligler-Vilenchik, and Arely M. Zimmerman, 61–101. New York: New York University Press, 2016.

Singhal, Arvind, and M. Rogers Everett. "A Theoretical Agenda for Entertainment-Education." *Communication Theory* 12, no. 2 (2002): 117–35.

Smith, Marc. "6 Kinds of Twitter Social Media Network Structures." *Social Media Research Foundation*, March 2, 2014, https://tinyurl.com/2p8vpeax. Accessed April 5, 2023.

SMK. "[STUDY] Facebook Video Watch Time: 4.57 seconds on Average." *SMK* (Website), March 2, 2020, https://tinyurl.com/5h7y6j2p. Accessed April 12, 2023.

Snow, David A., Rens Vliegenhart, and Pauline Ketelaars. "The Framing Perspective on Social Movements: It's Conceptual Roots and Architecture." In *The Wiley Blackwell Companion to Social Movements*, edited by David A. Snow, Sarah A. Soule, Hanspeter Kriesi, and H. J. McCammon, 392–410. Oxford: Wiley-Blackwell, 2019.

Socialbakers. *Social Media Trends Report Q4 2019*, 2019, https://tinyurl.com/2ps6tf3u.pdf. Accessed May 15, 2023.

Social Media & Politics. "#140: Social Media and the War in Ukraine, with Prof. Joshua Tucker." Lund University, April 7, 2022, https://socialmediaandpolitics.org/social-media-ukraine-war-russia-disinformation-putin-zelensky-politics-podcast/. Accessed November 3, 2023.

Solanas, Fernando E., and Octavio Getino. "Towards a Third Cinema." In *Movies and Methods*, edited by Bill Nichols, 44–64. Berkeley, CA and Los Angeles, CA: University of California Press, [Spanish 1969] 1976.

Sorg, Christoph. *Social Movements and the Politics of Debt: Transnational Resistance Against Debt on Three Continents*. Amsterdam: Amsterdam University Press, 2022.

Spier, Shaked. *Collective Action 2.0: The Impact of Social Media on Collective Action*. Cambridge, MA and Kidlington: Chandos Publishing, 2017.

Spivak, Gayatri Chakravorty. "Can the Subaltern Speak?" In *Marxism and the Interpretation of Culture*, 271–313, edited by Cary Nelson and Lawrence Grossberg. Chicago, IL: University of Illinois Press, 1988.

Squires, Catherine R. "Rethinking the Black Public Sphere: An Alternative Vocabulary for Multiple Public Spheres." *Communication Theory* 12, no. 4 (2002): 446–68.

Srnicek, Nick. *Platform Capitalism*. Cambridge and Malden, MA: Polity, 2016.

Srnicek, Nick. "The Challenges of Platform Capitalism: Understanding the Logic of a New Business Model." *Progressive Review* 23, no. 4 (2017): 254–7.

Stahl, Lesley. "How Does YouTube Handle the Site's Misinformation, Conspiracy Theories and Hate?" *CBS News*, December 1, 2019, https://tinyurl.com/5ckmrkr4. Accessed April 5, 2023.

Stalder, Felix. *The Digital Condition*. Translated by V. A. Pakis. Cambridge and Medford, MA: Polity, 2018.

Stegemann, Patrick, and Sören Musyal. *Die rechte Mobilmachung: Wie radikale Netzaktivisten die Demokratie angreifen*. Berlin: Econ, 2020.

Stephansen, Hilde C., and Emiliano Treré, eds. *Citizen Media and Practice: Currents, Connections, Challenges*. London: Routledge, 2020.

Stewart, Nicole K., Ahmed Al-Rawi, Carmen Celestini, and Nathan Worku. "Hate Influencers' Mediation of Hate on Telegram: 'We Declare War Against the Anti-White System'." *Social*

Media + Society 9, no. 2 (2023), https://doi.org/10.1177/20563051231177915. Accessed December 29, 2023.

Stoknes, Per Espen. *What We Think about When We Try Not to Think about Global Warming: Toward a New Psychology of Climate Action.* White River Junction, VT: Chelsea Green Publishing, 2015.

Stoldt, Ryan, Mariah Wellman, Brian Ekdale, and Melissa Tully. "Professionalizing and Profiting: The Rise of Intermediaries in the Social Media Influencer Industry." *Social Media + Society* 5, no. 1 (2019), https://doi.org/10.1177/2056305119832587. Accessed December 29, 2023.

Stratil, Jasper. "'Ja es ist wieder Zeit für so ein Video.' Zur audiovisuellen Adressierung und rhetorischen Situation des Rezo-YouTube-Videos *Die Zerstörung der CDU.*" *Mediaesthetics—Journal of Poetics of Audiovisual Images* 3, 2019, https://www.mediaesthetics.org/index.php/mae/article/view/83/207. Accessed December 31, 2021.

Strick, Simon. "The Alternative Right, Masculinities, and Ordinary Affect." In *Right-Wing Populism and Gender: European Perspectives and Beyond*, 207–30, edited by Gabriele Dietze and Julia Roth. Bielefeld: Transcript, 2020.

Strick, Simon. *Rechte Gefühle: Affekte und Strategien des digitalen Faschismus*, Bielefeld: Transcript, 2021.

Strick, Simon. "Reflexive Facism in the Age of History Memes." *Journal of Modern European History*, 20, no. 3 (2022): 335–51.

Suler, John. "The Online Disinhibition Effect." *Cyberpsychology & Behavior* 7, no. 3 (2004): 321–6.

Sunstein, Cass R. *Echo Chambers: Bush v. Gore, Impeachment, and Beyond.* Princeton, NJ: Princeton University Press, 2001.

Sunstein, Cass R. *#Republic: Divided Democracy in the Age of Social Media.* Princeton, NJ and Oxford: Princeton University Press, 2017.

Taylor, Diana. *Performance.* Durham, NC and London: Duke University Press, 2016.

Taylor, Keeanga-Yamahtta. *From #BlackLivesMatter to Black Liberation.* Foreword by Angela Davies. Expanded 2nd ed. Chicago, IL: Haymarket Books, 2021.

Tedjasukmana, Chris. "Das Netzvideo als Flaschenpost: Sylvia Rivera und queere Filmgeschichte." In *Queer Cinema*, 56–67, edited by Simon Dickel and Dagmar Brunow. Mainz: Ventil, 2018.

Terranova, Tiziana. *Network Culture: Politics for the Information Age.* London: Pluto Press, 2004.

Torchin, Leshu. "*KONY 2012*: Anatomy of a Campaign Video and a Video Campaign." In *The Routledge Handbook to Cinema and Politics*, edited by Yannis Tzioumakis and Claire Molloy, 123–33. New York: Routledge, 2016.

Tretyakov, Sergei. "Art in the Revolution and the Revolution in Art (Aesthetic Consumption and Production)." *October* 118 ([Russian 1923] 2014): 11–18, https://doi.org/10.1162/octo.2006.118.1.11. Accessed April 11, 2023.

Tseronis, Assimakis. "Documentary Film as Multimodal Argumentation: Arguing Audiovisually about the 2008 Financial Crisis." In *Building Bridges for Multimodal Research:*

International Perspectives on Theories and Practices of Multimodal Analysis, edited by Janina Wildfeuer, 327–45. Frankfurt am Main: Peter Lang, 2015.

Tufekci, Zeynep. "'Not This One' Social Movements, the Attention Economy, and Microcelebrity Networked Activism." *American Behavioral Scientist* 57, no. 7 (2013): 848–70.

Tufekci, Zeynep. *Twitter and Tear Gas: The Power and Fragility of Networked Protest.* New Haven, CT: Yale University Press, 2017.

Tufekci, Zeynep. "YouTube, the Great Radicalizer." *The New York Times*, March 11 (2018): 6.

Tuttle Ross, Sheryl. "Propaganda and the Moving Image." In *The Palgrave Handbook of the Philosophy of Film and Motion Pictures*, edited by Noël Carroll, Laura T. Di Summa, and Shawn Loht, 757–80. London: Palgrave Macmillan, 2019.

Urman, Aleksandra, and Mykola Makhortykh. *My War Is Your Special Operation: Engagement with Pro-and Anti-regime Framing of the War in Ukraine on Russian Social Media.* 2022, https://osf.io/67snk/download. Accessed December 29, 2023.

Vaidhyanathan, Siva. *Antisocial Media: How Facebook Disconnects Us and Undermines Democracy.* Oxford: Oxford University Press, 2018.

Valkenburg, Patti M., Jochen Peter, and Joseph B. Walther. "Media Effects: Theory and Research." *Annual Review of Psychology* 67, no. 1 (2016): 315–38.

van Dijck, José. *The Culture of Connectivity: A Critical History of Social Media.* Oxford: Oxford University Press, 2013.

van Dijck, José, and Thomas Poell. "Understanding Social Media Logic." *Media and Communication* 1, no. 1 (2013): 2–14.

van Dijck, José, Thomas Poell, and Martijn de Waal. *The Platform Society: Public Values in a Connective World.* Oxford and New York: Oxford University Press, 2018.

Verma, Mimansa. "India Has Blocked 14 Mobile Messenger Apps on Security Fears." *Quartz*, May 1, 2023, https://tinyurl.com/bdd9hyyk. Accessed May 3, 2023.

Voß, Malte. "Videoaktivismus und Soziale Medien: Eine Bestandsaufnahme der Gegenöffentlichkeit durch Video im Internetzeitalter." In *Protest—Film—Bewegung: Neue Wege im Dokumentarischen*, edited by Kay Hoffmann, Erika Wottrich, Ursula von Keitz, and Thomas Weber, 161–73. München: Edition Text + Kritik, 2015.

Waldman, Diane, and Janet Walker, eds. *Feminism and Documentary.* Minneapolis, MN: University of Minnesota Press, 1999.

Walsh, Alistair. "TikTok Censoring LGBT, Nazi Terms in Germany: Report." *DW*, March 23, 2022, https://tinyurl.com/yxuwuucs. Accessed April 29, 2023.

Warner, Michael. *Publics and Counterpublics.* New York: Zone Books, 2002.

Waters, Richard D., and Paul M. Jones. "Using Video to Build an Organization's Identity and Brand: A Content Analysis of Nonprofit Organizations' YouTube Videos." *Journal of Nonprofit & Public Sector Marketing* 23, no. 3 (2011): 248–68.

Waugh, Thomas. *"Show Us Life": Towards a History and Aesthetics of the Committed Documentary.* Metuchen, NJ and London: Scarecrow Press, 1984.

Weibel, Peter, ed. *global aCtIVISm: Art and Conflict in the 21st Century*. Cambridge, MA: MIT Press, 2015.

Weizman, Eyal. *Forensic Architecture: Violence at the Threshold of Detectability*. New York: Zone Books, 2017.

Welles, Brooke. *#HashtagActivism: Networks of Race and Gender Justice*. Cambridge, MA: MIT Press, 2020.

Wessels, Josepha Ivanka. *Documenting Syria: Film-Making, Video Activism and Revolution*. London: Bloomsbury Publishing, 2019.

Weyler, Rex. *Greenpeace: How a Group of Ecologists, Journalists and Visionaries Changed the World*. Vancouver: Raincoast Books, 2004.

White, Katherine, Rishad Habib, and David J. Hardisty. "How to SHIFT Consumer Behaviors to Be More Sustainable: A Literature Review and Guiding Framework." *Journal of Marketing* 83, no. 3 (2019): 22–49.

Wiehl, Anna. *The Digital Moment in Interactive Documentary: Polyphony and Collaborative Storytelling Between On-Line and On-Ground Action*. Hamburg: Avinus, 2019.

Wike, Richard, and Sneha Gubbala (on behalf of *Pew Research Center*). "Social Media Seen as Mostly Good for Democracy Across Many Nations, but U.S. Is a Major Outlier." *Pew Research Center*, December 6, 2022, https://tinyurl.com/yrr3cdkh. Accessed April 19, 2023.

Wike, Richard, and Sneha Gubbala (on behalf of *Pew Research Center*). "Social Media Seen as Mostly Good for Democracy Across Many Nations, but U.S. Is a Major Outlier." *Pew Research Center*, December 6, 2022, https://tinyurl.com/yrr3cdkh. Accessed April 19, 2023.

Wikipedia. "Comparison of Video Hosting Services." (n.d.), https://en.wikipedia.org/wiki/Comparison_of_video_hosting_services. Accessed April 5, 2023.

Wimmer, Jeffrey. "Counterpublic." In *The International Encyclopedia of Political Communication*, edited by Gianpietro Mazzoleni, 1–5. Hoboken, NJ: John Wiley & Sons, 2015.

Winskell, Kate, and Daniel Enger. "Storytelling for Social Change." In *The Handbook of Development Communication and Social Change*, edited by Karin Gwinn Wilkins, Thomas Tufte, and Rafael Obregon, 189–206. Chichester: John Wiley, 2014.

Winston, Brian. "The Tradition of the Victim in Griersonian Documentary." In *Image Ethics: The Moral Rights of Subjects in Photographs, Films, and Television*, edited by Larry Gross, John Stuart Katz, and Jay Ruby, 34–57. New York and Oxford: Oxford University Press, 1988.

Witness. "Deepfakes, Synthetic Media and Generative AI: Dossier." WITNESS (2023), https://www.gen-ai.witness.org/. Accessed November 29, 2023.

Woolley, Samuel, Martin Riedl, and Josephine Lukito. "TikTok has a Political Influencer Problem Targeted at Gen Z Voters." *The Hill*, June 6, 2023, https://tinyurl.com/4wjdekh5. Accessed July 16, 2023.

Yékú, James. *Cultural Netizenship: Social Media, Popular Culture, and Performance in Nigeria*. Bloomington, IN: Indiana University Press, 2022.

Yuan, Elaine. "Publics (and Networked Publics)." In *Routledge Encyclopedia of Citizen Media*, edited by Moma Baker, Bolette B. Blaagard, Henry Jones, and Luis Pérez-González, 1–7. London and New York: Routledge, 2020.

Zimmermann, Patricia R., and Helen de Michiel. *Open Space New Media Documentary: A Toolkit for Theory and Practice*. New York: Routledge, 2019.

Zimmermann, Peter. "Camcorder Revolution—Videoaktivisten und internationale Öffentlichkeit." In *Referenzen: Zur Theorie und Geschichte des Realen in den Medien*, edited by Harro Segeberg, 256–61. Marburg: Schüren, 2009.

Zuboff, Shoshana. *The Age of Surveillance Capitalism: The Fight for a Human Future at the New Frontier of Power*. New York: Public Affairs, 2019.

Zuckerman, Ethan. "The Cute Cat Theory Talk at ETech." *Ethan Zuckerman* (blog), March 8, 2008, www.bit.ly/2VMZKHG. Accessed April 24, 2023.

Zulli, Diana, and David James Zulli. "Extending the Internet Meme: Conceptualizing Technological Mimesis and Imitation Publics on the TikTok Platform." *New Media & Society* 24, no. 8 (2022): 1872–90.

Zutavern, Julia. *Politik des Bewegungsfilms*. Marburg: Schüren, 2015.

www.ingramcontent.com/pod-product-compliance
Ingram Content Group UK Ltd.
Pitfield, Milton Keynes, MK11 3LW, UK
UKHW051802070625
459301UK00002B/3